INTERNATIONAL SIX-DAYS'TRIAL

INTERNATIONAL SIX-DAYS' TRIAL

Mick Walker & Rob Carrick

This book is dedicated to the memory of Phil Mellers,
gentleman and life-long motorcyclist, for whose
friendship, wisdom and guidance, so many of us are so
grateful

FRONTISPIECE
**Austrian KTM rider Strossenreuther airborne during
the 1977 ISDT in Czechoslovakia**

Published in 1992 by Osprey Publishing
59 Grosvenor Street, London W1X 9DA

Cataloguing in Publication Data is available for this title upon
request from the British Library

Editor Shaun Barrington
Page designer Geoffrey Wadsley
Filmset by Tradespools Ltd., Frome, Somerset
Printed by BAS Printers Ltd., Over Wallop, Stockbridge, Hants.

Contents

About the Authors

Mick Walker is an enthusiast for all forms of motorcycle sport. He is one of the best tuners around, and rode a variety of racers during the classic era, including an AJS 7R, Manx Norton, Greeves Silverstone and a brace of BSA Gold Stars. Today he heads a company specialising in the supply of spare parts to Ducati owners and racers around the world. He is one of Osprey's most prolific authors, producing titles as diverse as *Classic Italian Racing Motorcycles* and *BMW Twins Restoration*.

Rob Carrick spent 22 years in the RAF, specialising in explosives and bomb disposal. He has been a motorcycle enthusiast from the classic era of the late 1950s onwards and over the years has owned and competed on Velocettes, Vincents, Matchless and AJSs, and lately a 200 Greeves. He has always been interested in the 'dirty' (offroad) side of the sport, but now has found a new passion for road racing. He is a motorcycle restorer whose company is right on the spot, at Snetterton race track.

Acknowledgements

This particular book came about as a direct result of the close working relation which Rob Carrick and Mick Walker found they had enjoyed so much in the preparation of their earlier title, Greeves (Osprey Publishing) which was published in 1988.

It was not always possible for two authors to share common interests, let alone to work happily alongside each other; but this has been the case between fellow East Anglians Rob and Mick.

So another 'joint venture' was planned, this time covering the famous 'Six Days'. As before it was agreed that each author would write half of the chapters, with Rob compiling the appendices, and Mick taking responsibility for the picture captions (which included the task of finding the photographs in the first place!).

The amount of research needed was extremely comprehensive; and took over two years to gather by both parties. The reasons for this are not only the number of years to be covered, but also the many different countries represented. To the best of both authors' knowledge, this is the very first work to cover the history of the ISDT and ISDE in a single volume; so there was much virgin territory to be explored.

Many kind people from all corners of the globe helped in some way, but none more so than Peter Brushwood. A former Major in the British Army Edu-

Mick Walker (far right) has direct links with both the ISDT and the ISDE through his association with the Italian Cagiva marque in the late 1970s and early 1980s as their British importer. Gwyn Barraclough (seated) rode this RX250 as part of the official British Army team in Elba, 1981. Also in photograph are Tony Davis, mechanic (left) and MW Cagiva manager Peter Brushwood; without whose help this book would have been much the poorer

cation Corps, Peter left the military during the late 1970s to pursue his great love of motorcycles; taking up the post of general manager at Mick Walker Motorcycles in Wisbech. Subsequently, he took charge of the Cagiva UK enduro team – the British importers being the Mick Walker Group. This entailed Peter travelling with the squad to the 1980 French ISDT and 1981 Elba ISDE events.

Besides being a competent off-road rider, he has a life-long interest in the 'Six Days', considering it the finest of all forms of motorcycle competition. This knowledge and background has played a vital role in the production of *ISDT*.

Another big thanks must also go to Ken Heanes, a veteran of many ISDT battles, both as rider and later as British team manager, for agreeing to compile the foreword. Although Ken sold his Fleet, Hampshire motorcycle business a few years ago, he has lost none of his enthusiasm for the sport.

Gwyn Barraclough has been a top British Army teamster in both the ISDT and later the ISDE, winning a clutch of medals along the way. He has been kind enough to share his fund of knowledge, dedication and photographs.

Further help came from John Collard, George Chapp (Czechoslovakia), Sammy Miller, Mick Noyce, Phil Mellers, Nick Nicholls, Doug Jackson, Eddie Crookes, John Craigie and Ralph Venables, to name but a few.

Photographs came from a variety of sources including the EMAP archives, Nick Nicholls, Doug Jackson, several private enthusiasts and Mick Walker's personal collection.

The manuscript was typed by Joan Carrick (Rob's mother), Margaret Brushwood and Kim White – a big

Co-author Rob Carrick. A great enthusiast for the event, Rob has brought his own special talents to the ISDT story

thanks to all. Thanks also goes to the Osprey editorial team including editor Shaun Barrington and Publisher Nick Collins.

Finally, a tribute to all those men and women who down through the years have made the International Six Days' Trial (now Enduro!) the premier motorcycle challenge in the world.

Rob Carrick   Mick Walker
Downham Market,   Wisbech,
Norfolk   Cambridgeshire

Foreword

It was with great pride that I accepted the job of writing a foreword for this book on my favourite subject – The International Six-Day Trial – an event in which I have been active since 1951. Readers today may well consider my name synonymous with the Triumph marque alone, but it was on different makes of machines that I first competed.

My father Jim Heanes rode for Ariels in the thirties, and it seemed only natural that I would get interested in motorcycling at an early age. At the age of 11, I would come home from school and secretly remove from our shed a 1914 flat tank Royal Enfield (which dad had been trying to sell for £4.87½p) and get a friend to push me up and down a track in the woods adjoining our house. It was not long before I got the hang of it and fired it up, only to end up headlong into a tree. Surprisingly, my father was amused by this episode and decided to piece together a WD type 250 Matchless for me to ride. From then on, throughout my career, Jim gave me assistance,

advice and encouragement without any pressure. In my early years (my apprenticeship) I learned a great deal from him, especially the art of hacksawing lugs off an old frame, filing and making up various brackets.

My first real event was to be in 1947 (aged 13) at a speed hill climb, held at Buster Hill, Petersfield. In those days there were no events for 'schoolboys' and to my horror and disappointment, the organisers decided on the day that I was too young to ride. However, at the end of the meeting they allowed me a 'demonstration' ride. To the amazement of all concerned I set the fastest time of the day and received a memento, which I still have to this day.

After this I rode in various trials and scrambles on a BSA Bantam, a 125 Royal Enfield Flying Flea and the

Ken Heanes in action during the final day's speed test, ISDT 1956. Machine is a 175cc Triumph Cub. In this his second 'Six Days' Ken gained a gold medal

Ken Heanes with the works 504cc Triumph he rode in the 1966 event, which is now encased in his home as a reminder of the happy relationship he enjoyed with the Meriden factory. Photograph taken November 1991

250 Matchless for about four years, until in 1950 Jack Stocker (7 ISDT gold medals) provided me with a semi-factory supported Royal Enfield 350 Bullet to ride in the ISDT held that year in Wales. The first two days went well and I stayed on time, then a puncture put me in a panic, and when trying hard to get back on time, I crashed into a brick wall. It was raining, the bike was ruined, but I remember my only concern was 'where's my cap?'. Fortunately, I was uninjured, and later retrieved the cap – of the cheesecutter style cloth variety – for helmets were yet to become compulsory. The ride in Wales whetted my appetite, and I was determined to ride in an event again one day and win a gold. My father had ridden a Royal Enfield in the 1949 and 1950 events, winning 2 silver medals, having lost 1 mark each year for timekeeping.

I continued my career in trials and scrambles, with semi-works support from the Matchless factory, on the recommendation of Geoff Ward my scrambling idol, and rode twice in the Scottish Six-Day Trial, but I was more interested in speed events. It was then that lady luck (in the shape of Ralph Venables) took a hand. He whispered in the ear of Triumph's competition manager Ivor Davies, which led to my first Triumph works ride in 1954. I had various successes on 500 and 650 scrambler twins, then I was given a 175 Tiger Cub to ride as a member of the Vase B team at Garmisch in

1956, which earned me my first gold. My taste for the event had been rekindled, and so it was for the next 17 years, whenever the ACU entered teams in the event, I rode as a member of the Trophy team, gaining 10 golds and 2 silver medals.

The event has changed a lot in recent years, to the detriment of the original idea. Nowadays the bikes are purpose-built racers which bear no resemblance to a factory's wares, riders receive outside assistance, and time can be made up to counteract previous lateness in the day. My 2 silvers would have turned to gold if these rules were in force when I dropped a mark in Czecho-slovakia in 1959, for failing to kick start the bike in the 1 minute allowed, and being 30 seconds late – stuck in the mud on the biggest bike in the trial – on the Isle of Man in 1965. However I can only advocate the rules as they were in the fifties and sixties, when the event was a true test of a riders ability, stamina, mechanical knowledge, and a test of the machinery, without any outside assistance.

Throughout my term with Triumph (1954–1966) credit must go to Henry Vale and the late Vic Fiddler, who assisted me in every possible way from within the factory's competition department. It was from the factory, in 1966 after the Swedish event, that I purchased my last 504cc works machine, which is now encased in my home as a memento of my happy relationship with the Triumph marque.

I continued to ride in the ISDT (sponsoring myself) with my last ride in the Isle of Man in 1971. I had always hoped to be a member of the winning Trophy team, but this was not to be, so I carried on as team manager for a further four years, which included arranging and building the team's machines. My ambition was never fulfilled, as our Trophy team only managed runner-up twice, to East Germany in 1964 and the USA in 1973.

Needless to say, during my ISDT years I made a considerable number of friends, and now some 20 years on from my last competitive ride, I still meet a number of officials, helpers and teamsters from all over the world and it is to these I say thank you for the ISDT.

KEN HEANES
10 gold medals 2 silver medals 1956–1970
British Team Manager 1971–1975
Farnham Surrey

CHAPTER ONE

The early years

In December 1897 the Automobile Club of Great Britain and Ireland was founded to look after the interests of the early motorist. No distinction was made at that time between four-, three- and two-wheeled vehicles! In the 'Emancipation Run' to Brighton in 1897 the only British-made vehicle to complete the course was a tricycle. Sport has always been a major interest of motorists and in 1900 the ACGBI promoted the 'Great 1000 Miles Trial'. Among the entrants were two quadricycles, two motor tricycles and one tricycle with a trailer. A couple of Werner two-wheelers were also entered but did not start. By 1903 the development of the motorcycle was such that 93 members of the motorcycle branch of the parent body set up the Auto Cycle Union. In the very first year of its existence the ACU organized a 1000-mile trial which became an annual

The forerunner of the ISDT was the ACU Six Day Trial. LS Partler, Scott (leading) and H E Ashley, LMC 3½ hp are seen here climbing Kidstones Pass during the 1911 event

event as the ACU Six Days' Reliability Trial. The object of the event was to satisfy the sporting urge to demonstrate the advantages of one machine over another. In 1913 it was decided to incorporate in the event, and under FIM rules, the first International Touring Trial.

This event in 1913 is generally regarded as the first International Six Days Trial and the ancestor of the events with which this book deals. Although the international element was only a class in the ACU's 1913 trial it set the pattern for the future. Its purpose was to provide a prolonged test and demonstration of the reliability and efficiency of the motorcycle. Needless to say it was also important to the manufacturers as an indication of the quality of their machinery, and to the riders as a test of fitness and skill. The organization of the 1913 event, under ACU direction, was in the hands of the Westmorland and the Cumberland County MCCs. In the light of experience gained in the Kendal-based ACU Autumn Reliability Trial in October 1912, regulations were issued for 1913. Basically the format

was to remain similar for many years. Riders were required to maintain a set speed schedule during the mileage covered over the six days and also to undertake speed trials and flexibility tests. Marks were lost for:

Deviation from schedule

Stopping in non-stop sections

Use of spare parts not carried by the rider or passenger

Defective condition of the machine

Dirty or untidy machines or riders

Although penalties for stopping in non-stop sections were subsequently confined to more specialized trials and the dirty rider and machine has been relegated to history, even the riders of today's much more specialized events would recognize 1913. The only national

teams in 1913 were from Great Britain and France. Each country was represented by one passenger carrying machine (i.e. sidecar outfit or three- or four-wheel cyclecar), and either two 500cc solos or one 500 and one 350. International teams were to be mounted on machines manufactured within their own national borders. It was hardly surprising that Great Britain won the new International Trophy (value 200 guineas) donated by the Motorcycle Manufacturers' and Traders' Union. The team comprised W.B. Gibb (348 Douglas), Billy Little (499 Premier) and Charlie Collier (7/8 hp Matchless and sidecar).

The 1914 event, which would have been the first full International, was cancelled for obvious reasons, although the timing of the event and its proximity to the outbreak of the war caused some consternation to the British contingent who were already en route! The event was not revived until 1920 and even then this was

RIGHT **Starters number board for ACU Six Days, Drill Hall Yard, Taunton circa August 1912**

LEFT **N.O. Soresby (LMC) at Porlock, Devon during the ACU Six Day Trial, August 1912. Note stationary Scott competitor on the left**

An international class was introduced in the ACU's 1913 trial. The only foreign team was the French shown here

a major anti-climax since lack of interest by manufacturers and the casualty figures in the war ensured that there were only 15 starters in that year. Bearing in mind the fact that 162 riders competed in Britain in 1913, the entry for 1920 can only be regarded as disastrous. Based in France, Switzerland took the first genuine team trophy using Motosacoche machinery. Despite the poor turn out in 1920 the event played its part in determining the basic format of its successors, and it might be as well to outline it at this stage.

Essentially the ISDT, as it came to be known, was a reliability test for standard production motorcycles. It was not designed to produce a new breed of highly specialized machinery and it enabled manufacturers to test, demonstrate, improve and publicize their roadgoing machinery as purchased by the general public. Indeed it could be argued that the gradual departure from this ethos transformed the event into something very different, recognized eventually by the change of title in 1981 to the International Six Days *Enduro*. The format, even as early as 1913, was the completion of a lengthy course within a set average speed. Moreover, the ISDT was essentially a team contest. The trophy was awarded to a group of national representatives riding nationally manufactured machines.

The 1913 event
attracted 162 entries;
here are two sidecar
crews, MC Marston
Triumph 3½hp (left)
and W Laud-Dibb
Rex 6hp

No ISDT took place in 1919; only the ACU Six Day
Trial in September that year. The Scott team is shown
here; left to right; H O Wood, B Alan-Hill, C P Wood
and W L Guy

In order to ensure that the test would be formidable,
the distances to be covered were considerable, and the
road and track conditions were to be difficult enough to
pose a severe, but not impossible, test. Indeed, according to the regulations the course was to consist of
'roads that are passable in all weathers for every kind of
motorcycle'. Time-checks were introduced to monitor
the progress of competitors and to enable organizers to
include difficult time sections which would cause all but
the best to incur penalty marks. Penalties were also
incurred for inability to start machines within a limited
time period at the start of the day. In order to ensure
that machines were fully tested and could not undergo
major repair, a number of regulations were imposed.
Careful mechanical scrutineering before the event
included the marking of all major components to prevent their replacement during the trial. These parts
were marked and sealed. The only spare parts which
could be used were those carried by the riders, who
were also confined to tools which were carried with
them. External assistance was not allowed. Access to the
machines for maintenance and repair was only allowed
during the riding day and for a limited period before the

start. All competing machines were confined in a *parc
fermé* after scrutineering and there they remained outside the riding time. The ISDT thus became an attempt
by national teams to maintain often cruel schedules
against the clock over long distances and frequently on
atrocious surfaces, riding basically production road
machines. In this form it became internationally known
as the 'Olympics of Motorcycling', a title which was
fully justified.

One factor of major importance was the relationship
of the trophy to national motorcycle manufacturing
industries. Although undoubtedly unfair to smaller
nations without a manufacturing basis of their own, it
ensured manufacturers' support for the event for many
years and was regarded as vital for prestige. Nevertheless, the FIM recognized the necessity for a second team
award which did not require a national industry and, in
consequence, a second International Cup was intro-

duced in 1924 for national teams riding motorcycles manufactured outside their own borders. In 1925 this became the International Silver Vase, but it remained of secondary importance even after 1970 when the requirement for national machinery was lifted from trophy teams. It was not until 1985 that this situation was finally resolved when the Vase became the Junior Trophy for teams of riders under 23 years of age.

One of the outcomes of the quite complex structure of the event was the inevitable development of a mass of rules and regulations which have been continuously amended and updated. Unfortunately, the nature and complexity of the rules led to the development of widespread cheating which has constantly bedevilled the event throughout its history. Frequent amendment has made the regulations even more complex. For example, from the very beginning riders have been awarded gold, silver and bronze medals in the event. In the earlier years a gold medal was simple to understand, for it was awarded to riders who incurred no penalties and who completed a final speed test in a minimum time determined by the engine capacity of their machines. Similarly, silver medals were awarded to all riders who lost up to 25 marks and bronze for up to 50. The unfortunates who completed the event but were not excluded altogether for being more than one hour behind schedule, received no awards.

The trophy and vase contents were determined by finishing with teams in which all members were unpenalized. If more than one national team was in this category, ties were decided on the results of the final speed tests. More recent events have their results calculated in a much more complex manner and medals are awarded in capacity classes, based on the performance of the class winners and incorporating the results of special tests, for example timed motocross, cross-country and acceleration tests. The team contests are decided in a similar way.

Some milestones along the regulation road were as follows:

Until 1937	4-man trophy teams including one sidecar outfit.
1938–1947	5-man trophy teams including one sidecar outfit.
1939	Two different capacities mandatory for solos in trophy teams.
1948	Five solo machines in trophy teams from three capacity classes but no sidecar outfits.
1956	Six machine trophy teams from at least three capacity classes; four machine vase teams from two capacity classes.

The 1922 ISDT was held in Switzerland. Here Robmann (Frera) negotiates the Klausen Pass

1960	Special tests introduced.
1970	Requirement for trophy teams to use machines made in their own country revoked.
1975	Complete reorganization of penalty system. Penalty points replaced by classification system.

Of course the ISDT was never an event held exclusively for the benefit of the trophy and vase competitions. Any motorcycle manufacturer was able to compete with three-man teams for an FIM gold medal for manufacturers. There has always been a Club Team award for the best three-member club entry and, perhaps most important of all, it has always been possible for courageous individuals to compete independently.

However, to return to the early years of the event, the 1920s was a period of technological development and progress and there was a parallel growth in the size and prestige of the event. Of course it has to be remembered that World War I had decimated almost an antire generation of young men throughout Europe. It was really quite surprising that it was possible to restart the event

as early as 1920 and the small entry reflected a dearth of riders as well as some lack of interest. From 1920 to 1924 the trophy was won, rather unexpectedly, by Switzerland on three occasions and by Sweden in 1923. In 1921, following their success in the previous year, the Swiss hosted the event and this time there were 51 entries with 24 British-made bikes. Only two teams, Great Britain and Switzerland, entered the trophy competition. The 39 successful entrants covered a total of 1156 miles, ending the Six Days with the customary speed test. As well as winning the trophy the Swiss collected a manufacturer's award through the efforts of Motosacoche. For Great Britain, Eric Williams (AJS) won a gold watch for the best performance for a visitor, in addition to his gold medal, and Douglas collected a manufacturer's award.

The line-up for 1922 in Switzerland still comprised only a small number of entrants. However, the 45 starters represented five nations and the trophy was contested by three: Britain, Sweden and Switzerland. This, of course, was the era of the multi-purpose motorcyclist

Typical AJS 2hp side valve single as used by a number of British riders during the early 1920s

RIGHT **German riders
at Southampton
prior to the start of the
1925 event**

BELOW **Part of the 1925
ISDT took in the
Brooklands race circuit**

and the British team included two former TT winners!
As an indication of the machinery used, the teams were:

Great Britain
G.S. Davidson (249 Levis)
A. Bennett (492 Sunbeam)
F.W. Giles (800 AJS sc)

Switzerland
J. Morand (248 Condor)
A. Robert (496 Motosacoche)
E. Gex (994 Motosacoche sc)

Sweden
B. Malmberg (494 Husqvarna)
G. Göthe (494 Husqvarna)
P. Swanbeck (995 Husqvarna sc)

Surprisingly there was no French team although two
individuals entered in addition to two Dutchmen and
an Italian. Twenty-five per cent of the entry was from
Great Britain. Nevertheless, the Swiss won, albeit by

only one mark, from the British team. Manufacturer's
awards went to AJS, Harley-Davidson and Motosacoche; the Club Team award to the Zurich MCC with
Worcester & District in second place. G.S. Davidson on
his Levis was the best foreign competitor. Particularly
noteworthy in this year was that, despite the small number of entrants, scrutineering of the machinery, which
included weighing in bike and rider and the marking
and sealing of components, occupied two full days.

The 1923 event was held in Scandinavia and proved
to be very tough indeed. Held from 6 to 15 August
(including pre-trial formalities and post-trial festivities!) it covered 1237 miles in Sweden and Norway,
starting in Stockholm. Forty per cent of the entrants
were forced to retire, in many cases following accidents.
As in 1922 Great Britain, Sweden and Switzerland contested the trophy but this time Sweden, with a definite
home advantage, won. Although still not a major event
in terms of numbers, it remained truly international and
the Swedes put up a first-class performance. The prize-

giving celebration was held in the Stockholm town hall following dinner at the Grand Hotel, and the foreign competitors were given an impressive send-off with brass bands and cheering crowds.

1924 marks the beginning in ISDT history of one of those periods when a single nation appears to be invincible. What is perhaps more surprising is that the dominance which Great Britain was about to display should have been delayed for so long. The British motorcycle industry was powerful and diverse, its manufacturers were anxious to demonstrate their superiority and there were many first-class riders. Despite this, 1924, although it saw a British trophy win, was neither auspicious nor decisive. The event was based in Belgium, centred on Liège, and entered the territory of Holland and Luxemburg. History records that an individual entry cost £5 6s and a trade entry £10 13s. The average speeds required on the course were between 21 and 24.85 mph, although allowances were made for the more difficult sections. The winning British team comprised G.S. Arter (499 James), C. Wilson (499 Sunbeam) and F.W. Giles (348 AJS sc).

For the very first year the International Cup II was introduced for the best team result by a nation using machinery constructed outside its borders, and this was won by Norway with C. Vaumund (499 Triumph), O. Graff (550 Husqvarna) and J. Juberget (989 Harley-Davidson sc). Most controversial was the fact that the Norwegian team put up a better performance than the British but were debarred from the trophy contest by the 'national machine' rule. Equally dramatic was the fact that the Belgian team, mounted on Belgian FN and Saroléa machinery, would also have finished ahead of the British but were ineligible because their team had no sidecar entry. Saroléa and FN both won manufacturer's team awards and, all in all, the British victory was rather empty.

The 1925 event was held in Great Britain, centred on Southampton and finishing with the speed test on the Brooklands circuit. Most of the mileage was found in the west of England and in Wales. More than 100 entries were accepted although only 87 started. Of these 64 completed the six days and 36 gold, 12 silver and 3 bronze medals were awarded. This time the British win in the trophy competition was convincing. F.W. Giles (498 AJS sc), B. Kershaw (346 New Hudson) and G.S. Arter (499 James) formed the winning team. In this year the Trophy II became the International Silver Vase for the first time and this competition was also won by Great Britain. Rowley, Simpson and Williams won the 350cc manufacturer's award for AJS and Arter, Kimberley and Lidstone, riding James machines, the 500cc

LEFT **First day of the 1925 ISDT saw competitors travelling from Southampton to Taunton. H S Perry (85) and P Cranmore (86), both BSA mounted, pass through the famous Cheddar Gorge**

award. A perfect indication of the increasing importance and international significance of the event is to be found in the list of competing machines:

AJS, Ariel, Brough Superior, BSA, Douglas, D-Rad, Dunelt, Harley-Davidson, Gillet, Humber, Indian, James, Matchless, Morgan (3-wheeler), Neander, New Gerard, New Hudson, New Imperial, Norton, OEC – Blackburne, OK, P & M, Raleigh, Royal Enfield, Rudge Whitworth, Saroléa, Scott, Sunbeam, Triumph, Velocette, Victoria, Zenith.

In 1926 the number of competitors was still growing at 113. On home territory, starting from Buxton in Derbyshire, British riders once again swept the board. Seventy-seven gold medals, eight silver and seven bronze were awarded. The British 'B' team comprising J. Lidstone (495 James), P. Pike (588 Norton sc) and that well-known personality (and father of Murray!) Graham Walker (493 Sunbeam) won the trophy. Notable performances were put up by the German A team, who lost Guberla's 820 Mabeco sidecar outfit midweek but the survivors, Roth and Schleicher on 498 BMWs, performed superbly. The Dutch also went well, finishing second to Britain in the vase contest, riding British machinery. This was also the first year in which Britain entered a women's team for the vase. Marjorie Cottle (348 Raleigh), Edyth Foley (494 Triumph) and Louie McLean (348 Douglas) rode well although they did not feature in the results. Indeed Louie McLean, née Ball, had just celebrated her marriage and she and her husband both competed in the event as a sort of honeymoon tour!

In 1927 Great Britain's run of success continued in the event based on Ambleside in the Lake District. Germany and Sweden provided the opposition in the trophy contest, while Denmark, Belgium and Austria were also represented in the entry. The fact that there is nothing new under the sun may be a truism, but the German machinery in that year was a revelation. The DKW factory produced two 175 and one 496cc two-strokes. The 175s were supercharged, watercooled singles. Supercharging was effected by a second cylinder and piston mounted underneath the crankcase. The 496cc model was a watercooled twin. The British team, this time including L. Crisp (349 Humber), Graham Walker (495 Sunbeam) and F.W. Giles (498 AJS), again took the trophy by a clear margin of 91 marks from Sweden.

However, the most remarkable achievement of the decade was the success of Marjorie Cottle, Louie McLean and Edyth Foley, entered as the British vase C team. Given no chance by contemporary critics, the girls quietly set about winning the competition by two marks from the Danish team. This success was followed by a triumphant 7000-mile tour of Europe (on bikes of course!) organized by a Dutch barrister. Having been more or less ignored in the event itself, they were subsequently fêted in the European capital cities.

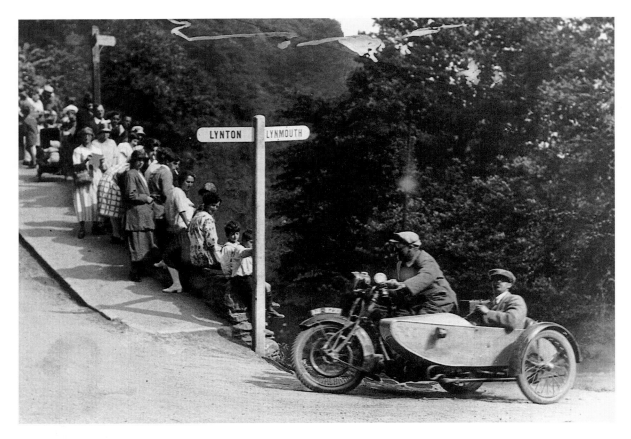

Also worthy of note was the first appearance in this year of the Tiffens of Carlisle. From 1927 to 1935 Billy Tiffen senior won consecutive Gold medals in the six days and his son, Bill junior, continued this performance from 1936 to 1938! In 1938 the family motorcycle business in Carlisle carried the slogan '17000 miles without losing a mark!'

A hundred and eight riders set out from Harrogate in Yorkshire in the first event to be held in September as opposed to August. The weather in 1928 was perfect and, partly in consequence, 92 entrants completed the Six Days. Once again a British team won the trophy, but in very controversial circumstances. V.C. King (348 Douglas), F.W. Neill (495 Matchless) and H.G. Uzzell (493 BSA sc) actually lost more marks than the Swedish team 'on the road' and, not surprisingly, the Swedes expected to win. At the final machine examination Ericsson's and Malmberg's machines from the trophy team were found to have fractured rear brake operating arms and, in consequence, were docked 11 marks each. The British team, which was penalty-free after the final inspection, was awarded the trophy. The controversial rules of the event were once again the cause of much discontent. The British B team won the vase competition, having lost no marks at any stage. The ladies team entered once again but could not repeat the 1927 performance. In the manufacturer's classes Excelsior

ABOVE **W Edwards and passenger (Rayleigh Sidecar) on the Lynton/Lynmouth road during the ISDT in August 1925**

RIGHT **A lunch stop for hungry (and thirsty) competitors during the 1927 ISDT based in the English Lake District with its headquarters situated in the town of Ambleside**

won the 250cc award, BSA the 350, Ariel the 500 and Scott the 750.

The 1929 event ended the decade in quite spectacular fashion, justifying the optimism of all those who had organized and taken part in the Six Days since 1920. The FIM had decided to run a truly international event, at least as far as Europe was concerned, both in riders and the route which was set out for them. When entries closed at the end of July 168 had been accepted, and this later increased to 175. At long last the entry list exceeded the 1913 total. Of these Great Britain entered 64 riders, Germany 53, Holland 12, Switzerland 12, Austria 8, Ireland 6, Italy, Hungary Romania and Czechoslovakia one each. Britain, Switzerland and Sweden entered trophy teams and the vase was contested by two teams each from Britain, Ireland, Germany, Austria, Holland and Switzerland, while

Denmark and Sweden each entered a single team. Twenty-nine manufacturers' teams were entered. Starting on Monday 26 August and finishing on Saturday 31st, the course covered a total of 1053 miles through Germany, Austria, Italy, Switzerland and France. The entire route passed through magnificent mountain scenery and included the routes along the shores of lakes Maggiore and Geneva.

That year it was called the 'International Six Days Trial-Munich-Geneva' and was generally regarded as the greatest motorcycle reliability trial ever held. It may seem carping to criticize the event at all, but, in the light of the organizational problems which bedevilled the event throughout its history, it has to be said that in some respects it came close to being an administrative disaster! The history of the ISDT records many examples of problems with accommodation for competitors, and the difficulty of providing adequate overnight facilities in a different centre every night can be imagined! Moreover, the competitors' baggage and equipment had to be transported to a new location each day by the organizers and, in the 1920s, trucks tended to break down frequently. Moreover, the officials' cars

also broke down frequently and in those days before the EEC hassles at frontier crossings without the support of the organizers were complicated and frustrating. Finally, and most unhappily, the officials at the all-important time-checks were often incompetent.

All in all, however, the British had no complaint for they won both trophy and vase once again! In the trophy contest G.R. Butcher (499 Rudge-Whitworth), and that great all-rounder and AJS man George Rowley, lost no marks, while the third team member, F.W. Neill, lost only one. Since no other team finished intact this meant an easy win for Great Britain. The British vase A team lost no marks at all and won the competition from the French team which lost 24. The manufacturers' awards contain famous names. Unfortunately only two of these companies are still actively producing motorcycles and neither is British:

250cc   1st Puch 2nd BMW

350cc   1st AJS 2nd Raleigh

500cc   1st Rudge-Whitworth 2nd BSA

Sidecar   1st Rudge-Whitworth 2nd BMW

Some of the superb scenery encountered by competitors in the 1929 event which ran through Germany, Austria, Italy, Switzerland and France

Despite the criticisms which can be levelled at the organization of the 1929 event, its reputation as the greatest event of its kind up to that time must surely be justified. Any shortcomings were the result of a design which was perhaps too grand for the organization to cope with. Indeed, any attempt to organize a similar event today, despite all the advantages which modern officials have, would probably encounter all manner of problems. All in all, 'International' provided a fitting end to a period of continuous progress which set this remarkable event well on the road to its 'Olympic' status.

CHAPTER TWO

The 1930s

1930

The 1930s saw a decline in the fortunes of Great Britain's trophy teams; if only because they did not achieve the overwhelming success of the previous decade. Great Britain, in fact, took the trophy on four occasions to become top scorer, but it was the formidable German teams – coming from nowhere with one entrant in the 1930 event – who dominated the proceedings just prior to the outbreak of war. Naturally, it was the top scorers who shared the venues, but for the 1930 event the honours went to France. Centred on the ski resort of Grenoble, the course took in the Swiss and Italian Alps, and was christened the Alpine TT by many riders, due to the high average speeds required by the organizers. The *Union Motocycliste de France* headed by the energetic M. Printamp, saw to it that no one could fault the organization, for indeed it was deemed as excellent with not one protest all week.

On the first day, descending from the top of the Col de Tourniol, it was a trio of Brough Superior riders who were amongst the early retirements. F.P. Dickson, on his 980 Brough, was involved in a serious crash and to his aid came none other than the manufacturer, George Brough, assisted by Eddy Meyer, another rider of the marque, who immediately retired themselves and dashed for help.

After the rain on the first day, sunshine greeted riders as they headed northwards on the second day into the Savoy Alps. Great Britain and Italy jointly held the lead in the trophy contest, both with clean sheets, as did the British A team and the French B team in the vase, but shortly after leaving Chambery Howard Uzzel's BSA outfit disintegrated, eliminating the British. It was here too that Maurice Greenwood performed the miracle of freeing off the gearbox of his 350 New Imperial after a bearing seizure, carrying on without penalty.

Luigi Gilera (driving a Gilera of course!), during speed test section of the 1930 ISDT. He was a member of the winning Italian Trophy team that year. The event was staged around Grenoble, France

More high-altitude riding greeted riders on the third day when they stormed the Col du Glandon pass. Climbing to a height of 6400 ft (the last 4000 ft climbed in 16 miles) snow and ice were encountered. It was on this stretch that the rear wheel of Harry Perry's Ariel sidecar outfit collapsed, and with it, the hopes of the British trophy team. Soon after, the remaining riders crossed the Italian frontier, en route to Turin and the overnight stop at Stresa, except Baron von Krohn – the lone German – whose Zündapp outfit developed so many punctures he was forced to retire. The following day, riders returned to Grenoble via the Col du Simplon in the Swiss Alps, down the Rhône valley and over the Col de la Forclaz to the French frontier. It was on the home run from the border that many riders picked up a particular type of nail in the vicinity of St Pancrasse, laid by a local anti-motorcycling group.

The last two days saw more Alpine runs within France ending up at the Circuit du Dauphine, near Grenoble, for the final one-hour speed test. The test was a foregone conclusion for the Italian Gilera-mounted trophy team, for they were the only trio still intact, and they toured round to collect the premier award. Lady riders also figured highly in the results with Marjorie Cottle, Margaret Newton and Betty Lermitte gaining gold medals for their week's work. 1930 also saw the first participation of a Czechoslovakian vase team, only one member surviving the ordeal to gain a souvenir. Forty years later this result would be stood on its head.

1931

The Alpine TT theme was again used by the Italians when they hosted the 1931 event, centred on Merano and run predominantly in the Italian Dolomites region. The pace was hectic at times, the daily mileage high and the climbs numerous. On the first two days alone, 430 miles had to be covered in 16 hours, and climbs made equivalent to 30,000 ft over the mountain passes. This high average over mostly unmade roads, took its toll of riders. Harry Perry of the British trophy team retired when a key sheared in the timing gear of his Ariel sidecar outfit, and Welch went out after a prang on his Royal Enfield. These two retirements effectively dropped Great Britain from the two major competitions. Melzer of the Czech vase team was another first day casualty when his BSA broke down irreparably. Peter Bradley of the British vase B team had a hectic third day, he had a puncture, broke a shackle bolt, and ran out of petrol on a tight section, but by driving the sunbeam outfit hard he retained his clean sheet.

Italian artfulness was at work, even in those far-off

days, in an attempt to help the home team. Oxford undergraduate, W. Clarke, riding a Vincent HRD into one of the third day controls, arrived early and duly stopped short of the official marker flag. The flag was held by a small boy who walked past Clarke, instantly the rider was pounced upon by the timekeeper, who punched his card debiting his score by one mark for early arrival. Baron von Krohn of the German trophy team, hit a car on the fourth day and was helped on his way by the enthusiastic Italian crowd who assisted him in straightening out the 350 Zündapp. The Italian teams demanded exclusion for outside assistance but the organizers – impressed by the fairness of the French the previous year – ignored the protest saying that the assistance was in no sense organized. The Baron carried on only to drop marks for timekeeping which relegated the Germans to second place. The Italian Gilera-mounted team still retained their clean sheets. Another German trophy rider penalized for timekeeping was Ernst Henne, who dropped three marks on the run over the Stelvio pass. The pass, which rises to an altitude of 9000 ft and was the highest motor road in Europe, gave little trouble to other riders who stormed it in great style.

The fifth day saw riders leave Merano en route to the Gardone night stop ready for the final day's speed test at the Monza Autodrome, but in the centre of the village of Ponte Alle Arche, the Rudge of Betty Lermitte caught fire. The flames threatened other parked machines but the quick thinking of Scotsman, Bob MacGregor saved the day, who jumped aboard, kick-started it, and rode off until the carburettor was dry. Disaster did hit the trial on the last day when the course was hit by hurricane force winds. Trees were uprooted, roofs blown off, and debris lay everywhere. The rain which came with it, drowned many engines, including the four-cylinder Matchless of Bert Collier, only two miles from the Monza circuit. Worst of all, the luncheon table – which bore a feast for the riders arriving at Monza – was completely blown away. When the winds abated, receding as quickly as they arrived, the speed test got underway, one hour late. First group out included the Italian vase B team who needed to set a faster pace than the stated average, in order to beat the Dutch A team, for both still had clean sheets. The Italian Mas 175s were no match for Rudges and Eysink of the Dutchmen, and had to settle for second place. In the trophy contest the Italian team only needed to finish in order to win, for all other teams had lost marks. This the Gilera-mounted team of Luigi Gilera, Miro Maffeis and Rosolino Grana did in fine style.

At the prize-giving dinner when all 67 finishers (88 riders started off) received their rewards, Baron Ricci of the *Royal Moto Club d'Italia* presented an extra award to the four British lady riders. Betty Lermitte, Chris Herbert, Edyth Foley and Marjorie Cottle, each received a suitably inscribed gold bracelet, in honour of, firstly, their performance in the event, and secondly, because they were ladies. The Italians do love motorcycles and speed events, but they also have an eye for the ladies. Nothing has changed.

1932

In 1932 the International Six Days Trial became a Seven Day event, in that the final speed test was held on the seventh day, presumably to let riders recover after six gruelling days on the road. Held again in the northern Italian Dolomites, and centred on Merano, the Italian organizers laid out a tortuous 1300-mile course, using some of the previous year's route and some new hitherto unused mountain passes. Of the 128 starters, 99 riders finished the trial, which was reckoned to be the toughest yet in the series – each country striving to be known as the organizer of the most testing event. Four teams now contested the trophy: the Italians, British and Germans, with new boys the Czechs, competing for the premier award for the first time on a trio of Jawas.

The first trophy team to lose marks were the Germans on the second day when Mauermayer buckled the sidecar wheel of his BMW outfit on the Col Broccon. He carried a spare but this was only interchangeable with the back wheel, and by the end of the day he was

minus many spokes and 33 marks for lateness. The wheel was repaired on the third day at the cost of eight more marks lost.

The infamous military road, the Passo di Campogrosso, was tackled by riders on the fourth day. Mile after mile of rough stone track, with its numerous hairpin bends, a one in six gradient, and a climb to 5000 ft, all of which had to be covered at 25 mph, saw many riders fall off and lose marks for lateness. However, the three remaining trophy teams still remained clean. By comparison, the fifth day was easy with many stretches of real tarmac road, but on one rough section Jaroslav Kaiser lost the sidecar wheel of his Jawa outfit, losing 26 marks in the repair.

On the last day the Gavia pass was stormed by the remaining 101 riders. Closed to traffic and with an official warning that the road was unprotected by fences, contestants feared the worst, but this 9000 ft climb was not as demanding as the Campogrosso. On this section old timers, Billy Tiffen on his Velocette, and Maurice

BELOW **Bob MacGregor (standing, centre), member of the British vase winning team in 1932, with other competitors that year. Patterson and Nelson to his right.**

ABOVE **Irish B vase team, 1933. From left to right:
J. Stewart, G. Thompson, G. Campbell.**

Greenwood on his Douglas, excelled themselves clearing the hill and going on to collect gold medals for their efforts. Len Crisp fell from his Triumph and Doc Galloway pranged his Rudge outfit, both losing marks in repairs and their chances of gold.

The final speed test this time was held on a two-mile street circuit on the outskirts of Merano, and saw the fight for final honours in the vase contest between both Italian teams and the British A team. The British had to complete 23 laps each, against the 21 of the 175 and 250 Guzzi-mounted Italians. The racing type Guzzis were holding out against the 500 Rudge mounted British, and at times were gaining. Then Fumagalli suffered a puncture on his 250 Guzzi and slowed down, letting the British team of Graham Walker, Jack Williams and Bob MacGregor, take the lead and the vase.

In the final shoot out for the trophy the British team of Bert Perrigo (499 BSA), George Rowley (498 AJS), and Peter Bradley (599 Sunbeam sidecar) were up against the Italian team of Maffeis, Gilera and Grana, all mounted on very swift side-valve Gileras. From the start of the test, which took place in pouring rain, the British led the field, but at the half-way point Bert Perrigo went missing. Suffering from plug trouble Bert had slowed but after the plug had unfouled itself the British team again took the lead which they held to the end, beating the Italians by 2 minutes and 13 seconds.

Once more the British had showed that they were in command, taking home both major awards, as well as two manufacturer's team awards, going to Marjorie Cottle, Bert Perrigo and George Povey of the BSA team, and MacGregor, Walker and Williams of the victorious Rudge vase team. When the festivities and prize-giving were over, riders packed their gear together for the return home wondering if Britain would be capable of organizing the next trial to match the demands of the Italian Alpine event. Riders had to wait and see as the area chosen was a hitherto unknown venue and based on an unheard of town hidden away in the western part of the country.

1933

Llandrindod Wells in central Wales was chosen as the centre of activity for the 1933 International, the first of seven such visits to this Radnorshire town, in the heart

of the Cambrian mountains. The route used was mainly on second- and third-class roads, which in themselves were not difficult, but to keep to the right time schedule meant that riders could not afford any holdups. Many of the local one-day trial hills were used, the toughest being Dinas Rock, but this time not as an observed climb, for the International is not a *feet up* event.

Four countries contested the trophy; Czechoslovakia, Germany, Great Britain and Italy. Great Britain started out as favourite, but a win eluded them when one of the team dropped two marks for timekeeping, allowing the Germans to snatch the lead and the trophy, on which *Deutschland* was engraved, for the very first time. The first day's run was a very wet affair, on narrow lanes which saw one-third of the starters fall off at one stage or another, the majority of riders having fitted standard tyres in preference to the competition variety, to cope with the high proportion of road work. Some of the high mountain roads were no better than cart tracks and many riders wished that they had fitted knobblies in order to find grip and stay on. Italy went out on the first day when Bianchi rider, Pigorini, lost his way and clocked in late. The retirement of Kaiser also pushed out the Czech team, for he sustained injuries

ABOVE **The British A vase team for 1933 repeated the preceding year's victory by the Rudge vase team of MacGregor, Walker and Williams. From left to right: Povey, V. Brittain, J. Williams.**

following a spectacular crash which rendered both him and his 500 Jawa combination in need of repair.

The major obstacle of the second day was the descent of Dinas Rock, whose loose and stoney surface unseated many riders, but it was the third day when the rock was tackled uphill that most problems occurred. After heavy showers of rain, the climb was in prime condition and brought out many different techniques in an endeavour to reach the top. Many British riders – used to observed trials – made feet up ascents, but it was the Germans, using intermediate tread tyres, who showed the way, using full power and footing where necessary.

After many more climbs and descents, and the odd encounter with roaming flocks of sheep, the riders finally set off from Llandrindod on the final morning on smooth major roads en route to Donington Park for the final speed test. Before they were allowed to proceed many riders had to repair the damage sustained in the unforgiving Welsh mountains. Both Billy Tiffen and

Marjorie Cottle changed damaged fork springs. The repairs took Marjorie over half an hour to complete, but by superb riding she was back on time at the first time-control. Sidecar driver, Harry Perry, changed a front wheel while H.F. Edwards had to lash the sidecar body solidly to his Panther chassis before stewards would let him proceed.

After two practice laps of the Donington circuit, riders waited for their group to be called forward for their one-hour speed test, in which they had to attain specific averages in order to qualify for a medal. During the test, which included the two surviving trophy teams, the rain began to fall again slowing the riders and, at one stage, unseating Mauermayer's passenger from the BMW outfit and dragging him along the track for 50 yards. It was at this stage that Graham Walker, who was commentating on the test, noticed that the BMW outfit was falling behind schedule and became very excited. Nothing could be done as the British team could not signal their riders the news, unlike the Germans who had a full

BELOW **The Scott team on their twin cylinder two-strokes. From left to right: A. Jefferies, G. Milne, H. Wheeldon.**

pit crew. When the rain ceased the BMW speeded up and came back on schedule. The test, which included three vase teams, each with clean sheets, was a different matter for this was a race to see who could make the highest average speed. Great Britain A, Ireland A and Germany A each battled on over the hour, but it was the superb riding of the British trio and the slowing of Oettinger's NSU that gave Britain the vase.

1934

The jubilant Germans, responding to their first international win, promptly chose Garmisch-Partenkirchen in the Bavarian Alps to be the showcase venue for the 1934 event. Under the shadow of the mighty snow-capped Zugspitze, the area lent itself to the spirit of the event, with much varied terrain, from leisurely valleys to tortuous mountain passes. With their usual teutonic efficiency, the organizers laid out a 1200 mile course, which encompassed many local beauty spots as well as hazards, many of which were known only to riders from the host nation.

The German trophy team, clad in fresh white overalls for each day, again used 750 BMWs. Mauermayer piloted the sidecar outfit, while Stelzer and Ernst Henne – holder of the world speed record – looked after

the solos. The British trophy team of Bradley on the 600 Sunbeam outfit, Vic Brittain on a 350 Norton and Bert Perrigo on a 350 BSA, looked as if they were in with a chance of winning, but a pulled out tyre valve on the first day dropped Bert Perrigo a mark putting the team in third place at the end.

The climb up Somerberg hill on the second day, was the first major obstacle encountered. The organizers had specified that this hill would be observed, and that any rider unable to climb the hill under his own steam would be forfeited 50 marks if pushed up. First riders to tackle the climb found it relatively easy, however later arrivals found the way up blocked by bogged down and fallen riders, a fate which claimed three-quarters of the field. Of the lady riders, Marjorie Cottle on a 250 BSA and Frau Thouret on a 250 DKW, made excellent climbs, but Miss Crow on a 250 Levis was badly baulked and had to be pushed up. Because of the chaos and subsequent delays the section was scrubbed and all marks were reinstated.

Day 3 brought riders to the foot of the Ettalerberg, a three-quarter mile loosely surfaced climb up a steepening gradient which had caused so much havoc in the 1929 event. This time the going was a little easier, but Doc and Mrs Galloway had to have their Rudge outfit pushed to the top. The yellow Morgan of Henry and Barbara Laird had no problem, the supercharged 1100 JAP motor blasting them to the top in fine style. Maurice Greenwood – a veteran of the first International – was not so lucky for he had to stop and change the plug of his 350 New Imperial, within sight of the top.

On the fifth day riders tackled the Schindelberg Hill, a four-mile climb to within 20 yards of the Austrian border. Having been ridden downhill the previous day, riders feared the worst on the uphill run. The hill saw the retirement of Edyth Foley. After losing first and second gears on her 500 Zündapp the climb was too much for third gear. Out too went Kroll and Klopfer, their diminutive 98cc DKWs crying enough. Even the mighty Mauermayer stopped on the hill with water on the BMWs plug leads, but soon got going again to reach the top unaided.

The last day saw riders heading towards Füssen, for the final speed test. Run over a fast 5½-mile triangular course, the test was to be a shoot out between the German and Italian teams who were still clean. On the way to Füssen Baron von Krohn turned his 791cc Zündapp outfit completely over twice, badly bending the bike frame and sidecar chassis, resulting in the chair wheel leaning outwards some 20 degrees. However, he managed to complete the run and take part in the speed test, to be awarded a gold for his efforts.

When the speed test started, the Italians – mounted on 500cc Gileras – knew that if they kept the German trio in sight, they would win, for they had six minutes in hand over the 750 BMWs. But it was not to be, for Grana – on the solo Gilera – was having trouble with his brakes. Grana was meant to be shadowing Stelzer, but in the end Stelzer lapped the Italian, thereby ensuring the trophy stayed once again in Germany. In the vase contest, the British B team of Thacker, MacGregor and Heath beat the Irish B team by seconds, again decided on the speed test as both teams were still clean. It was a fine finish to a hard but wonderfully organized trial, set in some of the best scenery that Europe can offer. To date, the trial has been based at Garmisch four more times but on each occasion it was a visiting team that returned home with the coveted trophy.

1935

By winning the 1934 International, the Germans played host once more to a gathering of 254 riders from all over Europe to compete in the 17th event of the series. Centred on the town of Oberstdorf in the Bavarian Alps, the route took in not only the Alps, but the Black Forest further to the north, with riders having to complete daily runs of 300 miles or more. The high mileages and the high average speeds required certainly took their toll on riders and machines, with the sidecar entrants receiving more than their fair share of troubles. One major problem throughout the week was one of blinding and choking dust, caused by the absence of rain for a long period. The sun shone brightly every day, but the evenings were cold – below freezing point – which caused many early morning starting problems, due to thickening oil.

The first day's run through the mountains saw Great Britain, Italy and France all lose marks for timekeeping, due to the rough going and the high average speed required. The highlight of the second day was a 25-mile thrash up the newly constructed Munich *autobahn*, with the supercharged BMWs leading the way. This test was not without its mishaps as some riders came to grief, mainly due to collisions and contact with other riders. On the third day, it was the sidecar drivers who suffered most. Peter Bradley of the British trophy team retired with engine trouble on his 599cc Sunbeam. Gilera of the Italian trophy team fractured the sidecar chassis of his 600 Gilera outfit, and was also forced into retirement. The supercharged 600 BMW outfit of Kraus and Müller was involved in a spectacular spill, upending the outfit and rendering the passenger, Müller, unconscious. Kraus, one time passenger to Mauermayer, righted the outfit and placed his helpless passenger in the sidecar and drove the remaining six miles to the end of the day's run. On seeing Kraus and his apparently sleeping passenger clock in, rumours began to spread that the Germans were having an easy time.

Titisee, the finish of the day's run, lay on the shores of a beautiful lake in the heart of the Black Forest, where the locals dispensed throat-burning schnapps to the tired riders. It was this medicine that finally revived the unconscious Müller. The return run to the Bavarian

Even the chef comes out to watch H Laird (1096cc Morgan) roar by under the shadow of the fairytale-like castle at Hohen-Schwangan during the final speed test session of the 1935 ISDT in Germany

Alps the following day saw more sidecar crews in trouble. Doc and Mrs Galloway retired, not for mechanical problems, but from sheer exhaustion, for the rough going had caught them unprepared and out of training. Henry and Barbara Laird tore off a front brake anchorage on the yellow Morgan, but managed to keep going. Kraus once more turned his BMW over, this time breaking two of his ribs. This time Müller was unharmed and the pair carried on to complete the run unpenalized.

On the fifth day riders tackled the Oberjoch, a climb to 4000 ft within sight of the Austrian border with 105 tight bends. Excellently surfaced and closed to traffic, riders used every inch of the road and enjoyed the experience. Baron von Krohn on his four-cylinder Zündapp outfit was first man up, before the sun had risen, with spectacular full throttle three-wheel drifts. The BSA of Marjorie Cottle had been spitting back through the carburettor for some time, and Marjorie had got used to dowsing the flames, but at the control on top of the hill, when the machine was restarted, it did it again. This time an efficient German timekeeper leapt into action and emptied the contents of his fire bucket over the

carburettor. It contained cement dust and promptly stopped the engine for good. Marjorie, none too pleased with the episode, retired.

On the last day – a 150-mile run to Füssen for the final one-hour speed test – the Germans were in the lead with zero marks lost to the Czechs' 22. But on the run in Stelzer smashed the cam box of his supercharged 500 BMW when he came off on a corner, the resulting repairs cost him 25 marks and reversed the result. During the speed test this result was reversed when Vitvar blew up the engine of his 350 Jawa and saddled the Czechs with a further 40 marks, giving the Germans the trophy for the third time. In the vase contest Geiss, Winkler and Kluge, riding 250 DKWs – with zero marks lost – secured Germany's first win with Czechoslovakia runners-up.

Tribute must go to the 130 finishers of this arduous event, held in a truly beautiful part of southern Germany, for riders had precious little time to view the glorious scenery as the high daily averages meant that they had to put all their concentration into staying on the road. When it was all over participants relaxed, some taking a ride on the funicular railway to the 6000 ft sumit of the Neibelhorn, oblivious of the fact that the manufacturer's three-year guarantee had run out a week previously. This fact meant little to them, for it was a far more dangerous and demanding task to actually compete and survive the International.

The 1936 event was also staged by Germany, but this time with its centre at Freudenstat. Note Nazi storm troopers on right of picture

1936

Der Deutsche Automobil Club took on the responsibility of organizing the 1936 International Six Days Trial, which was based on the Black Forest town of Freudenstadt. Against tradition, the event started on Thursday 17 September, the first half being based in the Black Forest, but on the Saturday evening riders reported to the Olympic Stadium near Garmisch, which was to be the base for the second part. With an event of such importance, military manoeuvres were curtailed for the duration, freeing the vast resources of the German Army to help with organizational and marshalling duties. German military teams even entered the event, top club honours going to Kraftfahr Lehr-und Ver-

suchs – Abtig Wünsdprf. a trio of army BMWs. It is not surprising that of the 249 starters, 138 were on home ground, the second highest contingent being from Great Britain and Ireland with 53 riders. Of the trophy teams entered, the German trio of Kraus, Stelzer and Henne were the most formidable but up against Brittain, Rowley and Waycott of the British team. Czechoslovakia again entered a Jawa-mounted team, but this time without Frantisek Brand who had been killed in a road accident.

The first day was a disaster for the sidecar outfits, as Czech trophy driver, Dusil, retired after crashing his 595cc Jawa combo, and both the French and Italian trophy sidecar crews retired after spills. Doc Galloway did not have an easy day for he lost marks repairing a broken fork spindle, caused by the rough going. The terrain and the tight time schedule soon saw Stanislav of the Czech trophy team crash out, and Walfried Winkler of the German vase A team losing many marks after damaging his gearbox footchange mechanism. Heiner Fleischmann, of the German vase B team, suffered three punctures in a row and also lost marks for subsequent lateness.

Day 2 was an easier run through mainly flatter areas within the forest, but danger lurked in the gloom under the trees. Hidden rocks and tree stumps were waiting to catch the unwary. However, it was not a rock which caused the retirement of Henry Laird but a mechanical disaster, for he blew the big-end of his yellow Morgan.

Saturday saw riders tackle the Ziegelwasen, a loosely surfaced hill, which was timed, but this caused little problem even in pouring rain. It was the timed road section later in the day that saw many riders drop marks for timekeeping. This was not the case for Stuart Waycott, piloting the Velo outfit for the British trophy team, who romped through it enjoying every minute. The route headed southwards into the Bavarian Alps, via Füssen and Oberammergau – scene of the passion play – to the Olympic Stadium at Garmisch, which became the new trial headquarters.

Day 4 saw riders heading down the new Munich *autobahn* to the Konigssee, a huge lake where riders took a lunch break and a boat trip, or just lay in the now brilliant sunshine. On the return to base, riders had to complete a 6½-mile high speed test on the *autobahn* at Siegsdorf, followed by a speed hillclimb at Kesselberg. Halfway through the climb a thunderstorm broke and drowned the track, but this again was no problem for Stuart Waycott who matched the times of the fastest BMW outfits. The final run back to base via Berchtesgaden, was completed in brilliant sunshine once again.

The sun shone again on the Monday when riders tackled the Ammerbrucke hillclimb. Again timed, it was only a mile in length but very dusty. Up until this point Germany and Great Britain had been level, but this changed when Henne seized his BMW not once, but twice, during the climb, losing two marks. Other riders to fall off were Alan Jefferies of the British vase team, and Villa of the Italian trophy team who parted company with his 500 Gilera.

The run to Füssen on the last day saw the trophy safe in the hands of Great Britain, but in the vase contest four teams still had clean sheets. Great Britain's A and B teams, Holland A and Austria B had to fight it out on the speed test to see who was to take home the vase. Before leaving Garmisch in the morning Henne fitted a new piston to his BMW in an endeavour to stop any further seizures, but in doing so dropped a further 15 marks which put Britain further in the lead. During the one-hour speed test, teams lapped with no problems, and it was the all Rudge-mounted Scottish trio of MacGregor, Leslie and Edwards who made the best average and took the vase for the British B team.

So the three-year domination of the event by the highly efficient German teams came to an end. Participating riders remembered the venues, the scenery and the organizational prowess of this very enthusiastic host nation. Even the heightened military presence did not appear to bother them for it was now Great Britain's turn to put on the next event.

1937

Having lost the trophy on home ground in 1936 the Germans were determined to win it back at all costs – an edict from the headman in Berlin – and descended on Llandrindod Wells in force. Having arrived in Southampton by sea the previous week, the German contingent (79 riders and 60 back-up crew), made their way to Wales where practice and course recce began in earnest. Military personnel abounded from all echelons of the German army, their units recognizable by the riding outfits worn. Field-grey leathers of the normal army units, light-brown one piece suits of the Storm Troopers and the black leathers of the SS. The trophy trio comprised of Stelzer and George Meier on 500 BMWs, with Kraus piloting the 600 BMW outfit. Henne had been dropped due to injuries received whilst racing cars. Up against the Germans were the British trio of George Rowley on a 350 AJS, Vic Brittain on an overhead cam 350 Norton, whilst Stuart Waycott again drove the Velo outfit which had been enlarged to 600cc especially for the event. The cylinder head finning of the over-sized Velo was so massive and the spark plug so inaccessible, that a tube was inserted into the petrol tank body to enable an extra long tube spanner to reach the plug.

Traditionally, the International is always held in September but this year it was brought forward to July in the hope of beating the wet weather that prevails in Wales at that time of year. The change of date meant that riders would have to be extra wary of the tourist holiday traffic as well as the problem with spectators and wandering sheep. Generally during the event the weather was fine, except for the first morning when teeming rain greeted the 213 starters who collected their bikes from the covered *parc fermé*. Anticipating the weather, the ACU had thoughtfully provided another covered area so that riders could wait in comfort before claiming their machines. Dead on 6 am the first riders got away and it was not long before the first casualty was reported. Dutch Harley-Davidson sidecar driver, H.M. Persoon, had taken a right-hander too quickly and clouted his passenger's head against a wall. After a quick stop to assess damage, the pair carried on but the passenger had a nasty cut over his eye. The two major climbs of the day were Allt-y-Budy and Doly-wern, Klopfer distinguishing himself on both with his diminutive 98cc DKW. Marjorie Cottle, on her 250 BSA, and Frau Thouret, on a 245cc DKW, both received standing ovations from the appreciative crowd for their efforts, but Harold Tozer turned over his 500 BSA outfit and retired.

LEFT **German Trophy team for the 1937 ISDT at Llandrindod Wells. Left to right; L Kraus, J Stelzer, G Meier. All rode BMW flat twins**

BELOW **The 1937 Irish Vase 'A' team who lost no marks. Left to right: R C Yeates, H L Archer and C W Duffin**

The first three days were very easy, with policemen out in force clearing the holiday traffic in favour of the International riders. Early going was not difficult and offered little excitement, but was interesting and of great scenic value.

On Thursday the pace hotted up but was marred by dust and low cloud up in the mountains. Conditions, or poor route marking – for this was criticized at times – caused Vitvar of the Czech trophy team to go off course

and run out of petrol before he could return to the route. Stewart, of the Irish vase B team, also got lost but only forfeited marks for their errors. Doc Galloway, too, was a victim of poor route marking but realized his error and got back on course without penalty. Retirements were beginning to mount, with Tommy Meeten going out after a prang on his 172 SOS, and Dutchman, Eysink, breaking the frame of his 122 Villiers-powered Eysink. After the day's run back at Llandrindod, 19 riders took the opportunity to change tyres with Stelzer completing the job on the rear of his BMW in under two minutes due to the special detachable rim flanges used by a number of the German entrants.

After Friday's mainly uneventful run both the British and the German trophy teams were still clean, together with the British vase A team, Ireland A, Holland B and both German teams. The final speed test – held again at Donington Park – was once more going to be the decider. After a week's punishment in the mountains it was a welcome respite to be able to ride on flat roads, but some bikes cried enough. Marjorie Cottle's BSA blew up in the middle of the speed test, but she still gained a bronze medal. With five teams still clean, the speed test for the vase contest became a needle match. Mohrke and Forstner of the German vase A army team, both dropped their BMWs at Coppice corner, but remounted and took the chequered flag. However, a protest from the Dutch team reversed the result as it was discovered that Moejes had been missed by the lap scorers on lap twelve. The vase then went to Holland. In the trophy speed test it was the solos that the result hinged on, the 500 BMWs having to complete 19 laps against the 18 of the British 350s. George Meier led for most of the test but George Rowley and Vic Brittain stayed with him to take the trophy for Great Britain by the merest margin of ten seconds.

The Germans returned to the Fatherland to rethink their strategy, to practice and to try harder next time, after all, the national pride of the German people was at stake . . . they had to win the trophy the following year.

1938

Having been denied the trophy by the smallest of margins for the last two years, the Germans mounted another all out effort in 1938. As in the previous year, the team arrived in Southampton – on board the Europa – a week before the start and headed straight for Cheltenham for a two-day stay to acclimatize themselves. From there, they moved to Nottingham for a further three days to get in some practice at Donington Park and the last few days were spent in Llandrindod Wells with more practice in the Welsh hills. As the British trophy team used thinly disguised TT machines – all ohc racers – the Germans decided to tread the same path, equipping their team with a trio of 175 blown DKWs and a 600cc BMW outfit, for the rules had been changed to three solos and a sidecar in the trophy contest. The DKWs were chosen for their turn of speed – comparable to a 250 – and to take advantage of the lower speed averages required of the smaller machines. They were ridden by Demmelbaur, Fähler and Scheizer, while the BMW was piloted by Kraus. Up against the Germans were the Czechs and the dominant British team of George Rowley, Jack Williams, Vic Brittain and Stuart Waycott.

In addition to the rule change governing the trophy

team riders, two further awards were to be competed for by three-man club teams. *Korpsführer* Adolf Hühnlein, who was leader of the sport in Germany, donated a trophy to be competed for by clubs, regiments and organizations whose riders were not members of the trophy, vase or manufacturers' teams. Percy Butler – a staunch supporter of the trial – also donated a British trophy called the Club Challenge Trophy, to be contested in a similar way by three-man teams, with the exception that no rider was debarred for being a member of the vase, trophy or manufacturers' teams.

With these new awards in mind, 209 riders set off from Llandrindod Wells at 6 am on 11 July in driving rain and mist, heading for the Black Mountains and day one of the trial. Flooded roads and swollen rivers caused riders many problems, but it was the condition of the many hills that had to be climbed which led to the loss of marks and retirements. Conditions were so severe that over the week 127 retired. Of the 82 finishers only 32 brave souls gained a gold medal. The sidecar crews found it particularly gruelling as only two of the original 37 starters finished the course. Day one saw many holdups on the hillclimbs, but it was on the second day that the hopes of both Czechoslovakia and Germany were dashed. The 590 Jawa of sidecar man Juhan, went out with engine problems, Kraus retired when he broke the sidecar chassis of his BMW, and Fähler split the tank of his 175 DKW. Other sidecar men in trouble were Baron von Krohn, who dislocated his shoulder when he turned his Zündapp outfit over, and H. Croucher who retired after upending his Panther outfit. Stuart Waycott dropped five marks for bad timekeeping on the third day, but was not unduly perturbed for the British trophy team was well in the lead at this stage. Waycott lost a further four marks that afternoon, again for lateness, but at least he was getting through where other drivers were failing. Harold Taylor was forced into retirement at the same control, with a broken chassis on his 997 Ariel outfit, sustained after taking risks to make up time after stopping to render assistance to J. Hecker who was trapped under his upturned Zündapp outfit. The going was getting tougher and by the end of the day, only seven outfits remained in the running. The third day also saw Scheizer retire when his DKW split its fuel tank, relegating the Germans to third place, with 503 marks lost.

On Saturday the British vase A team dropped one mark which let the German A team into the lead as they were still clean. Great Britain dropped a further seven marks the following day which relegated them to third place, behind Sweden. But the German trio captained by George Meier, remained clean to the end.

The final speed test at Donington Park was an anticlimax, after what many riders considered to be the most arduous International since its beginning in 1913. Run in wet conditions, many riders rode fast enough to retain their medals, but slow enough to stay out of

trouble. Hero of the test, for running more than half an hour on a flat rear tyre, was Vitvar of the Czech trophy team, this feat earning him a gold medal.

The German effort had failed to regain the coveted trophy which stayed in Great Britain for another year, but they did not go home empty-handed, for with them went the vase, the Hühnlein Trophy and the Club Challenge Trophy. The latter two awards were won by the SS team of Patina, Mundhenke and Zimmerman, mounted on 494cc BMWs. Runners-up in both these contests were the similarly mounted NSKK (Mobile Storm Troopers) team.

As far as resuls go this event marked the end of the decade, but one further event was to take place before Europe was plunged into war. Now known as the 'Salzburg incident' is related in the next chapter. The decade will best be remembered for the effort poured into the event by the German government and motorcycle industry to win the trophy three times against the masterful British teams. The sheer weight of numbers of riders and teams, the technical expertise and the excellent machinery which the Germans fielded, showed what a professional approach could achieve. This professionalism was not lost during the dark days of war but was to emerge again some two decades later with the loyalties of the German people separated by the Iron Curtain.

ABOVE **Group of riders at Redgate Corner, Donington Park during 1937 ISDT speed tests. Numbers 85 and 143 are German Vase teamsters**

BELOW **The British rider Tyrell-Smith at the start line with the 350cc Excelsior Manxman which he rode in the 1938 ISDT. At the moment the photograph was taken Tyrell-Smith is counting off the seconds to go before his starting time**

CHAPTER THREE

The Salzburg incident

Nothing demonstrates more clearly the truly international nature of the ISDT than the dramatic political events with which it has been associated. Despite claims to the contrary, history does have a habit of repeating itself and the event was associated with the circumstances surrounding the declaration of both world wars.

In 1914 the first truly international ISDT was to have been based in Grenoble in the south-eastern corner of France. (The 1913 'international' was really only a class in the English Six Days Trial.) Throughout the first six months of 1914 the crisis in Europe was deepening and the assassination of Archduke Ferdinand of Austria at Sarajevo on 28 June was only the spark which ignited a huge bonfire which had already been laid. Britain actually declared war on Germany on 4 August, in alliance, of course, with France. Not to put too fine a point upon it the south-eastern corner of France was not a healthy place to be in during the summer of 1914. *Motor Cycling* reported, however, that despite the ominous situation, a large party of British riders set out for the event. It can only be assumed that they were either blissfully ignorant of what was going on or, and more likely, they had the blinkers of the true motorcyclist with a major event in his sights. By the time the party reached Grenoble the event had been postponed, all foreigners had been given 24 hours to leave France and the French army had commandeered all petrol supplies, at least in cities and major towns.

Undaunted, all but two of the entrants set off back to Le Havre, obtaining fuel in villages which presumably had not been visited by the army. Most of them managed the journey on their own wheels in 27 hours. Maurice Greenwood and his friends had their machines confiscated by the French army in Lyons and finished the journey by troop train. Messrs Pressland and Chater Lea (yes, *the* Chater Lea!) decided that they would not waste the opportunity for a touring holiday and set off on their machines over the Col du Galibier. *Motor Cycling* was still wondering where they were several weeks later. They must have got back but their story remains untold. So much for 1914. It would seem that neither the ACU, the Foreign Office nor the competitors had memories of these events when August 1939 came around.

This book is not a history of Europe, but of the ISDT. Nevertheless the events of August/September 1939 and their forerunners had such a dramatic effect

on the event held in that year that they cannot be ignored.

By March 1938 Adolf Hitler's National Socialist Germany was rampant in European affairs. Committed to racial purity and therefore waging a frightful campaign against the Jews, Hitler was also seeking *Lebensraum* (living space) for the German people, and therefore seeking to take over all territories where there were significant numbers of people of German origin. On 14 March 1938 his forces marched into Austria which simply became another German province. This fact obviously confused the British motorcycle press which could not make up its mind in 1939 whether Salzburg, the headquarters of the ISDT, was in Austria or Germany!

On 24 March, Neville Chamberlain, the British Prime Minister, promised to support France and Belgium if they were attacked, but Germany's next victim was to be Czechoslovakia. An understanding existed between France and Britain to defend Czechoslovakia but it was a rather vague affair. In fact Britain was prepared to deal with Germany over Czechoslovakia and on 30 September Chamberlain, with Daladier of France, virtually handed the destiny of the Czechs to Germany and Italy with the signing of the infamous Munich Agreement. It was this which enabled Chamberlain to fly home with the famous 'peace in our time' agreement. Czechoslovakia was forced to surrender much of its territory to Germany, some also being lost to Poland and Hungary. On 5 October 1938 the German army marched into the Sudetenland. Of course this was not the end of the story and in March 1939 Hitler and his forces invaded and occupied the remainder of Czechoslovakia. It was clear that his next move would be against Poland and on 31 March Britain and France at last decided to make a stand if Poland was invaded. At last it seemed that Britain would be prepared to go to war to prevent further German aggression.

So, with the storm clouds clearly gathering over Poland, which Britain was committed to defend, weapon production and civil defence measures were taking increasing priority. However, the ACU continued with arrangements for British competitors travelling to the ISDT based in southern Germany. The fact that Germany would be the hosts in 1939 was due to the new FIM rule that no nation could host more than two consecutive events and the 1937 and 1938 events were based at Llandrindod Wells. Following high retirement rates and numerous casualties in 1938, the ACU was probably quite happy about this. It may also seem a little strange that the Germans should have continued with preparations to run the event in the light of their military priorities. It seems probable, however, that Hitler did not expect Britain or France to declare war on behalf of Poland. Britain had already backed down at Munich over Czechoslovakia, as she was patently not ready for war and the German leader knew that a non-aggression pact would soon be signed with Russia, freeing his forces to concentrate on the Western Front if necessary. The ISDT was a prestigious event everywhere in Europe except Britain, as it remains today. The patron and figurehead at Salzburg was to be *Korpsführer* (General) Adolf Hühnlein of the NSKK (motorized wing of the SA) and the clerk of the course *Standartenführer* Rühling of the SS! It was obvious that there would be no shortage of personnel or transport. It has been suggested also that the Germans would have preferred not to run the event but that 61 British entrants were too many to turn away when Hitler was seeking to avoid conflict with Britain. Whatever the truth of the matter the event went on as planned.

As far as the British entrants were concerned they were all assured by the ACU that the political situation would not become tense! The ACU could hardly be blamed for this because they had received this assurance from the Foreign Office. Just to be on the safe side, however, all competitors were issued with an official letter explaining why they were in Germany and asking for special consideration if there should be any trouble. Fred Perks, riding a 496cc BSA in the CSMA (Civil Service Motoring Association) team, recalls that the ACU advised competitors to reply to *Heil Hitler* with *Heil König* (Hail King) and a military salute!

Perhaps the best epitaph for this rather crazy situation is *Motor Cycling*'s editorial dated 23 August 1939:

> Whatever the result, it is a struggle which contains a moral for an insane world. At this time – when politicians issue threat and counter threat, when the Press of the world breathes suspicion and distrust – it is refreshing to escape from the frenzied outpourings of inspired propagandists and to view three great countries fighting a bloodless battle for natural prestige and world trade – the very things which threaten to plunge Europe into war.

In the end there were 278 entries for the event, including the British trophy and vase A and B teams. Three teams were to contest the trophy: Great Britain, Germany and Italy. The Italians were not mentioned in the early notification and there was some suggestion that they had been 'encouraged' by the German organizers. The vase was to be contested by these three nations together with Holland and Sweden. The full list was as follows:

The 1939 'International' entries
TROPHY TEAMS
BRITAIN

Entrant	Rider	Machine
Norton Motors, Ltd.	V. N. Brittain	490 Norton
Associated Motor Cycles	G. E. Rowley	347 A.J.S.
Triumph Engineering Co., Ltd.	A. Jefferies	498 Triumph
Norton Motors, Ltd.	H. J. Flook	596 Norton s.c.

GERMANY

L. Kraus (600 B.M.W. s.c.)	W. Fahler (250 D.K.W.)
R.. Seltsam (500 B.M.W.)	or
O. Sensburg (250 D.K.W.)	R. Demmelbauer (250 D.K.W.)

VASE TEAMS
BRITAIN 'A'

Ariel Motors, Ltd.	L. Heath	497 Ariel
Ariel Motors, Ltd.	G.F. Povey	497 Ariel
W. T. Tiffen and Son	W. T. Tiffen, Jnr.	348 Velocette

BRITAIN 'B'

C. N. Rogers	C. N. Rogers	346 Royal Enfield
Ariel Motors, Ltd.	W. A. West	497 Ariel
Triumph Engineering Co., Ltd.	J. H. Wood	343 Triumph

GERMANY 'A'

J. von Krohn	600 Zundapp s.c.
R. Grenz	600 Zundapp s.c.
J. Hecker	600 Zundapp s.c.

GERMANY 'B'

F. Lindhart	500 B.M.W.
J. Forstner	500 B.M.W.
H. Lodermeier	500 B.M.W.

HOLLAND 'A'

J. Moejes	500 B.M.W.
G. A. de Ridder	500 B.M.W.
J. E. Fyma	500 Ariel

HOLLAND 'B'

J. J. Bovee	350 Velocette
J van Rijn	350 Velocette
D. Rencoy	350 Eysink

SWEDEN / ITALY 'A' / ITALY 'B'

SWEDEN	ITALY 'A'		ITALY 'B'	
Carl Hedelin	Benzoni	Sertum	Cavanna	Guzzi
Folkë Larsson	Francone	Sertum	Ramazotti	Gilera
Seth Lindvall	Brunetto	Sertum	Ventura	Mas

ARMY TEAMS

War Office	Sgt.-Major B. Mackay	347 Matchless
War Office	Sgt. O. Davies	347 Matchless
War Office	B.Q.M.S. E. Smith	347 Matchless
War Office	Pte. J. L. Wood	496 B.S.A.
War Office	Cpl. A. C. Doyle	496 B.S.A.
War Office	Sgt. F. M. Rist	496 B.S.A.
War Office	Lieut. J. F. Riley	490 Norton
War Office	Sgt. J. T. Dalby	490 Norton
War Office	Cpl. G. M. Berry	490 Norton

* CLUB TEAMS

Civil Service		South-Eastern Centre	
L. Ridgway	496 B.S.A.	J. F. Whitfield	498 B.M.W.
F. C. Perks	496 B.S.A.	H. N. Toomey	498 Panther
F. A. Whitehouse	496 B.S.A.	T. N. Blockley	497 B.S.A.

Sunbeam 'A'		Huhnlein Trophy Team (Sweden)
G. Godber-Ford	347 Sunbeam	Carl Govan Dahl
Miss Marjorie Cottle	249 Triumph	Bertil Nilsson
A. A. Sanders	343 Triumph	Thor Lauren

RIGHT **British Army team riders 1939 ISDT. Their BSA singles were three of only 12 manufactured. Specification included hairpin valve springs and alloy cylinder heads. Army team was well in the running before it had to pull out of the trial on the Friday**

"The Motor Cycle," September 14th, 1939.

YOUR PETROL RATIONS: HELPFUL ADVICE

THE MOTOR CYCLE

3D

SALE THREE TIMES THAT
OF ANY SIMILAR JOURNAL

FOUNDED 1903.

CIRCULATES THROUGHOUT THE WORLD

No. 1901 Vol. 63

Thursday, September 14th, 1939

The British Army Team in the 1939 International Six Days Trial—

L/Cpl. A. C. Doyle, Sgt. F. M. Rist, Pte. S. Wood, who, at the time of their withdrawal on the fifth day

HAD NOT LOST A SINGLE MARK

riding

B.S.A

The B.S.A. Army Team was the only British Army Team with a clean sheet
The B.S.A. Team (J. Amott, J. Ashworth and H. Tozer) also had a clean
sheet when withdrawn

B.S.A. CYCLES LTD., 47, Armoury Rd., B'ham, 11

MANUFACTURERS' TEAMS

A.J.S.
T. C. Whitton	347 A.J.S.
D. A. Gulliford	246 A.J.S.
G. E. Rowley	347 A.J.S.

Ariel 'A'
G. F. Povey	497 Ariel
L. Heath	497 Ariel
W. A. West	497 Ariel

Ariel 'B'
H. R. Taylor	997 Ariel s.c.
S. E. Cunningham	497 Ariel
W. H. J. Peacock	997 Ariel s.c.

B.S.A.
J. H. Amott	496 B.S.A.
H. Tozer	496 B.S.A.
J. Ashworth	249 B.S.A.

Matchless
C. Edge	347 Matchless
G. E. Eighteen	347 Matchless
Wag. Bennett	347 Matchless

Norton
H. J. Flook	596 Norton s.c.
V. N. Brittain	348 Norton
J. E. Breffitt	348 Norton

Panther
J. S. Boote	349 Panther
R. Wilkinson	348 Panther
F. W. Whittle	598 Panther s.c.

Royal Enfield
C. N. Rogers	346 Royal Enfield
J. J. Booker	346 Royal Enfield
F. V. Chambers	346 Royal Enfield

Triumph
A. J. Jefferies	498 Triumph
J. H. Wood	343 Triumph
H. Sim	343 Triumph

OTHER ENTRANTS

Graham Oates	997 Ariel s.c.	E. Williams	350 Royal Enfield
J. White	348 Ariel	C. Jayne	348 Royal Enfield
J. H. Bryant	348 Ariel	Dr. R. L. Galloway	499 Rudge s.c.
T. Mooney	497 Ariel	L. E. C. Hall	499 Rudge s.c.
Lieut. R. C. K. Money	496 B.S.A.	R. Clayton	343 Triumph
C. R. Bates	348 B.S.A.	J. A. Hitchcock	249 Triumph
F. Fletcher	125 Excelsior	R. R. Meier	343 Triumph

Many and various methods of transport were employed for the route to Salzburg. Geoff Godber-Ford of the Sunbeam A team travelled by rail with Fred Neill and the AMC team. Their bikes were sent separately. The British Army teams travelled by staff car and trucks in convoy. The CSMA team had a variety of transport. Fred Perks dismantled his iron-barrelled 496cc BSA Silver Star and inserted it into his Standard 9 saloon from which some seats had been removed. Les Ridgway travelled by train with his bike. Fred Whitehouse carried his bike, which like Ridgway's was a 496cc M24 Gold Star from the BSA factory, on the sidecar chassis of his Ariel sidecar outfit. Harold Tozer, the BSA team's sidecar man, towed the outfit behind his car on a trailer and travelled in company with Perks and Whitehouse. Fred Perks had decided that the conditions would favour the 'softer' iron motor of the Silver Star which he had had fully equipped with extras. In addition to the new Dunlop competition front tyre he carried a CO_2 bottle and a clock, spare spokes (taped to forks and chainstays), spare bulbs (taped inside headlamp), extra long tyre levers (clipped under fuel tank) and the usual plasticine to waterproof the electrics.

On arrival in Salzburg there seems to have been little to complain about apart from the continental breakfast at the Pitter Hotel. The atmosphere seemed relatively relaxed, despite the presence of large numbers of uniformed SA men (brownshirts), although petrol was in short supply for non-competitors. 'Cyclops' report in the 23 August edition of *Motor Cycling* spoke of beautiful scenery, a most hearty welcome and 'utmost hospitality and respect'. Indeed, he went as far as to say that, 'if the political situation could be settled as easily and as

amicably as the Six Days, wars would never occur again in the history of the world!'

Of particular interest was the welcome given to the three Army teams commanded by Lt. Col. Bennett. He was full of praise for the wonderful reception given to him and his men. In stark contrast, only a week later *Motor Cycling* commented: 'The 1939 International Six Days Trial – the twenty-first of the series – will go down in history as the biggest tragedy that has ever befallen a British contingent competing in the world's classic.' In fact it was a case of international sport being swept away by international politics. In a curious way the event itself continued to function in a vacuum for several days before the political crisis overwhelmed it and, as the accounts of riders, team managers and even journalists testify, there was little obvious cause for concern. After all, up to 300 miles a day of tough going can blot out everything else!

The event itself was held in mountainous terrain ranging far and wide from Salzburg and often on poor second-class roads and unmade tracks. Daily mileages varied from 230 to almost 300. On Monday 21st, the first day, the route went into the Sudeten area of Czechoslovakia around which the 1938 crisis had revolved. The second day was spent in the Salzkammergut area. On Wednesday the riders tackled a route which included the famous Grossglockner Pass, while on Thursday and Friday they competed respectively in the Austrian Tirol and the Bavarian mountains.

Politically speaking it does seem that the British

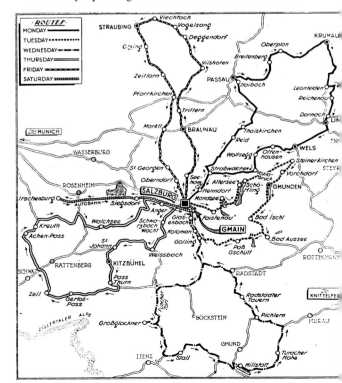

German and British competitors sit side-by-side in the sun at Salzburg in late August 1939...a few days later the two countries would be at war. Number 52 is Allan Jefferies (Triumph Speed Twin)

entry was very naïve for no one seems to have noticed that the first day – 21 August – was also marked by the signing in Moscow of the Nazi-Soviet non-aggression pact which virtually made World War II inevitable. However, the event started as planned.

The two innovations for 1939 were the introduction of the mandatory requirement for two different capacities of solo machines in trophy teams and a cross-country speed test on the final day. The latter was of considerable interest. The test, at Gmain near Salzburg, was 6 miles long and set in terrain resembling Bagshot Heath, which suited the British riders very well. Three laps were to be covered and Britain hoped to do very well on it, especially with the new competition tyres that were available.

Monday 21 August offered a 295-mile route into Czechoslovakia and back! The weather was excellent and the poor second-class roads and tracks were mainly

dry and dusty. The British entrants mostly seemed to prefer wetter conditons to lay the dust and bind the loose, gravelly surfaces into a consistency more to their liking. Presumably this meant more like home! There was not much difficulty with the times set and the British trophy and vase teams remained 'clean'. Not everyone had an uneventful day, however. B.Q.M.S. Smith of the Army team hit a bus and finished the day with badly bent forks and front wheel. Cpl. Berry collided with a dog and completed the day operating the throttle of his Norton by pulling on the inner cable. To complete a sad day for the Army, Lt. Riley's Norton suffered a split fuel tank which he repaired temporarily with a bar of soap. The CSMA team had a good day. Perks, Ridgway and Whitehouse were all on time. Geoff Godber-Ford also had a good day on his Sunbeam and remembered that it was hot and dusty but the organization was 'marvellous'.

Tuesday's 230-mile route into the Salzkammergut was also blessed with a good deal of sunshine although there was a thunderstorm late in the day. The unhappy B.Q.M.S. Smith attacked his Matchless front wheel and forks with a sledgehammer at the start, but failed to make it roadworthy. Berry's replacement twistgrip suf-

One of the Italian overhead cam 250 Sertum's which were so successful in the Salzburg event

fered sticking problems and, having been cast off several times, he was forced to retire. Lt. Riley's petrol tank proved impossible to repair. Sgt. Dalby was riding the only surviving Army Norton and it, too, had a leaking tank. In all there were 24 retirements that day, making a total of 39 over the two days. These included Billy Tiffen jun. from the British Vase A team whose 348cc Velocette also sprang a leak in its fuel tank. The Italian Trophy team was docked two marks when Macchi, on a 500cc Gilera, lost time. Harold Taylor, taking avoiding action with a car, put his 1000cc Ariel outfit in a ditch, bending the front end severely and retiring. This made a total of nine British retirements. Meanwhile, Alan Jefferies (Triumph 500) of the trophy team punctured but managed to stay on time. The CSMA team found this a harder day but managed to stay on time. Geoff Godber-Ford also found it harder but succeeded in maintaining the tight schedule. He also recalled a German sidecar outfit diving into a lake, where it probably still remains.

This day was also marked by the seemingly inevitable disputes over rules. It was not at all clear whether lights must work or not and, as a result of protests, the jury decided on Tuesday evening that the rule that lights must work would apply. There were also disputes about tools, resolved by a jury statement that only tools, spares and materials carried by the riders or on the machines could be used but that these could be exchanged between riders. Repairs to the machines could only be carried out by the riders, or the passenger

in the case of sidecar outfits. Incidentally, on the Wednesday evening the jury rescinded the rule about lights, thus relieving a lot of worries.

Wednesday's route took in the 14½-mile climb of the Grossglockner Pass. The climb was timed and its innumerable bends and hairpins seemed daunting. In fact the times caused little difficulty. There were many comments about the 'tidy' style of the British riders on the cobblestone surfaced bends, and riders commented on seeing numerous footrest and control levers lying about! At the end of the day the British and German trophy teams remained clean, together with six vase teams including Great Britain B, known to the other British riders as the 'boys' because of their relative youth. The Army BSAs were still clean and going very well indeed. The BSAs of Pte. Wood, Cpl. Doyle and Sgt. Fred Rist were of particular interest, so much so that Bert Perrigo, BSA's competition manager, was with the Army team to look after their interests. The 496cc M24 Gold Stars were really the ancestors of the post-war all conquering 'Goldies'. Twelve prototypes with alloy cylinder heads with hairpin valve springs were rushed through in 1939 and some of these went to the Army and to Les Ridgway and Fred Whitehouse of the CSMA team. Fred Perks, the third member of the CSMA team, preferred to use the iron-engined M23. With a combination of excellent machinery, Perrigo's expertise and the administrative backing of the large Army team, the BSAs were well in the running to win the Hühnlein Trophy for Service, Police and Club teams.

Godber-Ford thought that although Wednesday's

route sounded easier, a combination of early mist, slippery wooden bridges and dangerous level-crossings conspired to make it quite difficult. Unlike many of his compatriots, he found the Sunbeam losing power on the climb of the Grossglockner Pass and remembered clocking 80 mph on the descent to make up time. A number of riders complained about the high speeds necessary to keep up with the time schedules. Wednesday was a black day for the CSMA and Les Ridgway lost 11 marks for late arrival. Also on this day Norman Brockley, their 'travelling support' rider, went missing and was not traced for some time.

Unhappily, while the riders continued to do well, the political situation was deteriorating all the time. On Wednesday evening there were major discussions about courses of action, including the possibility of immediate withdrawal and a return home. Strange to say, the major source of information was the BBC News broadcast which announced that France had advised all of its nationals to withdraw from Germany within 24 hours. Moreover, Lt. Money, riding a BSA as an individual competitor, and a civil servant who was spectating at the event, had both received telegrams instructing them to return home immediately. The other side of the coin was the complete calm exhibited by the Army team management, who clearly intended to continue, and the strong position of our teams in all the major classes.

In the end the team managers decided to continue on Thursday but to keep bags packed ready for a quick departure. Of course it was not until the situation deteriorated further that it was realized that once the riders left the start, from 5 am onwards, it was virtually impossible to reach them until the end of the day.

Thursday was a difficult day both on and off the course. A 290-mile route in the Tirol proved to be the most difficult of all so far. The most serious incident caused the British trophy team to lose four marks. At a crucial refuelling point the organizers had provided only one truck and were issuing small quantities to riders. Harold Flook with the Norton sidecar outfit in the British team was given only five litres. Following a protest this was increased to an inadequate seven litres by officials who were not very helpful. Eventually he ran out of fuel and only managed to reach the finish late by borrowing petrol from a passing car. George Rowley was also forced to protest in order to obtain enough fuel to continue successfully.

It certainly seemed that the brownshirt organizers were becoming increasingly jumpy and less prepared to argue. At the end of the day the British vase B team was still clean, along with Germany and Italy A. In the Hühnlein Trophy contest the Army BSAs remained in contention with six German teams. The Birmingham, Bradford and Sunbeam clubs were all still clean and in the running for the Bowmaker Trophy while, in the manufacturer's competition, Triumph, BSA, Ariel and Royal Enfield were still in the running. On this day the CSMA team finally fell apart. Whitehouse lost 10 and Ridgway retired, leaving only Fred Perks running on time.

Geoff Godber-Ford, however, got the bit between his teeth on what he remembered as a very severe day. The 300-mile route, with 12 time-checks, featured mud tracks obstructed by tree trunks, steep climbs and descents with sheer drops at the side of the course. All of this was covered in 100°F temperatures. He finished with eight minutes in hand!

Meanwhile, back at HQ all hell had broken loose! Team managers were attempting to obtain official instructions and telegrams whistled backwards and forwards to the UK. Eventually the British Embassy in Berlin advised all British nationals to withdraw as soon as possible. The final decision came when two telegrams arrived. One was from the Norton factory instructing its team to withdraw and return immediately. The second was less ambiguous, from the President of the British Manufacturer's Union to its representative at the event, Major Watling: 'President instructs me to inform you British Consul General in Berlin has received instructions to warn all British subjects to leave Germany immediately.' There could no longer be any doubt. Preparations were then made for all the civilian British riders to leave Salzburg by 7 am on Friday morning. Astonishingly the Army teams had received no instructions from the War Office and proposed to continue with the event on Friday. In addition to the Army riders, four of the civilian contingent failed to receive the evacuation message. In consequence, Colin Edge, Hugh Sim, Alan Sanders and Marjorie Cottle all stayed on to ride on Friday.

Marjorie Cottle's story indicated the confusion which arose. She had been provided with a 250cc Triumph by the factory who were also paying her expenses and she had ridden the bike from the ferry port to Salzburg! At about midnight on Wednesday a female friend who was riding as a sidecar passenger came to her room too tell her that most of the competitors were leaving the next day. She duly packed her bags and was en route to collect her bike from the *parc fermé* when she recalled, 'I thought, well, this is a damn silly business. Triumph pay my expenses to come here and I arrive back early saying that Peggy told us we were having a war. They'll think I'm a bit soft in the head.' Consequently she consulted Lt. Col. Bennett who put her on the list to stay and ride on Friday!

Even at this late stage the SNKK organizers continued to protest that these arrangements were unnecessary, that there would be no trouble and, in any event, they would guarantee the safety of all competitors, arrange for their exit to a neutral country and provide fuel en route. Marjorie Cottle remembers being in Hühnlein's office on Thursday when he telephoned Hitler asking for assurance that the riders would be given safe conduct. Since no communication had been

Miles of rough tracks passing through magnificent wooded country were a feature of the 2nd day of the 1939 event. Here L Ridgway (496 BSA) is on his way to the St Koloman check point

received from the War Office the Army teams, less Sgt. Dalby whose leaky tank might have stranded him in Bavaria, set off, starting the day's route at the customary 5 am.

In the dramatic aftermath details of the day's activities seem to have been lost! The four civilian riders also rode on that day. Marjorie Cottle fell off her Triumph and blacked both eyes when she suddenly realized that, with a war imminent, she was in the wrong place! The inevitable recall telegram from the War Office arrived after breakfast. Apparently it had been sent on Thursday afternoon but had been misdirected. Perrigo waited for the riders to return, fill their tanks and sign off for good while Lt. Col. Bennett dealt with the administration. At 5 pm their convoy left for Switzerland, ac-

companied by Col. Grimm of the *Luftwaffe* who acted as escort to the border. All the civilian riders were with the military convoy of two lorries, fifteen bikes and three cars.

So the 1939 ISDT was over as far as the British contingent was concerned. At the time of the team's withdrawal it stood a fair chance in the trophy contest with 4 marks dropped. The winning German team eventually lost 30 marks. It would be reasonable to say that the British also stood a good chance to winning some, or possibly all, of the other sections including manufacturers' team prizes for Ariel, Royal Enfield, BSA and Triumph. In the end, of course, it did not matter since the results were declared void by the FIM in 1946. What is more important is that all the competitors should have successfully got back to the UK in the very nick of time. All their stories are fascinating, here are some examples . . .

Bert Perrigo, travelling with the Army teams, seems to have taken the whole thing in his stride. It was a most remarkable story and few people can have realized at the time, or subsequently, that just before war was declared a small detachment of the British Army was driving towards Munich on the *autobahn*! As well as two trucks and Lt. Col. Bennett's Humber staff car, the convoy included Bert's BSA car and J.A. Woodhouse's car. Woodhouse, and English garage owner from Cologne, had been spectating and was forced to make a run for it direct to Switzerland. With him were Marjorie Cottle, her bike in the back of a truck, and Miss Bunce of the ACU. Most of the riders seem to have been riding the bikes, on which they had started the fifth day, at 5am that morning. It was obviously especially tough for them and several fell asleep while riding through the night in the pouring rain. Fortunately no one had been injured.

Travelling via Munich and Bregenz they recalled passing convoys of military vehicles, including tanks, moving East along the other side of the *autobahn*. On one occasion they were stopped and questioned by German soldiers, which was hardly surprising, but Col. Grimm, their German liaison officer, was able to sort the problem out. The supply of fuel might also have been difficult but Herr Jaeger, from the German branch of Shell which had been looking after fuel arrangements at Salzburg, made stocks available at his Munich depot. Sometimes it pays to travel with the Army!

Saturday night was spent in the safety of Zurich and thence on Sunday into France at Versul. Travellig via the seething military traffic in the vicinity of the Maginot Line they eventually arrived at Calais on Tuesday, crossing the channel on Wednesday 30 August. Since war was declared on Sunday 3 September it was a very close run thing.

In the 30 August issue of *Motor Cycling* Peter Chamberlain recalled the experiences of some of the civilian riders. By 7.30 am on Friday almost all of them had left Salzburg. The largest group was organized by Len Heath, all on bikes collected from the *parc fermé*. The organizers, helpful to the last, offered to send a truck along the route to Switzerland with petrol, but it was not seen by Chamberlain and no one seemed to know where to expect it. In the end everyone found fuel in the normal way. They successfully travelled into Switzerland via Feldkirch in the pouring rain and, once on netural soil, divided into small groups for the dash to the Channel ports.

Fred Perks recalled the rather more haphazard arrangements made in haste at the *parc fermé* on Friday morning. With insufficient time to strip his BSA for transport in the Standard it went, with Jack Breffitt's Norton, on the trailer behind Harold Tozer's car. Fred then drove Tozer's sidecar outfit while Jack Breffitt drove the Standard. The ingenuity of this arrangement was positively mind-boggling but Fred's account does not record who worked it all out! Having had trouble obtaining fuel on the outward journey Fred had thoughtfully filled up his car, the BSA and a 10-litre can, which was just as well for his party also failed to find the fuel truck promised by the organizers. Travelling via Innsbruck they spent Friday night at St Gallen. The whole party got back to the UK safely, but not before Fred had restored the Silver Star, dismantled again, to its proper place in the Standard 9.

At least one bike failed to return. Norman Brockley, the team's travelling support rider, crashed and broke his leg on the Wednesday route. Although he got back safely to the UK his BSA was never seen again!

Geoff Godber-Ford of the Sunbeam A club team could obviously not take his 350 Subeam home on the train. Riding the bike, and forced to leave behind in Salzburg everything except the leathers he was wearing, he was one of the few to find Hühnlein's promised petrol truck at Innsbruck. The group he was with crossed the border into Switzerland at Feldkirch one hour before it closed until 1945! The main group split up in Switzerland and he travelled with Gilfinnan on an Ariel via Zurich, Basle, Nancy and Luxemburg. While following the general direction of the Maginot Line they were stopped and strip-searched by French soldiers. Fuel and food was a real problem on the Sunday and they were rescued by a Belgian enthusiast near Brussels, who gave them five litres of petrol each from a china jug. At Ostend, where they met some other competitors, they had to bribe their way on to a crowded ferry.

Obviously there are as many stories as there were riders. Billy Tiffen jun. on his Velocette and Dr Galloway with his son, on a Triumph sidecar outfit, crossed into Switzerland without trouble but had problems obtaining fuel in France. For one thing the French were not keen on accepting German Marks in payment! They also found some difficulty crossing direct from Germany into France but in the end managed to convince the French that they were not spies. For them the fuel situation eased when they were issued with vouchers enabling them to obtain petrol at military depots.

So the weary band, by various ways, found its way back home. At least 1914 was not repeated in that no bikes were confiscated. Perhaps the best epitaph to the whole affair was Fred Perks' attempt to enlist his Silver Star as a despatch rider's machine. It was turned down but when Fred went to the Chilwell depot to collect his DR machine, he was issued with another Silver Star! Within a week of the war being declared Fred Perks was sent back to France, from whence he eventually returned after the fall of Europe via Marseilles, Gibraltar and Newfoundland. After all, for a competitor in the 1939 ISDT that was only to be expected.

CHAPTER FOUR

Aftermath of war

1947

With the cessation of hostile activities, Europe was beginning to get back on its feet by 1947, and it was with this return to relative normality in mind that the FICM San Remo conference of April decided to reinstate the ISDT, giving Czechoslovakia its first opportunity to stage the event. The organization and running of the event was put into the capable hands of the *Autoklub Republiky Ceskoslouenske*, who initially drew up the schedules. Centred on the town of Zlin, each day's course would take the riders into the Slovak, Moravian and Silesian mountain ranges, with a total event mileage of about 1325 miles (2200 km). With a new organizing committee, a few changes to the basic concept of the event were instigated, one of which was a speed test, run on the last day over a 2.627-mile closed road course within the confines of the town of Zlin, instead of the traditional cross-country run last seen in 1939.

The chief press steward appointed by the Czechoslovakian organizers, did his best to keep participating countries informed, but all he could give was general information as the more detailed regulations were still being formulated.

The delay in the issuing of the regulations had the British ACU champing at the bit as they wished to sew up the loose ends with regard to entering a British trophy and vase team. Without the detailed rulings it was impossible to pick the squad from the 23 hopeful riders who were due to meet at the BSA works on 19 July for the selection tests. When the regulations duly arrived during the very same week as the selection tests the ACU had to do some rapid thinking as there were more changes to the event format than originally envisaged. The trophy and vase teams had to comprise three solos and one sidecar or three-wheeler as before, but now there was no mention of any different capacity classes. The major shock was the average speeds that these intrepid riders had to attain in order to stay in the running. For example, machines of between 350cc and 1000cc had to maintain a minimum and maximum speed of 24 and 43 mph respectively, some 8 mph faster than the Salzburg event. Even during the speed test scheduled for the last day, the 500cc machines were expected to attain an average of 56 mph over the stipulated 21 laps, with the 350cc bikes being required to average 55 mph, the smaller capacity machines (which the Europeans favoured), requiring greatly reduced

averages. The ACU had some serious misgivings over the averages required but, nevertheless, went ahead with the organization.

One major headache for any British private rider, wishing to participate in a foreign event, is the chore of actually getting there. To this end, the ACU planned a return rail trip for the national team and invited private riders to accompany them on the two-day trip at a fee of £35, plus £10 for a solo machine. If one added to this the entry fee of 5000 crowns (£25), plus accommodation, the cost of a privateer must have been around the £100 mark, about 20 weeks' wages in those far off days, a daunting financial burden for even the most well-heeled motorcyclist. This offer was soon rescinded when the secretary of the ACU, Mr. S.T. Huggett, issued a statement on 15 July calling off the team selection tests. The very same day Major Watling, the director of the *British Cycle and Motorcycle Manufacturers' and Traders' Union*, issued the following statement:

> British Motorcycle Manufacturers very greatly regret that they are unable to participate in the 1947 International Six Days Trial. They find themselves in a particularly unfortunate position this year due to production and other difficulties, and the necessity for concentration on exports in the National interest. Even so, they would have made every endeavour to compete but the Regulations unexpectedly differ in certain important details from those in force for the 1939 Trial and there is not now sufficient time to ensure the preparation of the machines to their satisfaction. They greatly regret that they will not have the opportunity of meeting their Czech friends but look forward to a greater measure of time and opportunity in 1948.

With no trade entrants to represent Great Britain, the private entrants who had expressed a wish to attend became very worried. The ACU, in an effort to quell any unpleasantness, then stepped in by issuing another statement which, in essence, said that they would give limited help to any British rider who wished to participate. Once the Czech organizing club had sensed the misgivings of the British ACU and trade barons, they promptly promised to produce a supplement to the regulations blaming the capacity classes and average speed rule changes on an unfortunate error in the English translation. This change of heart was of little comfort to the three British riders, who finally decided

These Czechoslovakian riders have every right to look happy – they are part of a squad which carried off both the Trophy and Vase contests in the first post-war ISDT in 1947. This was the Czechs first taste of glory and was to be repeated many times over in coming years

to enter. Listed as an ACU club team, the British contingent comprised of, L. Sheaf (250 SOS), A.A. Sanders (500 Triumph) and J.A. Hitchcock (500 Triumph).

So it was with some trepidation that 105 competitors weighed in for the start of the 22nd International whose headquarters was the nine-storey, 400-bedroom, *Spolecensky-Dum* building in the Moravian town of Zlin, a town better known for its Bata footwear factory, than for a centre of motorcycle trials activity. Only two countries fielded trophy teams, probably due to the short notice of the event. One, naturally, was the home team of V. Stanislav (350 Jawa), J. Simandl (250 Jawa), R. Dusil (250 Jawa), and J. Bednar (600 Jawa sidecar), who seized the opportunity to show off the qualities of their new Jawas which had been secretly designed and developed during the war years. Also representing the host country were two vase teams, together with other teams from Holland, Poland, Hungary and Italy. Austria was allowed to compete but not as a national team, for they were not yet re-elected as members of the FICM. By the

simple expedient of enrolment in a Czech club, the three Puch 125 riders were able to ride and put up a creditable performance in their wonderful little split-single twin-carb two-strokes, which were capable of well over 60 mph.

The first day of the event was a 280-mile mixture of easy and tough going which nevertheless claimed its share of casualties. Jock Hitchcock managed to get round unpenalized but with very little time to spare at checkpoints, and on checking his fuel tank back at base found it to be nearly empty. If the run had been five miles longer he would never have made it. The other two members of the British contingent did not fare so well, for Len Sheaf got a puncture and was penalized five marks for lateness, whilst Alan Sanders on his standard 1938 Speed Twin, suffered so many punctures, it delayed his return to Zlin to 11 pm and retirement. The afternoon run took riders up the Harmanec pass with its 129 sharp bends. Conditions were very dusty due to the nature of the surface and the lack of rainfall, and it was these hazards that caused the Italian trophy 500 side-valve Sertum sidecar outfit of Grieco to crash, badly damaging both rider and passenger, and machine, but they remounted and carried on. It was the same dusty conditions that caused rumours to spread that Bednar, on the 600 dohc twin Jawa chair outfit, was missing, but it was later confirmed that he had been overlooked at one of the numerous telephone points being used to monitor the progress of the riders. At the end of the day 71 clean sheets were recorded, but 13 riders found it too much and retired.

The second day was a little easier, for the first 100 miles were run on good roads before the Harmanec pass was re-attacked in the opposite direction. Grieco was allowed to start after a visit to the doctor, for he had sustained damaged ribs and lacerated knees and back, as a result of his spill on the Harmanec pass the previous day. Both the Italian and Czech trophy sidecars were reluctant to start in the morning, but after a few minutes they got away. Unfortunately, Grieco had to retire later in the day when a sidecar connection failed. A further eight riders retired on the second day but the Czech trophy team came home clean again as did the Czech vase A and the Polish vase A teams both mounted on 250 Jawas.

The third day was another relatively easy ride northwards, mainly run on good roads with the odd few miles of rough going thrown in for good measure. It was one of these cross-country sections that caused the head stock welding on Len Sheaf's 250 SOS to fracture. The SOS prepared by T.G. Meeten, was the same machine rode in the 1938 event in Wales, but now sported a set of Dowty oleomatic forks and an Amal carburettor, and was by now, some ten years old.

The fourth day saw the steady disintegration of many of the lesser machines with wire string and sticky tape much in evidence, to hold many machines together. Some riders had lost mudguards and rear lamps, but Nessor had managed to save his 250 Sertum rear mudguard, completing the day with its strapped across his knees. Day 4 also saw the testing of the excellent medical back-up provided by the organizers when Dutch Jawa 250 rider, A. Thomassen, collided with a Czech rider, and sustained a fractured collar bone. C Ries, the Swiss 250 Jawa rider also required medical attention for cuts and abrasions he received when he ran out of road on a cross-country section.

Saturday's run will always be remembered for its two special sections run over woodland tracks of one and four miles in length, into which had been laid tree trunks of about six inches diameter. These sections produced a surface akin to a choppy sea and produced some spectacular action with riders attacking the section with gritted teeth taking everything the surface could hurl at them. It was shortly after one of these tracks that Jock Hitchcock called it a day with rear axle problems on his new sprung hub Speed Twin.

The last day's run prior to the speed test was a mere 119 miles in length, but this still caused problems to some riders. The Swiss sidecar driver, E. Haller, finished the run minus the rear tyre of his 1000cc Harley-Davidson, and H. Veer rode the whole distance on one cylinder of his Triumph twin. At this point the Czech trophy team still had a clean sheet, against the 671 marks notched up by the Italian team, but the Czechs

British team members/reserves for 1948 ISDT. Left to right: J Brefitt, T H Ellis, C N Rogers, V N Brittain, J Stocker, A F Gaymer, J Williams, P H Alves, C M Ray, A Jefferies, F M Rist, G Eighteen. Major H R Watling Director of the Manufacturers Union is sixth from right. Great Britain won both the Trophy and the Vase that year

still kept the pressure up. In the speed test Stanislav's 350 Jawa would prove a problem for it was known to be exceptionally slow compared to the 250 Jawas of his team mates. The 350 Jawa did, in fact, finish the test but dropped six marks for failing to keep to the schedule. But the highlight of the test was the Jawa sidecar crew of Bednar and Hanzl, for at half distance the sidecar strut snapped, the whole outfit being held together by the brute force of the crew using their hands and feet while still circulating at 50 mph. Despite their heroism they dropped three marks, but this was enough for the Czech team to win the trophy for their country. The Czechoslovakian vase A team of Pastika Kohlicek and Marha all riding CZ 125 machines won the silver vase, with 17 marks lost. However, had the gallant Austrian team, on their fast Puch 125 machines, been members of the FICM they would have taken the vase, as they were still together and had lost no marks at all.

1948

As the Czechoslovakian team had won the trophy on home ground in 1947, the prerogative was extended to the runners-up to stage the next event. So it was that the *Federazione Motociclistica Italiana* organized the 1948 event centred around the Mediterranean resort of San Remo. Actually, the start finish-line plus the *parc fermé* and trade encampment was at Ospedaletti, some three

miles out of San Remo, but this was no problem as the organizers had enlisted the help of the local tram company to convey the riders and officials from the teams' hotels in San Remo to the start-line on a daily basis, free of charge.

The course took the riders inland each day, into the mountains which shielded the coastline from the harsher climate further north. Rising at times to a height of 4500 ft, the mountain roads would not be easy as the routes used a mixture of old military roads and mule tracks weaving their way up and down the steep slopes. None of the competitors underestimated the severity of the course as word had spread that this was going to be the toughest event yet held, and reconnaissance runs over the area backed up these initial worries. Road surfaces in the lowland areas were bad enough, but higher up in the mountains the routes consisted of nothing more than deep sand and rubble strewn tracks with unprotected hairpin bends, and sheer drops.

Great Britain, after the withdrawal the previous year, rose to the occasion and fielded not only a trophy team, but also two vase teams and a manufacturer's team. The trophy team consisted of Vic Brittain and Charlie Rogers on Royal Enfield 350s, Jack Williams on an International Norton, Hugh Viney on a 500 AJS, and team captain, Allan Jefferies, on a factory-prepared Triumph Speed Twin, for the Italians had seen fit to increase the team size to five members on two different capacity classes and forget about sidecars.

With many thoughts about the severity of the conditions ahead, the first two riders (Corbetta on a 50cc Motum and Gvasco on a 65cc Guzzi), were flagged off at 7 am on Tuesday 14 September, by Count Albert Bonacossa, the FICM honorary president. At two-minute intervals the rest of the field got away, the only notable exceptions being a team from the local *carabinieri* who failed to turn up, and a pair of Frenchmen who went home in a huff at being fined for late arrival.

The first day's run took the riders up and over the 4533 ft (1381 metres) Colle Di Casotto where they encountered mist and rain. After the lunch break at Alba riders headed back home via another 4000 ft pass, the Galleria Di Tenda, and then after a short excursion into France, returned to San Remo and a well-earned rest.

Results issued that night indicated that only two trophy teams had completed the day's run unpenalized and they were the hot favourites: Czechoslovakia, and the as yet outsiders, Great Britain. Day one had been hard going, for it saw the retirement of six out of the eight 50cc Motoms, but of the dozen scooter entries only one Vespa and two Lambrettas failed to finish. The Austrian and Belgian trophy teams had each lost six marks, but the home team had lost 100 marks when Benzoni (250 Sertum), was excluded for lateness due to fork problems sustained in a fall.

Day two saw further retirements, mainly caused by crashes due to the high average speeds demanded on some of the more severe stretches. Two British riders retired after hitting spectators' cars which were out in force to view the event. George Eighteen on his AJS pulled out after one such crash, but it was Olga Kevelos who ended up in hospital with a broken arm and leg that made other riders take notice. Latterly, Olga recalls that her time in hospital was not too bad, with plenty of local wine to ease the pain, but it was the bill for her stay which caused concern, as Olga was by now nearly broke, her local money used up. Peter Chamberlain, the British ACU jury member, bailed her out, accepting no repayment for he had made more than enough on one of his trips to the San Remo casino.

Sidecar crews were having a hard time running to the same schedule as the 250 solos, and it was this schedule, and a spate of punctures, that caused Doc Galloway to pull out, which then allowed him to take on the full-time duties as the British team medical officer.

Of the 151 original starters some 114 tackled the third day, which was a reversal of Tuesday's run – up and over the Colle Di Casotto and the cross border run through French territory again. At one of the border posts, Jack Williams bent the forks of his Norton when he ran up the back of Jim Alves who had unexpectedly stopped, but he carried on to retain his clean sheet. The day ended with Czechoslovakia and Great Britain still sharing the lead for the trophy, but at one stage it looked like the Czechs would be out as Kohlicek was seen carrying out frantic repairs to his Jawa after a prang. Apart from Williams bending his forks, Charlie Rogers lost his time card, for which he was fined 10,000 lire (£5.00), but the team remained clean and intact.

Day four saw the eventual tumbling of the Czech trophy team from the leaderboard when Pastika retired in the early stages with gearbox problems. Jack Blackwell of the British vase B team, finally blew up the engine of his Norton which he had been nursing for two days. The team had been laying in third position, but now their hopes were dashed for the team was out. The sole survivor of the Irish vase team, Manliff Barrington, fell from his BSA late on in the day breaking his collarbone, but bravely rode the remaining 50 miles to the finish-line. The 65cc Guzzi rider, Gvasco, had been putting up a brave fight having been on full throttle for four days, attacking smooth and rough going alike flat on the tank, finally admitted defeat when he clocked in one minute over his maximum time allowance.

At the end of the day Great Britain remained 25 marks clear of its nearest rival, the Austrian Puch-mounted team, in the trophy contest, but the vase A team was neck and neck with the Dutch A team, both with zero marks lost, with Czechoslovakia in third place, with only two marks lost.

On Saturday the run was less punishing to both riders and machines, staying mainly in the lower altitudes of the Ligurian range, but its length of 250 miles made it the longest trek yet. More clean sheets were lost, and destinies altered, when H. Veer of the Dutch vase A team was plagued by punctures on his 250 Jawa, losing 16 marks and relegating his team to third position. Riders were beginning to feel the heat in more ways than one. Some even began to feel sleepy, and this caused a few mishaps. Bob Ray bent the brake lever and footrest on his Ariel in a brush with a lorry, Charlie Rogers hit a submerged rock in a mud patch and ended up flying over a low stone wall into a field where he passed out. On coming to he remounted and carried on to the next control where he was administered brandy and wet sponges by local nurses.

The final day started with an 88-mile dash which was deemed to be the hardest test of the whole week. After a 6.30 am start – a time not relished by the one-legged

Fresh from victory in the road racing Grand Prix des Nations at Monza, Gilera works rider M Masserini poses with his 247cc Gilera Nettuno before the start of the 1948 ISDT at San Remo. . .

. . .Masserini in action. He went on to win a Gold medal

Tropical background to the check-point at Albenga during the 1948 event. J C de Wit (125 Eysink) of the Dutch Trophy team is at the table. Other riders await their turn to check in

Vincent sidecar driver, Harold Taylor, who had been up all night with a bout of the local tummy trouble, riders headed out into the hills for the last time. On the final run in, over a downhill section of hairpin bends and unguarded precipices, many riders came to grief. One rider T. Ellis, actually went over the side, but came to rest on the only available patch of grass a few feet down. Bandirola touched the brink but other riders like Ray threw their bikes down in the dust to avoid going over the edge. At the finish it was found that Jack Stocker had fractured a fork leg on his 500 Enfield, so with a few hours to go prior to the final speed test, a clamp was designed and made to hold the leg together. The clamp had a minimal effect on the poor handling of the sick Enfield, but Stocker carried on, wearing two leather suits just in case of a spill. All the British teams had to do to gain the trophy and vase was to complete the speed test which they did in style, putting in the requisite number of laps on the 2.412-mile course at Ospedaletti. The effect and effort on riders was so great that Harold Taylor actually fainted when he dismounted from the Vincent at the end of the test.

So Great Britain scooped all the major prizes at the prize-giving, the trophy going to the team of Jefferies/Rogers/Brittain/Viney/Williams, with no marks lost. The Silver Vase went to the A team of Alves/Ray/Stocker, again with no marks lost. Triumph won the manufacturer's prize with Alves/Jefferies/Gayner, and

the Sunbeam MCC took the club prize with Williams/Rist/Alves, all again with zero penalties.

After the gold, silver and bronze medals had been awarded, three extra cups were presented to riders who had put up a meritorious performance. The first going to the 125 Vespa rider, Mazzoncini, for his four-day faultless ride before incurring a penalty. The second went to Barrington for his 50-mile ride to the finish with a broken collarbone, and finally, to Olga Kevelos who had ridden to the event and was the only lady competitor before being eliminated by her tumble.

On the strength of this overwhelming success, the ACU officials returned home, happy in the thought that they would stage the next event on home territory and so repeat the victorious results achieved two decades previously.

1949

Having taken the trophy home from Italy the previous year, it was now Great Britain's privilege to host the 24th International trial. Centred at Llandrindod Wells in Radnorshire in the mountainous area of mid Wales, run under uncharacteristic blue skies, the event proved to be easy in comparison with the rigorous San Remo episode of 1948. The weather played a big part in that the absence of rain made the going easy, but this in itself put more loading on air cleaners and suspension systems, to the detriment of some riders. Normally the prevailing weather pattern is from the west, which brings rain in from the Atlantic, but during the week the breeze stayed easterly bringing sunshine to this predominantly soggy area.

Four teams were to contest the premier award, each

consisting of five riders on machines manufactured in their own countries. Switzerland was represented by a team mounted on a variety of solo and sidecar shaft drive, side-valve flat-twin Condors, while the Italians used a mixture of side-valve Sertums and ohv Moto Guzzis. Czechoslovakia fielded a formidable team mounted on Jawa and CZ two-strokes, whereas Great Britain used a diverse selection of its country's wares with one model representing each of the major factories. Triumph, Ariel, BSA, Enfield and AJS.

The event was made even more interesting, as a new ruling had been introduced, the average speeds required of the trophy, vase and manufacturers' teams was now increased by ten per cent. This may not sound a lot but it was to make a big difference to the riders as it meant that keeping on schedule was that bit harder over the rougher going. This two-tier system to sort the men from the boys at first sight seemed a good idea, but it did prove difficult to administer as highlighted by the late delivery of the results each evening.

Darkness greeted the 230 starters as they lined up for the off at 6.30 am on Monday, 12 September. The first to be flagged away by Peter Nortier, the Dutch president of the International Sporting Committee of the FICM, was F.H. Carey on his eleven-year-old 350 Enfield sidecar outfit, and the Hungarian, Hajdu, on his Csepel 98. The early morning gloominess and the 98cc Csepel's barely adequate lighting conspired to ensure that the third man, J. Reiszon, on another Csepel went

straight on at the very first turn. Attracted by shouts from the spectators, he did a swift about face and carried on unpenalized. Ten miles out, Swiss rider J.P. Roth, took a tumble from his big Condor twin, dislocating his shoulder and dashing the hopes of the Swiss trophy team. Later in the day, a further two members of the same team came off, damaging their machines. Hugh Viney, on his 498 AJS, who was following close behind, found his path blocked by the fallen Condors, and had no option but to lay the bike down to avoid joining the mêlée. He remounted and continued with no damage to rider or machine.

After the lunch stop where petrol was available, dispensed free of charge without need for ration coupons, riders continued once more into the mountains, at times encountering low cloud and visibility down to 10 yards. The route continued on to the infamous Dinas Rock, an observed section in the St David's Day trial, but now this obstacle was to be attacked downhill. Many riders of smaller machines actually dismounted and walked their bikes down, whereas other riders tobogganed down with locked rear wheels. Sidecar crews found this section particularly hard, with many ending up on their sides. Doc Galloway had a miraculous escape when his Triumph outfit was prevented from actually going over the edge by the flimsy wire fence which bordered the track.

Sidecar crews came in for another hammering on the second day, when the route took the remaining 214 con-

15   THE MOTOR CYCLE   SEPTEMBER 22ND, 1949

The International Six Days' Trial . . .

More international than any other motor-cycling event, the "Six Days" takes place in Britain for the first time since 1938. Again the headquarters are at Llandrindod Wells, a Spa town in the heart of the Principality, and the route is over the same sort of territory. Bleak mountain passes, winding tracks over the hills which were already old when the Romans were here, alternate with the well-surfaced but narrow Welsh lanes which carry the modern motor traffic. From the start to the finish of the trial absolute reliability of man and machine is essential, for marks lost through being late at a check cannot be regained by speeding to the next. This all-important element of timekeeping, with schedules for each class of machine so arranged that all must give their maximum performance, has been a feature of the "International" for many years. In all there have been 24 trials in the series, the first in England in 1913, others in France, Switzerland, Scandinavia, Belgium, Central Europe, Italy, Germany and Czechoslovakia. The International Trophy has been won by Great Britain on twelve previous occasions and the Silver Vase, first offered in 1934, on ten.

Congratulations to Great Britain's Team members on winning The International Trophy—

ALL ON DUNLOP

SUBJECT TO OFFICIAL CONFIRMATION)

testants over the Tregaron Pass. The 500 Enfield outfit of Christensen, after lashing the chair body to the chassis finally ran out of road. The driver sustained facial injuries and ended up in hospital, but the passenger drove the outfit back to the finish with an empty chair. The sidecar of the H. Juni Condor outfit, after fitting snow chains to aid grip, parted company from the bike, forcing the crew into retirement. The ex-Harold Taylor Vincent HRD outfit, now driven by F.C. Moldenhaver, also went into retirement with broken front forks. Clarke of the Irish vase B team also suffered fork problems, and limped in with one leg of his Matchless forks snapped clean off. Italian Morini team member, M. Vola, had to be transported down the mountain by ambulance after looping his 125, but before he boarded

he insisted that his machine be carried with him, and would not leave until the machine was loaded. Norton rider, Murray Walker, smashed his spectacles when he fell off at one stage, but gamely carried on without them, to remain unpenalized and finish the week with a gold medal.

Both Czechoslovakia and the Great Britain trophy teams, together with the Italian and Great Britain vase A teams, and the Swiss and Czech B teams, all started the third day with clean sheets. By the end of the day, the Italians had dropped 23 marks, and the Swiss 7, on the re-run over the Tregaron Pass. It was on this route that Doc Galloway stopped to offer assistance to W. Hemsley who had gone over the edge and fractured his thigh. The Doc initially lost marks for late arrival, but

Speed in the Brecon Mountains. J W Price (346 Enfield) and R T Dunn (348 BSA) leading a string of riders during the speed tests on the Eppynt circuit in the 1949 event

this penalty was quashed by the organizers on humanitarian grounds.

Thursday saw the Czech vase B team drop to second place when a member arrived late at a check, but the two marks lost were contested, which was upheld, and the Czech team was reinstated to equal first with Great Britain. The pace was beginning to hot up as the end of the event got nearer. The Czech trophy rider, Pastika, on his CZ 125, was nearly running out of his time allowance after a puncture, but survived the day, only to be plagued by ignition problems the following day, which put his team in second place. Bob Ray caused a few heartaches in the British camp, when after losing his way he attempted to make up for lost time. With one remaining brake, cooked and fading badly, he hit a car and dropped his card. On retrieving the card he clocked in, but he was over time by seconds, which meant one mark lost. Harold Taylor appeared to be in trouble on his immaculate Sunbeam S7 outfit when his single footrest was torn from the machine as he was hurrying to make up time after a puncture. Harold carried on clean to earn himself a gold medal.

The trophy contest had been decided by the time the remaining riders gathered at the Eppynt circuit for the final speed test, but the vase competition was wide open

and the Czech B team and the British A team still had clean sheets. Blaha Marha and Kremar set a cracking pace on their little CZs, their target being five laps in 52 minutes. Jack Stocker, who was feeling very ill with suspected pleurisy, had to manage eight laps in 60 minutes, and the Triumph-mounted Manns and Gaymer, nine laps in 63 minutes. The speed test was not supposed to be a race, but in the case of the vase contest, it had to be, for both teams were on zero marks, and the outcome would be decided on who made the best percentage increase over the laid down schedules. As was suspected, the advantage went to the smaller capacity machines of the Czechoslovakian riders, who took the Silver Vase home with them for the second time.

At the prize-giving held in the Llandrindod Grand Pavilion, the Lord Lieutenant of Radnorshire witnessed the handing over of the trophy to the victorious British team of Alves/Ray/Rogers/Rist/Viney. Matchless won the manufacturer's award, with Hall/Burnard/Usher, and the Sunbeam MCC B team took the club award away from the Sunbeam MCC A team, the result being decided on the final speed test.

Over 50 gold medals were handed out that night for some truly meritorious rides. John Brittain on his James 125 and Olga Kevelos on her Norton 500T, to name but two of the recipients.

So the third post-war event brought us to the end of the decade. In the following years fortunes were changed, supreme powers waned, unknown contenders emerged and venues changed, but the spirit of the event lived on, to be contested just as avidly as before.

CHAPTER FIVE

British decline

As this review of the 1950s begins it is important to remember what the ISDT was all about. Essentially it was a reliability trial for production motorcycles in everyday use. As Cyril Quantrill of *Motor Cycling* magazine pointed out at the time, bikes were, even then, becoming quite specialized. In this event, however, there should be, and organizers were still ensuring that there was, an equal chance for solos of all engine capacities and types, and for sidecar outfits. Bearing in mind the variation in speed schedules for different sizes of machine and the nature of the courses chosen by host nations, it should not be necessary to employ racing engines or one-day trials technology to ensure success. Ideally the trophy and vase would go to the nation with the fittest and most skilful riders on the toughest and most reliable machines. However, cracks were already appearing in this ethos and there is nothing new under the sun. Whereas today the motocross special tests are often criticized, the final speed test at the events was more and more frequently seen as unfair.

1950

A quick look at the British line-up for 1950 in Llandrindod Wells should throw some light on the technical aspects of the situation. The machines which appeared for the ACU team selection were in many cases familiar. The three AJS 347cc singles and the three almost identical Matchlesses had the new 'Jampot' rear suspension units. Four plunger sprung 499cc BSA Gold Stars and three 350cc Royal Enfield Bullets with swinging-arm rear suspension made up the complement of singles. The twin-cylinder contingent consisted of three 498cc Triumph Trophies, three Ariel Red Hunter 498cc machines, four Norton Dominators and David Tye's lonely 348cc Douglas. Although the bikes had detailed modifications in the light of experience, all were clearly recognizable as current catalogue models. The Ariel twins had the normal downswept exhaust systems. Of particular interest were the Norton Dominator twins which were taken off the road machine production line and modified to accept specially made quickly detachable rear wheels, upswept exhaust systems and a hinged dualseat with provision for spare inner tubes. There were some experimental features on other machines. The BSA Gold Stars, for example, were using an oil-damped and rubber-sleeved version of the plunger rear suspension. In another direction entirely the Triumphs

had sacrificed rear suspension altogether in order to retain quickly detachable rear wheels. General opinion at the tests was that all of the machines present would be excellent for hard touring.

Unhappily, despite the wealth of machinery and a high level of public interest, quite unexpectedly Great Britain was about to enter the doldrums. Of the 27 events held between 1913 and 1953 (excluding the fiasco of 1939) the British teams won the trophy competition on 16 occasions. The vase was won in 11 of the 19 events in which it featured. Despite this and a very healthy start to the decade including trophy success in 1950, 1951 and 1953, the following 36 years have been completely barren, indeed Britain's last win in the vase contest was in 1950. There are very many reasons for this, including the decline of the British motorcycle industry itself, but Britain has never ceased to produce world-class riders with a will to win so it would seem that the fundamental problems lay elsewhere.

However, the argue that success in the ISDT died with the decline in competitive status of the machines can last only as long as the rule which limited trophy team members to machines made in their own country. The answer must lie in a complex set of problems related to the riders, the machines and, most important of all, the nature and rules of the event itself. Fortunately the men and the manufacturers of the 1950s could not foresee the future and the epic story of the 1950s is perhaps the most exciting in the history of the ISDT.

The 1950 event is remembered by those who took part as being wet and tough. Indeed, some said that it was as strenuous as San Remo in 1948 and as wet as the Lake District in 1927: a formidable combination. In these conditions the British trophy team and vase A carried all before them, winning both competitions convincingly. Fred Rist, riding a 499cc BSA Gold Star, captained the trophy team with P.H. Alves on a Triumph Trophy, C.M. Ray on an Ariel Red Hunter twin, Jack Stocker on a 350cc Royal Enfield and Hugh Viney with a 350cc AJS. The vase A team also contained very famous riders: Bob Manns on a Triumph, Ted Usher on a Matchless and A.F. Gaymer also on a Triumph. The trophy competition was to be disputed with Austria and Italy since the Czechs had declined to enter a team. The vase was contested by Austria, Ireland, Holland, Italy, Sweden and, of course, the British B team

28 SEPTEMBER 1950   *THE MOTOR CYCLE*   17

BRITAIN WINS INTERNATIONAL TROPHY *Team Captain rides* AGAIN...

BSA

B.S.A. WON 9 GOLD MEDALS

FRED RIST, Captain of the winning British Team, on the B.S.A. 500 Gold Star.

For trials and scrambles LEAVE IT TO YOUR BSA

Fred Rist, Captain of the winning British Trophy team in 1950. His machine is a factory prepared 499cc BSA Gold Star

comprising Hall (BSA), Ellis (Royal Enfield) and Taylor (Matchless).

In the major competition the pattern of engine capacity for the decade was already set. The Austrians had an all Puch team, two 125s and three 250s. Italy was still very much a manufacturer of small capacity singles with three 125 MVs, one 250cc Sertum and a 250cc Moto Guzzi. In addition to this array of competitors the 232 entrants included 15 manufacturers and 30 club teams. Sidecar outfits remained quite popular. Thirty-one were entered, ranging in size up to a 1000cc Vincent. Particularly popular were the 350cc outfits which benefited from a 24 mph time schedule. One notable innovation for 1950 was that in order to ensure that the

lighting regulations were taken seriously, the event included a night run on the second day.

History records that Great Britain simply walked all over the opposition in 1950. What is much more remarkable is that this was achieved in a very difficult event, in truly awful conditions and the fact that the British trophy and vase A teams remained completely unpenalized ... an achievement matched by no other nation. In itself this is less remarkable than the fact that at the end of the decade, in 1959, British manufacturers withdrew their support from the event and the nation was forced to enter a team of private entrants backed by members clubs of the ACU. By this time its performance was so poor that the only publicity was bad publicity! On the very first day of the 1950 event, of the 213 starters 41 retired and only 87 retained clean sheets. On this, possibly the toughest and wettest first day recorded to that date, among the retirements were the two Italian trophy team 250s and Weingartmann of the Austrian Trophy team who was excluded for missing a checkpoint.

Thirty more riders retired on an equally tough second day even though the 10 per cent slower B time schedule for severe weather was in use. By this time only the Dutch A, Irish and Swedish vase teams were in the running with the British, and it is noteworthy that their machinery comprised BSA Gold Stars and Star Twins. The night run of 89 miles produced few problems as it was mostly run on tarmac roads but some riders, notably from Continental Europe, had problems passing the 100-metre 'reflector' test since their lights were only producing 'a dull glow'. This will not be unfamiliar to riders of Italian machines of that era!

The severe conditions continued for the rest of the week. At the close of play on Wednesday only 115 riders were still in contention and only 55 of these had clean sheets. In case it may be felt that conditions were impossible, it should be noted that Carancini's Lambretta

ISDT gold medal winners in the 1950's, Frank and Kay Wilkins pictured with their faithful Ariel 650 twin and sidecar which they still used in 1984, some three decades after their glory days

scooter was still in the event although he finally dropped out on Thursday. Thursday's run, traditionally into North Wales, proved even more difficult than usual and suggested worse for Friday when it would be in use in the opposite direction. The Bwlch y Groes, Eunant and Hirnant Pass sections over the Cambrian Mountains would have done justice to a one-day observed trial. Fred Rist, Bill Nicholson and Brian Stonebridge all won applause from spectators for their speed and skill. At the end of this day only five sidecar outfits were still running, and all of them were British. Frank Whittle's 598cc Panther outfit finally went out with a broken drive chain jammed around the sprockets, but for four days he had fought against the weather and the terrain on a 10 per cent faster speed schedule imposed on 'works' entries. Thursday also saw the loss of Dick Clayton and his Norton Dominator to the British vase B team. The unfortunate bike was drowned in a watersplash while Clayton was overtaking a Swedish competitor and the cylinder head lifted.

On Friday, after more heavy overnight rain, the ascent of the Eunant Pass in the opposite direction proved even more difficult. The great slabs of rock which the competitors negotiated were waterlogged and heavily rutted. Never let it be said by today's generation of riders that the ISDT of the 1950s must have been relatively easy. Basil Hall's BSA Gold Star was labouring very badly but it made it and remained on time. If anyone could stay on time as long as the bike ran, then Basil could, but he failed to reach the start of the speed test on the following day. Tom Ellis, also of the British vase B team, fell by the wayside when his 500cc Royal Enfield holed a piston. Vase B seemed to be experiencing all the failures which were in later years to plague the British teams. Desperately unlucky on this day was G. Pickering on a 125cc BSA Bantam who was the only surviving rider of a 125 who had not lost marks. He missed the route marking and was out of time. However, he had proved that a small two-stroke could do the job.

So the 1950 ISDT entered its last day with competitors making their way to the speed test. Only 83 of the original 213 starters were eligible to take part and only 39 of these were without penalties. However, despite the severity of the event, Molly Briggs on her 500cc Triumph, having survived the first day with a nine mark penalty, was about to complete the event without any further penalties. Matching her effort a young medical student named T.M. Tun, riding a 650cc Triumph Thunderbird, who had only begun riding motorcycles three months before the ISDT, finished with a bronze medal.

The speed test has often been seen as a notorious part of the event but, on this occasion, the British trophy and vase A teams had only to meet the minimum requirement over the Eppynt road race circuit, and this day did without bother. The FIM had always maintained that the object of this final test was to assess the mechanical

12 OCTOBER 1950   THE MOTOR CYCLE   3

19 **AJS** 50

INTERNATIONAL SIX DAYS TRIAL

A.J.S. RIDERS WIN
8 GOLD MEDALS
out of the 37 Awarded
and
A MANUFACTURERS' TEAM PRIZE
Riders—B. H. M. VINEY, T. H. WORTLEY, A. W. BURNARD
(Subject to official confirmation)

B. H. M. VINEY 347 c.c. A.J.S.
Member of the
WINNING BRITISH TROPHY TEAM
*For 12 times in succession A.J.S. Motor Cycles
have been included in the British Trophy Team*

AJS MOTOR CYCLES · PLUMSTEAD ROAD · LONDON, S.E.18.

LEFT **AJS riders won 8 gold medals and a Manufacturer's team prize in the 1950 event**

RIGHT **Night section during the 1950 ISDT. The sidecar driver is Harold Taylor (Sunbeam) and the solo rider B Nystrom (Royal Enfield of Sweden).**

conditon of machines at the end of the event. Unfortunately, it was also used to determine the winners when more than one team finished unpenalized. Moreover, the speed schedules set for machines of different capacity was on a sliding scale. In the event of a 'tie' the team which made the greatest percentage improvement on the times set for its class of machines would win. In years to come this was to be a cause of some concern for Britain. In 1950, however, there was no such problem. The British teams had the backing of a powerful industry. Their riders were extremely skilful and quick. The machines were, on the whole, strong and reliable, even in awful weather, and fast enough. They were, in short, the winners. What could possibly go wrong?

1951

The 1951 event was based in Varese in Northern Italy. The Czechs were again absent leaving Britain to cope with Austria and Italy. The British trophy team was unchanged. In the vase teams Evans moved from vase B to A, Ted Usher was demoted to first reserve and Tom Ellis joined the B team. Expecting a very fast event in the Italian style, the machinery for selection by the British squad was entirely composed of vertical twins. The trophy was therefore contested with Viney's 498cc AJS, Alves' 650cc Triumph, Ray's 498cc Ariel, Rist's 650cc BSA Star twin and Stocker's 496cc Royal Enfield twin. The vase teams comprised very similar machines. Certainly, from the point of view of service facilities, it

could not have been easy to look after five different makes in the same team. The Italian philosophy was similar in this respect if not in terms of cubic capacity with MV, Bianchi, Rumi and Morini 125s and a lone 250cc Gilera. By contrast the Austrians were relying exclusively on 150 and 250cc Puch split-single two-strokes.

Of course the choice of machines was dictated by the 'home grown' rule for trophy teams as well as the need to enter machines of two different capacities. This left Britain and Italy with a much greater choice than Austria or indeed, subsequently, Czechoslovakia. It could be argued, for example, that the concentration of effort in Czechoslovakia on the Jawas and CZs and the dedicated resolve to win, produced the marvellous line of ISDT specials in later years. Indeed, while European manufacturers were beginning to prepare serious single-purpose machines, Britian was still dedicated to the modified tourer. This concept produced some fascinating bikes. Dick Clayton's 497cc Norton Dominator for 1951 was installed in a 'Featherbed' frame and sported a Manx Norton front brake. Apart from its 'knobbly' tyres and high level front mudguard, it looked more like a road racer. The Triumphs for 1951 were still confined to rigid rear ends in the interest of quick wheel changing.

Unlike 1950 the 1951 event turned out to be a very close run affair. Great Britain won the trophy, but only just, while their vase A team lost out to the Dutch B. Most ISDTs have a predominant characteristic but that year it was not so easy to identify. Two hundred and twenty riders started the event and set out to cover 1250 miles of bumpy and often very dusty Italian back roads and tracks. Overall it must have been relatively easy for riders competing on the 'normal' schedule. In general, time allowances were fairly generous and 89 gold medals were won by those who were not required to follow the plus 10 per cent schedules.

Despite this the event was certainly not easy for the team riders. Riding on the faster schedule they encountered a number of sections during the week which required superhuman efforts to stay on time. The ISDT was seen as a test of *sustained* hard riding but this was not the case in 1951. It may be that we were seeing the development of events with a very distinctive national character and Italy, with its hot dusty hills and riders of fiery temperament, preferred bursts of almost insane speed and devil-may-care to sort out the eventual results. It is felt that a direct comparison can be drawn with the Elba event in 1981, in which the outcome was decided solely on the daily motocross special tests.

Another of the problems which bedevilled the event in 1951 is also characteristic of the ISDT as a whole. This was the difficulty caused by organizational and administrative errors. That year the British teams had special cause for complaint. They were allocated accommodation in the hotel Campo dei Fiori which was situated on the top of a 4000 ft mountain approached by nine miles of narrow road with many hairpin bends. Team manager Len Heath covered 400 miles during the week simply driving to and from event headquarters. Major Watling, the British representative on the FIM jury was, however, living in the HQ hotel itself and was thereby separated from effective discussion with the teams.

On the first morning, with the start at 6 am, the British riders found that the bus arranged to collect them from the hotel failed to arrive. The only alternative was the funicular railway and, in order to use this, the teams were forced to crawl from their beds at 3.30 am. All of this pales into insignificance by comparison with the events of the first day. The morning was relatively uneventful and the lunch check was in the small town of Biella. At this check the system was to collect riders' time cards and arrange them in re-starting order for return at the end of the break. In short, the official responsible became confused and so did the time cards. The result was pandemonium. Time schedules went out of the window and the numbers of marks lost were determined by the time spent in finding the card! Subsequently the jury scrubbed the entire afternoon's run from the results.

The second day began with disaster for the Italian trophy team. D'Ignazio was involved in an accident en route to the start from his home. The trophy was now a straight fight between Britain and Austria. Apart from this the day produced no special surprises. The Irish rider Terry Hill and Rozenberg of the Dutch A team demonstrated the incredible toughness of ISDT men. Both finished without loss of time, Hill having broken both upper and lower jaws and Rosenberg a leg! Needless to say, neither man started on the third day. Ted Usher, starting at the same time as Walter Zeller, the German road racer, had an interesting day. Allowing

Built to incorporate every refinement required by the competition rider the Triumph "Trophy" model has a long string of successes to its credit from every corner of the world. Easy and accurate to handle, thanks to its light weight (295 lb.) and a steering geometry evolved as a result of experience gained in fiercely contested competitive events. The engine, using the same unique die cast alloy head and barrel as the "Tiger 100," is designed to provide a high power output at low revolutions, yet give adequate top end performance when required. Riding standard "Trophy" models the Triumph team completed the 1950 International Six Days Trial without loss of marks, winning a Manufacturers Team Award—the third to be won in succession (1948-49-50).

O.H.V. vertical twin. Bore 63 mm., stroke 80 mm., 498 c.c. Dry sump lubrication. Air cleaner. Manual control magneto. Two-in-one exhaust. 6" ground clearance. 70° lock. Telescopic forks. Wide ratio four-speed gearbox. 2½ gall. petrol tank. Folding kickstarter. Quick release headlamp. Dunlop tyres 400—19 rear 300—20 front. Finished silver sheen and black. (For complete technical data see back pages.)

SPECIFICATION

Triumph Trophy. One of the most successful ISDT bikes ever. It won Manufacturers awards six years running in late 1940s and early 1950s. Rigid rear end enabled quick wheel changing – sprung hub could have been used but was too unwieldy

the BMW to go about its business ahead of him, Usher finished the day on time while Zeller lost four minutes before the last check as the result of a puncture.

The following day used Monday's route in reverse and proved to be a good deal more difficult. The main problem was the dusty conditons. In Italy beautiful weather means dust and 'ball bearing' surfaces on the minor roads and tracks. Jack Stocker later claimed that the event was, at this stage, as difficult as anything he had encountered, for it was like riding for miles with flat tyres. Machine problems were beginning to develop. Because of a filter problem the British Army's Gold Star BSAs were suffering from a faulty oil scavenging system, with Les Archer the worst affected.

The day was not entirely without administrative problems either! Early numbers at the start were given twice the normal working time for no apparent reason. John Draper of the BSA works team was having a famous week. On the first two days he had been issued

with a 'normal' time card instead of a plus 10 per cent. Having sorted this out, on Thursday he reached the penultimate check at Oleggio before the officials arrived. At first penalized with 100 marks he was later reinstated and fined £2 instead!

On Friday it became apparent that the Italian organizers were determined to introduce really difficult sections. The morning's 145 miles covered sections of dusty and rocky tracks with severe gradients, interspersed with easier road links. In order to stay on time riders found it necessary to 'get down on the tank' on the road sections. The 27 miles between Callazio and San Pellegrino were generally considered to be the most difficult to date. Many British riders compared the worst parts with the Devil's Staircase in the Scottish Six Days Trial. After these sections of the 1951 event, only 15 of the trophy, vase and manufacturers' teams remained unpenalized. Nevertheless the morning was far from impossible, for the German Zündapp sidecar team and the Italian Vespas (the latter exclusively *scoo-ter*- mounted) were still on time. By comparison with the morning the 105-mile night run, mainly on first- and second-class tarmac roads, was uneventful. Even so, fate was not on John Draper's side as he was involved in a collision with a car and retired injured.

Continuing with a similar pattern on the fifth day the organizers introduced two tight and very difficult sections early in the morning. The second of these, 21 miles of rutted and broken tracks across Monte San Michele to Laveno, cost more gold medals than any other part of the week and finally decided the destination of the trophy. H. Rauh of the Austrian trophy team simply could not get his 250cc Puch over on time and lost one mark at the next check. Later the Austrian team lodged a protest that the section was more than a mile longer than shown on the route cards. Actual measurement showed it to be a mile shorter! There seems little doubt that Britain deserved to win. In this area Bob Manns broke his throttle cable but still managed to change it and check in on time. Not all riders were as fortunate. On the descent to Laveno, Tom Ellis, of the British vase B team, catapulted over the bars of his BSA and ended up 50 ft down a cliff. Local spectators recovered him and the BSA but he lost a lot of time. Olga Kevelos, riding a 125cc Parilla provided by the factory, also went over the side, breaking two teeth and was forced to retire. S. Lindvall of the Swedish vase A team lost marks as the result of a split petrol tank.

The speed tests were held on Sunday at the Monza Autodrome and the story was once again of relative

schedules and percentage improvement on target times. Fortunately the British trophy team had only to satisfy the minimum requirement and this they did without fuss. The vase contest was a straight battle between Great Britain A and Holland A. In the club contest Newport and Gwent saw Gilchrist, Redmore and Dunn on their Triumphs against the Stockholm club. The British vase team stood little chance against the Dutch 250cc Jawas but they certainly tried! In the end the Dutch improved by 17 per cent and the British by 14 per cent.

The hard luck story of the event goes to Gilchrist of the Newport team. During a routine plug change before the test he broke a plug and could not remove it. Even on a Triumph the schedule cannot be maintained on one cylinder! The nature of the speed tests did highlight one of Britain's problems. While the test remained to sort out ties at the end of the event, the larger machines would always be handicapped. There was, moreover, little hope of changing to fairer schedules because of the very great popularity of smaller-engined bikes in Continental Europe.

As a footnote, and not without relevance, the Italian Vespas finished the week without penalty. Other manufacturer's teams to win FIM golds were Puch, Royal Enfield, Norton, Triumph and BSA (Holland).

1952

The event based at Bad Aussee in Austria in 1952 may well be seen in hindsight as the 'writing on the wall' year. The British teams were eliminated from the event by an unmitigated series of mechanical disasters. It is

British Army riders on 'parade' before departure to Italy for 1951 ISDT. Left to right: Lt W E Dow, 2 Lt L R Archer, S/sgt E Arnott, Capt D J Miles, Sgt V E Mark, Sgt J Whittingham, RSM H Broad, Sgt D G Rawthorn, Sgt J H Moore (mechanic), Capt L J H Jenkins and Major E R R Lloyd (Officer-in-charge)

The famous British woman competitor Olga Kevelos at the start of the 1951 ISDT at Varese in northern Italy. She was the only woman among 221 entrants. Olga rode a 125 Parilla provided by the factory, but her trial ended on the fifth day when she crashed over a cliff suffering painful facial injuries and wrecking her machine in the process

true that certain aspects of the trial such as the night run were particularly difficult, but in the main it was the sort of event in which British riders and machines would have been expected to do well. Of course the old problem of speed schedules and machine capacity was raised. The trophy was contested by Britain, Germany, Austria, Czechoslovakia, Sweden and Italy and of these only Britain entered machines of over 250cc. The Czechs had their usual CZs and Jawas, the Italians another rare collection ranging from a 73cc Alpino to a 175cc Guazzoni, the Germans 175cc Maicos and 98cc NSUs, the Austrians 175cc and 250cc Puchs and the Swedes the usual 125cc and 250cc NVs. Before the event the Germans maintained that a 500cc machine would be incapable of maintaining the speed schedule, but in the event there was little to suggest that this was true. Because of the apparent fragility of the British machines it is probably best to look at the event from the viewpoint of mechanical failures.

The weather played a significant part in the problems faced during the six days. Only on the fourth day could the weather be regarded as reasonable. Both immedi-

ately before and during the majority of the trial heavy rain fell and temperatures were very low. Bad Aussee is situated 5500 ft above sea-level. At the lower levels heavy rain fell and the tarmac surfaces were extremely slippery. This made it impossible to use the extra power of the larger engines to make up time. If anything the conditions favoured engine capacities of 175 to 250cc, powerful enough to tackle the gradients and favoured by the speed schedules. Sidecar outfits were also in a reasonably favourable situation, especially as the tracks were frequently wide enough to allow overtaking.

At the highest levels used during the event melting snow was frequently encountered, inhibiting the performance of the bigger machines. Between the two levels was one which consisted of sleet, rain and mud. Strangely enough many British competitors preferred this since it reproduced the conditions in which they always performed at their best. The yellowish limestone which provided the surface of many tracks was at its best in the wet for controlled sliding, braking and acceleration.

Although the British disasters did not really begin until the second day, by the end of the first day only Britain and Czechoslovakia remained without penalty in the trophy competition. Johann Kramer of the Austrian team dropped out when his 175cc Puch was fed with straight petrol. The German team lost Dolmann and his 98cc NSU in an accident and the Italians lost Serafini's 175cc Guazzoni with gearbox trouble. Sweden lost time although the team was still intact. Their NVs were simply underpowered for the severe climbs of the day.

On the second day the morning's run involved negotiating miles of narrow, muddy lanes in continuous heavy rain. Don Evans of the British vase A team had a

Weird looking 123cc Lambretta scooter with which Italian rider Mario Masserini won a gold medal in the 1951 ISDT

One of the 246cc split single Puch two-strokes with which the Austrians came so close to winning the Trophy contest in 1951. Puch machines also won the premier Manufacturers Award

disastrous time. Having stopped to repair a leaking fuel tank he crashed trying to make up time. Don Williams (497cc Norton) found him lying unconscious in the road and gave some help. Then George Buck went off to look for an ambulance, only to be passed by Evans on the Enfield revived and trying to decrease the 17-minute delay! The lunch stop was at Graz and the event then went into hibernation for six hours awaiting the start of the night run. The machines stood in the pouring rain for six hours. It was at this stage that Bob Mann's Matchless Twin refused to restart. Indeed it was still out of action several hours later. The Lucas 'Wader' magneto was full of water. Some accounts blame this on condensation but the magneto was fitted with a 'breather' pipe which had been especially lengthened but seems to have caused capillary action. In any case the British trophy challenge would fail after four successive victories. At this stage the Czech Jawas were still dealing easily with the time schedules and the riders were able to clean their machines before handing them in at the end of the day.

The night run itself was a horror. It comprised a 120-mile journey in rain, fog, snow and ice and incorporating a crossing of the 5000 ft Gaberl Pass with a four-mile section of hairpin bends coated with three inches of slushy snow. David Miles of the British Army BSA team sums it up: 'David Redmore and I took it in turns to lead each other as we groped our way agonisingly slowly from hairpin to hairpin up the slush covered, loose surfaced 1 in 5 gradient and down the equally steep and even more vicious descent. We seemed to be isolated in a world of our own, with no sign of life except for the wheel tracks of the riders ahead of us.' They made it to the last check with seconds to spare. Others in trouble included Howard Taylor whose Royal Enfield outfit went out when the distributor drive sheared at the top of the mountain. Molly Briggs, ever helpful, stopped to give a hand but then her Triumph's lights failed and she groped her way to the finish just inside the permitted hour of lateness.

The third day was slightly less eventful but Jim Alves' and Hammond's Triumphs were already beginning to show signs of the gearbox problems which were to put them out. Hammond was only able to select bottom and second gears but still managed to get along at up to 60 mph. At the end of the day his vase B team with the Dutch A were the only unpenalized vase contes-

ABOVE **Majestic scenery in the Italian Alps. S Mazzola (CZ) leads N Biasci and D Mazzoncini (Vespa's). Mazzoncini won a 'gold', helping the Vespa team win a Manufacturer's award**

RIGHT **Mario Visioli with his 60cc pull-rod Ducati four-stroke at Arona, the smallest machine in the 1951 ISDT. Although Visioli was destined to retire on the fourth day his team mate Umberto Tamarozzi on a sister machine went on to gain a bronze medal**

tants. Clearly this would not last for long for, in addition to Hammond's problems, Dick Clayton's Matchless was suffering from badly twisted forks and all that evening he practised changing the fork yokes on Bob Mann's retired machine. On the following morning, after struggling for 50 minutes, he broke the seal on the front numberplate and was immediately disqualified. Hammond only managed to get as far as the first check and shortly thereafter the Triumph gearbox failed completely. Jim Alves nursed his gearbox until the fifth day when it finally seized. All manner of reasons have been given for this problem but it seems that the sliding pinion seized on the layshaft. It has been claimed that the components included shafts from 1950 pattern gearboxes with later pinions and also that the case hardening of the layshaft splines was faulty. Be that as it may, the Czechs, even though they lost a couple of marks, remained the only intact trophy team.

More problems were still to come. On the fourth day Hugh Viney had great trouble starting his AJS. Although he managed to do so with a couple of seconds in hand, John Brittain did not and was forced to push start his Royal Enfield. Temperatures were so low that the heavy oil needed to cope with hard work was like treacle at the early start times. Subsequently riders were changing to lighter, 20 sae oil at the end of the day and then changing to heavier oil when the engines were warm. It may be that lubrication problems caused Brittain's Enfield engine to fail terminally 31 miles from home on the fifth day. Don Evans was still suffering from a leaking fuel tank and on day four his event ended when the bike caught fire and burned out. Jack Stocker's Royal Enfield also sprang a leak but he managed to contain the problem. David Tye's BSA suffered from a similar problem. By the close of play at the end of the fourth day 33 per cent of the entry had retired. Although this attrition rate was not uncommon, the state of the British teams certainly was. Nevertheless, British riders were still showing their real class.

On the fifth day there were amazing scenes at Wasserbogen, near Frauenstein, where a muddy lane led through a watersplash and then up a muddy hill with a clay surface. Machines and riders were everywhere, attempting to get to the top at all costs. Many took at least four attempts, arriving late at the lunch check, and the rule about outside assistance was severely bent. Into this mêlée charged Jack Stocker on his 700cc Royal Enfield, Molly Briggs on the 500cc Triumph and D. Murdoch on a 498cc AJS, and all of them climbed 'feet up' to the sumit! The Czech team, in contrast, stopped engines at the watersplash and pushed their Jawas to the top. The jury later decided to cancel all the penalties in this section as it had been 'too severe'.

On the final day the speed test was a formality for the Czech trophy team, who had lost only five marks to Austria's 600 and Britain's 700. In the vase competition only the German team was unpenalized at this time. Unhappily for them Roth's 590cc BMW refused to start, handing the win to Czechoslovakia. No manufacturers' teams finished unpenalized so no awards were made.

So it would seem that 1952 was all gloom, doom and disaster, but it was not so. Relatively unnoticed and unheralded, one of the most remarkable performances ever by British motorcycles was underway. At the end of August John McNulty from Neath, appointed as observer by the ACU, travelled to BSA's Small Heath factory and, from a batch of 37 498cc Star Twins on the production line, selected three at random. BSA had decided to make an attempt to win the coveted Maudes Trophy, awarded by the ACU for the most meritorious reliability performance of the year. The object of the exercise was to subject these three standard production machines to a lifetime of hard work within the space of a few short weeks. Since the ISDT was intended to be the

DKW entered their entire road racing team of Siegfried Wünsche, H P Müller and Ewald Kluge on RT125 models. Wünsche (shown here) won a 'gold', the other two 'silvers'

ultimate test of such machines, the event was included on the itinerary!

Having selected the machines, they were equipped with simple, but very important, modifications for the Six Days. Larger rear drive sprockets were fitted, lowering the overall gearing to that used when pulling a sidecar. A tank top toolkit and mapholder, together with a vital crankcase shield, was fitted to each machine, and the bikes were then sealed and locked up until the test commenced on 7 September. In the event itself air bottles to inflate flat tyres were carried and extra tyre security bolts were fitted to prevent tyre 'creep'. At the start on Sunday 3 September, the highly experienced trio of riders – Norman Vanhouse, Fred Rist and Brian Martin – were allowed to tailor the riding positions to their own requirements. The three riders were accompanied by one car carrying the ACU observer and George Savage (and for the second half Bert Perrigo) the factory representative and, initially, by a Golden Flash sidecar outfit with the official photographer. This unfortunate soul ended up in hospital at Tonnerre in France having his appendix removed! From the start, via an official send-off by the ACI in London, the trio

Keitel and Seeman won a gold medal with their Zündapp KS601 sidecar outfit. They are shown here on the 5th day of the trial at Lecco

crossed to The Hague and thence via Antwerp, Paris, Geneva, Zurich and Innsbruck to Bad Aussee. Having stopped briefly to see what was going on they then rode on to Vienna before returning to hand in their machines at the start in Bad Aussee on 16 September.

From 17 to 23 September the trio were engaged in serious competition. It was at this time that their head-gear changed from black berets to 'pudding basin' helmets. Also at this stage the riders became the Birmingham Motor Cycle Club's official entry for the Six Days. The prevailing conditions at the event have already been described and they were generally appalling. The British machinery was decimated. It has to be remembered of course that the three 'Stars' were not subject to the plus 10 per cent speed schedules of the top level of competition but, nevertheless, their performance was quite extraordinary. All three completed the event without trouble and penalty free. They were the only British team of any description to win three gold medals. Indeed, no manufacturer's team from any nation, albeit on the plus 10 per cent schedule, succeeded in completing the six days unpenalized and no FIM medals were awarded.

Immediately following this arduous test the three riders exchanged their helmets for the familiar berets and set off on the return journey via Stuttgart, Düsseldorf, Hannover, Hamburg, Kiel, Copenhagen, then ferry to Malmö in Sweden, thence to Gothenberg and Oslo, where they arrived on 30 September. Oslo was entered amid scenes of great enthusiasm and at this, the

ABOVE **Zündapp KS601 ohv flat twins (with sidecar attached) did exceptionally well in the ISDT during the early 1950s. The 597cc engine gave around 34 bhp in competition form**

BELOW **Italy's Carlo Bandirola (Gilera) stops for a well-earned drink during the final day of the trial on 19 September 1951**

For the 15th time, Britain won the ISDT Trophy in the 1240 mile event staged in Italy during September 1951. The victorious team compromised BHM Viney, PH Alves, CM Ray, WJ Stocker, FM Rist and team manager Len Heath

end of the line, the team had covered 4958 miles, including the 1265 miles of the ISDT. At this stage, to prove that there was still life in the machines, speed tests were held producing average speeds of 83 mph for the quarter mile. Brian Martin actually recalls 90 mph on one run.

Perhaps of all the events of the 1950s this epic performance recalls all that was best of the ISDT in its original form, as a test of the strength, stamina and performance of basic production machines. Certainly it puts paid to any ideas about the poor reliability record of British motorcycles of the 1950s.

1953

In some respects the event in 1953 was an anticlimax. Brilliantly organized by the Czechs and based at Gottwaldov, it was blessed with almost unrelieved good weather. As in Wales, and indeed anywhere in central Europe, the severity of the Six Days was dependent to a high degree on the weather, and a course which could be extremely difficult in the wet might just as readily be

innocuous in dry weather. This is not to say that any event can be easy for all competitors. There were still many who lost marks and some who were forced to retire, but for top-class riders on competitive and reliable machinery, there were no real problems. This was, of course, the last time that Great Britain was to win the trophy competition, and by the skin of its teeth. If the Czechs had not suffered from a mysterious bout of ignition trouble, they would not have lost a single vital mark. It certainly seems likely that the schedules in the speed test would have made it impossible for the 500s to compete successfully with the smaller machines. This was undoubtedly so in the vase contest in which four teams, including Britian and Czechoslovakia, were unpenalized and settled the contest on speed. Short of mechanical problems or accidents the smaller capacity bikes were bound to win and the Czechs did so.

In terms of machinery there were no great surprises. The British teams remained faithful to a trophy quintet of big Twins, Jim Alves as usual riding the largest, a 650cc Triumph. The vase teams were also 'twin' mounted with the solitary exception of David Tye's 350cc BSA. Among the other teams the absence of the Italians removed much technical interest, and the Austrian Puch-mounted team withdrew at the last moment. The German Trophy team had a trio of 590cc BMWs teamed up with two 175cccc Maicos, making an un-

LEFT Start of the 27th ISDT at Bad Aussee, Austria. Hugh Viney (AJS Twin) and Phil Mellers (Ariel). This was the latter's second ISDT for the Ariel works team and he was to be forced out through gearbox troubles later in the event. Meanwhile Viney went on to score a 'gold'

LEFT Start of the 27th ISDT at Bad Aussee, Austria. Hugh Viney (AJS Twin) and Phil Mellers (Ariel). This was the latter's second ISDT for the Ariel works team and he was to be forced out through gearbox troubles later in the event. Meanwhile Viney went on to score a 'gold'

likely combination. Sweden was loyal to its NVs, the Czechs were, of course, CZ- and Jawa-mounted, while the Hungarians were out once more on their home-brewed Csepels. Among the vase teams only Sweden and Holland were still following the British 'big banger' route. Notable was the fact that some British competitors were still loyal to the 350cc sidecar class with its relatively favourable time schedules.

No Six Days can be dismissed in a very short space but there was rather less interest in this year. The Hungarian trophy team lost a man on the first day but the crucial moment came on day two when Klimt's 250cc Jawa from the Czech trophy team refused to start for 15 minutes at the beginning of the day. Although he had recovered his 15 minutes by the time he reached the first check (which was in fact only 52 minutes away!), he had lost the one vital mark which would make all the difference. Strangely enough, the Swedish trophy team also lost a man at the start on this day when his NV completely refused to fire.

On Wednesday the two-hour night ride was almost all on good class tarmac roads and caused no problems. Thursday's route, although covering nearly 300 miles, was not especially difficult although two awkward hills were included. At Chavoz the chalk surfaced climb took

BELOW German Horex teamsters checking over their machinery. They won two silver and one bronze medals. The 1952 event was extremely difficult and no manufacturer's team finished without penalty and no awards were made

Gold medal winner Ted Usher among a snow covered landscape high up in the Austrian peaks. The going here was particularly tough with a skating-rink type road surface

a lot of marks and caused some retirements, although the British 350cc sidecar outfits managed to succeed. Another of the Swedish Trophy men fell by the wayside when he drowned his machine in a watersplash. The unfortunate Walter Zeller was eliminated from the German trophy team when a universal joint failed on the BMW's transmission. This was an unheard of problem and caused much heart searching back at Munich. At the end of the day Great Britain had the only unpenalized trophy team.

Friday and Saturday continued dry, warm and dusty, and presented no problems to most of the riders.

However, on Friday David Tye of the British vase B team damaged the front wheel of his BSA quite badly and lost nine marks. Hitchcock's 148cc Triumph Terrier also failed and joined the sole 123cc BSA Bantam in retirement. Clearly, if Britain was to enter the small capacity classes better machines were needed. By close of play on Friday 100 of the original 236 starters had lost marks or retired. John Giles of the British vase B team was once again afflicted by the one-cylinder Triumph syndrome and lost five marks. Olga Kevelos missed the route marking and lost five marks. After all the preparation and training which she had undertaken with the Czechs before the event she must have been very fed up.

On the final day it actually rained during the morning and this could have made things difficult for the British trophy team. Set to average 62 mph on the three-mile circuit in order to win, they might have been pushed in

the wet. As it was, the rain stopped and the surface quickly dried out. One minute on the second day had cost Czechoslovakia the trophy. Usher, Evans and Ray made mighty efforts to defeat the Czechs in the vase contest, but could not really hope to compete against the 44.7 mph schedule required for the smaller machines.

1954

Many expected Britain to win the trophy in Wales in 1954. After all, the team was on home ground and had all the advantages apart from time schedules. Yet in the end it failed in the attempt to secure trophy and vase and never won them again. Not that 1954 was a clear-cut victory for Czechoslovakia. The result went into the records as the event in which the only team to lose no marks at all came second! It also remains in the memories of many riders, team managers and administrators as an example of how *not* to run the event. This is all the more extraordinary because the 1950 Six Days, also based at Llandrindod Wells and with the same clerk of the course, had been a model of organization and had set the pattern for the Continental Europeans. It was also the year in which a distinction was made between 'Team Schedule (Special)' and 'Standard' gold medals. Moreover, Club teams, for the first time, had to include at least two different makes of machine, thereby removing the practice of manufacturers entering spurious club teams for advertising purposes.

Setting these factors aside for the moment, a brief review of the British team selection tests gives an indication of the approach to machinery. Expecting the event to be of the usual wet, muddy and difficult Welsh variety there was a general, although not universal, return to single-cylinder machines. AMC entered a mixture of twins and singles. Ariel reverted to 497cc singles. BSA continued to nail its colours to the 348cc Gold Stars, and once more a solitary 148cc Bantam appeared. Royal Enfield entered three 346cc Bullet singles while Triumph, of course, remained faithful to its 646cc twins. At long last, however, some serious factory attention was being given to small two-strokes. This year saw the introduction of a new class from 125 to 175cc and Francis Barnett and James were taking a real interest in this. For selection Francis Barnett entered two machines and James three. The James's were 125s uprated to 150cc and the Francis Barnetts modified 197s. Francis Barnett used Villiers 8E power units modified to use a 55 mm bore with a deep skirt Villiers 30 C piston giving 172cc. In the event itself three DMWs used this 172cc conversion. This class was hotly contested by the four-stroke MV Agustas, with more two-strokes including German Maicos and a large number of DKWs and Puchs. The British 172s were producing 10 bhp and tuned for top end perofrmance with little power below 2000 rpm. Speed schedules in the selection tests were set higher than for the event itself, i.e. 27.5 mph for the up to 175cc class and 350 side-

LEFT **Eddie Dow (500 BSA Gold Star) leads Phil Mellers (500 Ariel Twin). Captain Dow, as he was then, went on to win a gold medal for himself and the British Army team**

BELOW **Speed test on autobahn near Salzburg in 1952 event. Riders include Walter Zeller BMW (244), J E Breffitt Norton (208), DS Tye BSA (259) and BHM Viney AJS (233)**

BOTTOM **The victorious 1952 Czechoslovak Trophy Team. Left to right: C Kohlicek (150 CZ), J Pudil (150CZ), R Dusil (248 Jawa), J Kubes (248 Jawa) and J Novotny (248 Jawa)**

cars, and 33 mph for the bigger solos. The actual time schedules used during the competition were as follows:

50–75cc	20 mph	All + 10 per cent for all team members except club teams.
100cc	24 mph	
125–175cc and 350cc s/c	25 mph	
250cc solos and 250cc+ s/c	27 mph	
350cc+ solos	30 mph	

Machine reliability during the pre-event selection was not very encouraging. John Brittain damaged the front end of his Royal Enfield. Parsons' and Holmes' Ariels, Tye's BSA and Humphries' Norton sidecar outfit all went out with waterlogged magnets, and Jeff Smith's BSA was delayed by the same problem. The front brake

If 1952 was generally a poor year for the British, there was at least one truly remarkable performance. This concerned a trio of standard production 498cc BSA Star Twins. Not only did they complete the Six Days without trouble and penalty free (and were the only British team of any description to win three gold medals), but they also clocked up nearly 5000 miles apiece through 10 countries to win the coveted Maudes Trophy

anchorage of Smith's Francis Barnett gave trouble, damaging him and the machine. Ted Usher's Matchless got into difficulties when it inhaled water. Jackson's AJS broke its connecting-rod. Jack Stocker's Royal Enfield broke its rear wheel spindle. Povey's James and Baldwin's AJS sidecar outfit failed to complete the speed test and Sid Wicken's Triumph ran out of steam. Although this all seems rather awful it at least indicates the importance of discovering problems before an event rather than during it. After all this the selectors decided to retain the trophy and vase A teams from the previous year, to replace Brian Martin with David Tye in vase B

and to include Parsons with his 497cc Ariel and Smith with the 172cc Francis Barnett as first and second reserves respectively.

Recriminations about the organization began before the start on 20 September. Regulations seem to have been circulated late and, in some cases, in the wrong language, and a flood of entries were received at the last moment. The entry acceptances were increased from 200 to 300 but 375 entries were received and some riders whose entries had been returned turned up at the start and were accepted. Indeed it was necessary for the jury to meet on the night before the start in order to decide who should be allowed to compete! In some instances it was necessary to increase the number of riders starting together from two to three, thereby making the time-keepers' task more difficult. Moreover, to increase the competitors' discontent, the amount of hotel accommodation required was underestimated and there were problems.

By the end of the first day the worst incident of the week had already happened and the FIM representative was openly expressing dismay. At the start a member of the German trophy team started his engine before being given the signal and was penalized by five marks. Then the Swedes were upset by baulking on a slippery hill but much worse was to follow. On leaving the lunch check at Llandovery riders should have been directed right at an unmarked turn but the marshall responsible was missing. Many competitors turned the wrong way and then picked up the second day's route marking. The result was chaos with riders realizing their mistake and returning at high speed to Llandovery. During this period Martin's James collided with a Czech trophy rider travelling in the opposite direction with disastrous results as the Czech was unable to continue. One of the major factors involved in this confusion was the British route-marking procedure. This involved using cards: white indicating straight on, blue for 'left' and red for

An ISDT Jawa on the company's stand at the Swiss Show early in 1953

'right'. Clearly this meant that there was no indication as to which day's route the marking showed. The European method used arrows with a different colour for each day backed up with large-scale maps in the appropriate colour. At any rate the outcome of this appeared to be a daily penalty of 100 marks for the Czech team. What made the matter worse was the inclusion of another slimy, rocky hill near Talley shortly after the disastrous lunch check. The result was hundreds of protests and a jury session which lasted well into the small hours of Tuesday. The most important outcome was the reinstatement of the Czech rider, who was given time to repair his machine and remained unpenalized. Of course the Czechs then proceeded to finish the week without any loss of marks!

The rest of the week was separated into three categories. Tuesday and Wednesday remained relatively easy, the weather was reasonable and yet the organizers reduced the time schedule to the 10 per cent slower 'B' times reserved for exceptionally bad weather. One of the problems which caused this was difficulty in communicating with officials in the far flung parts of the course. Consequently, with a poor weather forecast on Tuesday afternoon for Wednesday, the decision to reduce speeds were made many hours before the start. It was unnecessary. The British team were recorded as saying that Tuesday was 'a pleasant jaunt through magnificent scenery'! This did not however, prevent the Swedish trophy team losing two marks for five minutes'

LEFT **The spectacular opening ceremony for the 1953 ISDT at Gottwaldov, Czechoslovakia**

BELOW **Weighing in at Gottwaldov, a group of Jawa 250 two-strokes**

late arrival at Tregaron. Although the route was more difficult on Wednesday there was plenty of time for able riders. However, the German team lost Ulrich Pohl (Maico) who broke his wrist in an accident, reducing the trophy teams with a clean sheet to four. There were complaints after the day's proceedings about the passage checks used to control possible by-passing sections of the route. Some of these were alleged to be located elsewhere than indicated on route cards, while some were missing altogether.

Thursday's route was in a separate category, i.e. difficult. Reverting to the faster time schedule the traditional route took competitors into the difficult territory of the northern Cambrian mountains. The worst area was the slippery rutted grass, deep water splash and severe gradients just before the second check at Bidno, only 43 miles from the start. Much time was lost in this area but the worst problem affected the Italian trophy team which lost marks when two riders (both on Mi-Vals) ran out of fuel. Again an organizational error was partly responsible. It had become normal practice for fuel to be available every day at the start and finish. However, on Wednesday evening announcements were made in English and German in the start/finish area, that fuel would not be available on Thursday morning and advising riders to fill their fuel tanks. This message was either not heard, or not understood, by the Italian teams. More disaster befell them when the vase B team lost Gandossi (98cc Ducati) after he was in collision with a car. This was certainly not an easy day. The Hirnant and Eunant Passes were as diffi-cult as ever and, on the roads to the lunch check at Bala, many riders were trying very hard. Even Jack Stocker claimed he was 'frightened to death'.

Nevertheless, the trophy contest was now a two-team affair. Two Army teams were still very much in the run-ning for the club award. It is worth noting that David Miles had damaged the front wheel of his Triumph quite badly. At the end of the day he records that it was suggested he replace it with one from the machine of a retired Scandinavian rider and, since it was a marked part, the marking would be altered. Miles declined the offer and finished the week with a wobbly wheel. Unhappily this was an indication of the growth of the great 'cheating' controversy which was to bedevil the event in the future.

If Thursday was in the 'difficult' category, Friday was something else. Riders recall parts of it as a night-mare. It was so bad that the jury, which had been exceeding its charter quite frequently during the week, ruled that the 250cc class should be given an extra minute! Frequent rain squalls, the normal time sched-ules and the problems of the previous day's course in reverse caused great difficulty. The 13 muddy miles of grass track overlooking Barmouth Bay caused such problems that many riders, finding virtually no traction, walked alongside their machines. The Bidno to Glas

W Aukthum (174 Maico) approaching the Myjava time-control point on the 4th day of the 1953 event. West Germany's hopes of winning the Silver Vase were dashed when Aukthum could not start his engine on the start line the following morning

Lyn section was even worse, especially around the Diluw watersplash. Three of the Austrian trophy team men lost time in this area. Nevertheless the British and Czech teams managed to stay on time. Brian Martin of the British vase B team drowned his engine and lost six marks. Olga Kevelos, still going strong on her 150cc CZ, couldn't restart after the Diluw splash and retired.

Although the last part of the week was quite severe all of the major classes were still to be settled by the results of the speed test. The British trophy team faced a formi-dable task. The two 350cc Royal Enfields of Jack Stocker and John Brittain needed to complete 22 laps of the Madley Airfield circuit. Hugh Viney, Jim Alves and Bob Manns needed 23 laps. The 150cc Czech Jawas were required to do 19 laps and the 250s 21 laps. The Madley circuit measured 2.1 miles with a bumpy sur-face covered in places with small stones, and five slow corners. The Czechs remorselessly improved on their speed schedules by 2 per cent more than the British team and that was that. The vase contest no longer included the British A team. Don Evans' Royal Enfield seemed to have a cylinder-head gasket problem. He lost a mark at the start and then crashed out en route to Madley, damaging the bike too badly to continue. This left the Czechs, Swedes and Dutch to fight it out. One of the Czech Jawas and a Swedish NV seized, leaving the Dutch B team with the vase. The three-man team comprised Schram (147cc Maico), den Haan (248cc Puch) and Jansema (148cc Jawa).

On this occasion even the club contest was decided on this last test since a number of teams, including two from the British Army, were still unpenalized. The German Maico Motorsport team came out on top. The

ABOVE **The Czech teams proceed to the weigh-in for the 1954 event through the streets of Llandrindod Wells**

FAR RIGHT **Riding a prototype 150cc BSA Bantam Major with the new swinging arm rear suspension, George Pickering (85) won a well-deserved silver medal even though he was saddled with the 10% faster 'team' schedule. Here he heads a group of competitors as they pass near a Welsh target range**

RIGHT **West German Rudolf Hessler gained a gold medal in the 1954 ISDT, riding a 246cc version of the Zündapp Elastic production roadster**

Riders strive to make up time on the tarmac sections of road on the route. Here, near Forest Lodge, above the Senni valley, J Pudil (148 Jawa) of the Czech Trophy team is followed by M Riva (124 Rumi), of the Italian Vase 'A' team, and G Bodmer (174 DKW), of the German Vase 'B' team

military team award went to the British AMCA no 2 team. British manufacturers among the awards were BSA, Matchless, Triumph and, for the first time, Francis Barnett.

1955

In 1954 it could be argued that Great Britain should have won the trophy as the only unpenalized team, or indeed as the only team to complete the entire course. As it was the trophy was lost by a whisker . . . and the British were never to come as close again. It seemed that in 1955 the rot really set in. In terms of machines and men the British trophy and vase teams were very much the same mixture. There were exceptions of course. Poor Hugh Viney, once more appointed as team captain after the selection tests, was injured in an accident in August and was unable to ride. His place was taken by

porated the usual BSA Gold Stars and Triumphs, with Fisher and Smith's 172cc Francis Barnetts in vase B. By and large the machinery was as seen before with detailed modifications. For example, the Royal Enfield Bullet was equipped for the first time with a crankshaft-mounted AC generator for lighting purposes and a separate Lucas racing magneto, and the Ariel Twins had full-width front hubs.

In fact the event was still playing an important role for manufacturers in the testing of prototype parts for the standard road machinery which the team bikes so closely resembled. Unfortunately there was still no concerted effort to produce smaller and lighter machines with reduced engine capacity to take advantage of the more favourable speed schedules. At last it seemed that the 350cc sidecar exponents were about to abandon their attempt for team selection. These heros had for years persevered with outfits taking advantage of the speed schedules, but the attrition rate was too great. This year A.J. Humphries was still trying with a 348cc ohc Norton International with a Canterbury sprung-wheel sidecar. In short it was about to be demonstrated that Continental European machines were becoming more suitable for the problem posed by the ISDT.

The event was based once more at Gottwaldov in Czechoslovakia and it proved to be a model of first-class organization. Rain, mud, severe conditions and tighter times played havoc with many of the entrants and combined, despite gallant attempts, to decimate many teams. The West German trophy team, on 175 and 250cc two-strokes, proved that even in an event as severe as this, light and nimble machines with a good power to weight ratio could stay on time.

On winning the trophy for the first time since 1935 the West Germans were the only team of the six entered to complete the 1320-mile course without penalty. The victorious team consisted of: J. Abt (174 DKW), O. Brack (175 DKW), E. Deike (172 Maico), U. Feser (174 DKW) and V. von Zitzewitz (245 Maico).

The first day, Tuesday, was difficult and at this early stage the British trophy team lost its first marks when Ted Usher had rear wheel spindle problems on his Matchless. However, difficult as this day was, it became insignificant after day two. On the afternoon of that day the combination of rain, mud and 'stopper' hills produced a chaotic situation. Some of the British riders, notably Jim Alves and Sid Wicken, were in serious trouble with mud jamming the close-fitting throttle slides. Wicken, for example, was forced to ride with the throttle jammed half open, using the ignition cut out to control his speed! The conditions pulverized the entry and eventually only approximately 50 per cent of the 243 entrants finished the week. By the end of the day all of the British 'privateers' except Cope had retired. Jim Alves had lost marks, George Fisher's Francis Barnett had seized solid, Parsons' Ariel was out, its engine clanking horribly. Stirland's Royal Enfield was suffer-

Bob Ray from the vase A team, and the first reserve, Gordon Jackson, took over in the vase team. Jack Stocker was also unable to take part because of injuries which he had sustained in that year's Welsh Two Day. The trophy team therefore comprised Jim Alves with a 500cc TR5 Triumph (the ACU had insisted that year on the model being identical to the kind that the public could buy), John Brittain on a 350cc Royal Enfield which had a 350cc top end grafted on to a strong 500cc bottom half, Bob Manns and Ted Usher on, respectively, 500 AJS and Matchless Twins and Ray on his usual mount a 500cc Ariel Twin. The vase teams incor-

ing from lubrication problems which would cause his retirement on the next day, and Smith and Ellis had both abandoned their BSAs with drowned magnetos. So dire was the overall situation that the organizers cancelled all of the afternoon penalties and allowed all survivors a 60-minute maintenance period before the start of the next day.

After these amendments it became clear that the British were 124 marks down, the Austrians 101, Czechoslovakia 3 and, amazingly, the Germans penalty free, demonstrating that it could be done. Only two vase teams, Czechoslovakia B and Poland A were still 'clean', from a total of 23 squads!

The rest of the week was modified by the organizers and it became much easier. However, despite the amnesty on Wednesday, Smith and Ellis failed to restore life to their BSAs and Jim Alves lost another mark on Wednesday with a recurrence of throttle slide problems. Nevertheless, as the days went by British hopes rose as doubts began to emerge about the condition of German and Czech two-strokes after the battering early in the week. On the fourth day the Czechs lost another 26 marks when Roucka had an accident. However, any hopes that might have existed were completely dashed on Saturday when Ted Usher's Matchless shed the retaining nut on its engine shaft shock-absorber, wrecking the primary chain and putting him out. Nor was the British team's chapter of disaster complete for on the final morning, preceding the speed test, Gordon Jackson discovered a broken front fork spindle clamp which put him out of the event, and Jim Alves' Triumph failed on the last lap of the speed test.

Only 119 riders of the original 243 came to the start on the last day. Nevertheless the West Germans did not lose a single mark and won the trophy handsomely from Czechoslovakia on 29 and Great Britain on 329. Austria and Sweden lost over 1000 marks each and the Italians, who had withdrawn, lost 2502. Amazingly enough Czechoslovakia B, Poland A and West Germany B were all unpenalized and fought out the vase on the speed test, the Czechs coming out on top.

Only four manufacturers' teams finished without losing marks and were thus eligible for team prizes; they were DKW, Maico, NSU 'One' and NSU 'Two'. This result illustrates to perfection West Germany's dominance in the 1955 IDST.

From a final entry of 248 riders, 243 actually started the event. No fewer than 97 retired and only 56 gained gold medals for completing the course without losing marks.

British medals were:

Gold
350cc   John Brittain (Royal Enfield)
500cc   Brian Martin (BSA), Mob Manns (AJS), N.S. Holmes (Ariel), John Giles (Triumph), J.E. Wicken (Triumph).

P H Alves (649 Triumph) during the speed test part of the 1954 ISDT. He won an FIM Special Gold Medal (no marks lost, riding to team schedule)

Silver
350cc   Pat Brittain (Royal Enfield).

Bronze
500cc   C. Cope (Ariel), G, Ray (Ariel), P. Alves (Triumph).

1956

The 1956 Six Days in West Germany is remembered for a number of special reasons. Based at Garmisch-Partenkirchen it was the first year in which trophy teams comprised six riders instead of five, mounted on machines which must still come from at least two of the nation's own factories and be of three different engine capacities. Vase teams were increased in size to four members. For the British, in particular, this caused even more problems for the trophy team. It was now more or less imperative to run 350s, 500s and 650s since the ACU and team management had little faith in smaller two- or four-stroke machines in this part of the competition. With Hugh Viney now in the post of team manager, the task was given to John Brittain (350 Royal Enfield) as team captain, Ted Usher (350 Matchless),

ABOVE Once again Triumph won a Manufacturers Team Award. Left to right: P F Hammond, P H Alves, J Giles. Alves' machine was basically a standard 650 Tiger 110 fitted with 2-into-1 exhausts and Trophy, front fork. Hammond and Giles rode similar machines, but with 500cc engines

BELOW The Dutch Vase 'B' team, winners of the 1954 Silver Vase. Left to right : S Schram (147 Maico), H Burik (manager), M den Haan (248 Puch) and B L Jansema (148 Jawa)

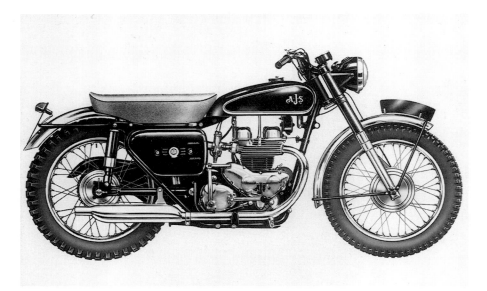

LEFT **The 597cc AJS Model 30 ohv twin of the type campaigned by Gordon Jackson on which he won a gold medal in the 1955 Six Days**

BELOW **The NSU Gelӓndemax was a real force to reckon within the ISDT. In 1955 the German Vase 'B' team was mounted exclusively on these 247cc overhead cam singles**

Brian Martin (500 BSA), Stan Holmes (500 Ariel), Bob Manns on an overbored 506 AJS and John Giles (650 Triumph). There was very little of new technical interest. The AJS and Matchless machines had dispensed with dynamos altogether, relying on the magneto and a battery. The Ariels and Royal Enfields were basically standard single-cylinder trials models, and, wonder of wonders, the Triumphs had new chromium-plated tank badges! The vase teams showed some concession to smaller engine sizes: George Fisher riding a 175cc Triumph in the A team and Ken Heanes a similar model in the B.

This was also the largest event held to date with 320 accepted entrants and 19 participating nations including, for the first time, the USSR. In addition to 7 trophy and 30 Vase teams there were no fewer than 44 manufacturers and 20 club teams. Unhappily it was also the first occasion when host country was involved in a major scandal.

The question of cheating has always bedevilled the ISDT and there have been times when it has threatened the whole future of the event. The general attitude seems to have been, and for that matter remains, that everybody does it and you can't win without breaking the rules. Indeed it has often seemed that there is nothing morally wrong in blatant cheating because that is what the Six Days is all about. It has, for example, been reliably reported that one of a team manager's responsibilities before an event begins is to secure a supply of the organizers' paint and seals, so that marked parts can be changed if necessary! It seems that the first dramatic example of this attitude was found in the 1956 event. There is no doubt that the event, as a whole, was quite difficult. It was, to quote contemporary journalists, 'severe yet sporting'. In other words it was a 'real' international and a tough test of machinery. At the finish of

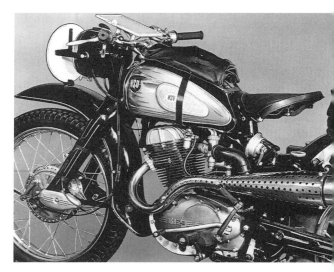

the second day it was noted that Gerhardt Bodmer's 175cc DKW, running in the German trophy team as number 226, was carrying plate number 224 with the 4 overpainted with 6. Then it appeared that H. Ott, number 226 on an identical machine, carried 226 overpainted 224! Count Johnny Lurani, the Italian FIM representative, queried this and then discovered that Bodmer's machine was still receiving attention in the paddock although his time card had been stamped and handed in. Lurani then demanded to know why neither 224 nor 226 was in the *parc fermé* and he was told that both riders had retired. It seems that, subsequent to this, both riders, the team manager and the official who had stamped the time card, all mysteriously disappeared and were not seen again during the event.

However, the incident was soon forgotten and made no difference to the domination of 21 out of the next 22 events by Germany (West and East) and Czechoslovakia. Notwithstanding this there was a taste of things to come as although Czechoslovakia won the event the Italian team was only one mark behind, having lost a single point on the second day. It had been thought that the basic reliance of Italy on small capacity four-stroke machines was a mistake, and that the bikes were too fragile. This no longer appeared to be the case. Certainly their machinery was fast and if the result had been decided on the speed test, the 100cc Laverdas on a 36.076 mph schedule and the 175 Gileras on 46.028 could have out-performed the Czech Jawas. The Italian 125 Mi-Val were of course two-strokes but also powerful performers.

In the event itself Great Britain had three days of unusual optimism. Happy enough in the difficult conditions their trophy team performed very well indeed. Bob Manns was able to change the chaincase on his AJS without losing time and despite the organizers' claim

At Hostalkava checkpoint on the 4th afternoon of the 1955 ISDT. Checking in is J Hradek (248 Jawa) with a rather slower form of transport passing by

that it was a part which could not be replaced within the rules, the jury overturned the verdict. Manns seemed to be out to prove a point because on the second day he also replaced the primary chain without loss of marks. The British sidecar outfits were not so fortunate. By the end of the same day only one, Carey's 350 Royal Enfield, was still left in the running. The days of the outfits were surely numbered. Wednesday was another very tough day. Hardly any of the national team riders had more than a couple of minutes in hand, but Britain was intact and 'clean'. However, this was too good to be true and on Thursday John Brittain's Royal Enfield broke a new fabricated head lug on the frame and, despite attempts to jury rig it, he was forced to retire. Precisely the same disaster afflicted Pat Stirland on the previous day and Sammy Miller on Friday.

So, by the close of play on the fourth day, only Czechoslovakia was still penalty free in the trophy competition. All of the British hopes were then placed on their vase B team comprising Dave Curtis (500 Matchless), David Tye (500 Ariel), Sid Wicken (500 AJS) and Ken Heanes (175 Triumph), who were still without loss of marks at the start of the speed tests.

Speed Schedules 1956

Solo	Road	Speed test
50cc	22.3	26.124
75cc	22.3	31.100
100cc	23.6	36.076
125cc	26.0	41.052
175cc	27.3	46.028
250cc	28.6	51.004
350cc	30.0	55.358
500cc	30.0	59.090
750cc	30.0	59.090
1000cc	30.0	59.090
Sidecar		
250cc	25.0	39.186
350	26.0	43.540
500	27.3	47.894

The 1956 speed test for the vase given a very clear indication of one of Great Britain's most urgent problems at that time. The other teams in contention were Holland B with a 175cc Jawa, a 175cc Maico and two 250cc Zündapps; Germany A with two 250cc NSUs and two 300cc NSUs; and Poland A with 150 and 250cc Jawas. A glance at the speed schedules, combined with the knowledge that the 250cc NSUs were good for 90 mph, will show immediately that the British team stood no chance at all. Indeed, Dave Curtis's Matchless was actually *passed* by Westphal's 250 NSU and it was only with difficulty that the Matchless rider could shake off the smaller machine. Even the Germans were forced to succumb to the speed schedules and they were defeated by the Dutch with Great Britain in last place. Poor David Tye, having disconnected the Ariel's dynamo from the Magdyno for the test, lost the dynamo en route and finished without it. Although not itself a marked part, it was part of the equipment with which the machine must finish and, with it lost, he was excluded and lost his gold medal. Consequently it proved to be another very disappointing event for Britain.

1957

Since so many of the ISDTs have been held in Central Europe it is hardly surprising that they have been affected by international politics from time to time. Having been dramatically affected in 1914 and 1939 it is no real surprise that, following the Anglo-French expedition to Egypt and the crisis involving the Soviet invasion of Hungary (both in the autumn of 1956), the ACU decided that it could not support the 1957 event which was based at Spindleruv Mlyn in Czechoslovakia. Despite this situation 246 riders started the event, which is

At the ski stadium Garmish-Partenkirchen riders prepare their machines in readiness for the 1956 ISDT. In the foreground is Piero Carissioni's 175 Gilera

BELOW **The Russian Victor Pylaew wheelies his massive side-valve 750 M72 flat-twin during the 1956 ISDT. He lost four marks over the six days and won a hard earned silver medal**

remembered as one of the toughest on record. The Czech organizers were determined to ensure that the event would be decided out on the course, without resort to the speed test to settle the finishing order. To achieve this they arranged a tight schedule in difficult country and frequently horrendous weather. The outcome was that by the end of the first day almost a third of the entrants had retired. Only East Germany and Czechoslovakia survived with unpenalized trophy teams, and not a single vase team remained 'clean'. In fact, at the start on the following day Polanka's CZ from the Czech trophy team went out with a gearbox problem, thus eventually ensuring an East German victory. Amazingly enough the Germans managed to finish the entire event without penalty. The Zündapps and Maicos, including 262 and 277cc models, proved extremely tough and reliable as well as swift. The Czech team lost 700 marks, the Italians – very unhappy with the rain and mud – lost 1613 and the Soviet team was totally outclassed. Jawa and Maico won manufacturers' awards, having finished unpenalized. As another sign of the times the Czechs would not accept any sidecar entries as they claimed to be unable to produce a suitable course.

The efforts of the handful of British riders who made this long trip unsupported must not go unrecorded. A.W. Glassbrook (500 BSA), J.S. Oliver (500 BSA) and E.D. Chilton (650 Triumph) represented the Birmingham MCC. The late Roger Maugling, nothing if not unconventional, started the event in the role of rider and journalist on a DMW powered by a twin-cylinder 250cc Villiers 2T engine. Unfortunately, he was unable to finish. In addition to this gallant band the Australian ACU entered Les Fisher from Sydney, on a 125cc CZ, with John Rock and Tim Gibbes on 250cc Jawas. Of this group only Aussie John Rock and Brit Eric Chilton

managed to finish the event, both receiving bronze medals. Such were the conditions that this was a magnificent achievement. Maughling and Glassbrook damaged themselves and their machines in accidents on the first day. On the same day Fisher damaged the spindle carrier on the rear wheel of his CZ and retired. Gibbes survived until Thursday, by whch time he was carrying many bits of his Jawa about his person and had missed a check.

Thursday's run was particularly traumatic. The event came near to collapse at one particularly steep and narrow climb up a muddy track in low cloud and heavy rain. More than 50 riders finished the day very late. So

Bulgarian Vase teamsters I Tschbrikoff 250 Jawa (65) leads J Toplodolski 350 Jawa (92). They won gold and bronze medals respectively. Their team finished in 11th place in the Vase contest (out of 29 teams)

late were the finishes that the start/finish area was floodlit. By 6.30 pm it was quite dark and 24 riders were still unaccounted for. In the end the jury was forced to cancel the penalties sustained on the most difficult section, but for many it was too late.

The outcome was certainly fair. The German performance in the trophy was little short of astounding and the Czech A team won the vase with the lowest number of penalty points (205). It is of course arguable whether such a tough event is justified. However, the penalty-free performance of the Germans suggest that it was. Nevertheless, as is always the case when an event is so difficult, the 'ordinary' riders found it almost impossible. One interesting change in the tightening up of the maintenance regulations was the sealing and marking of almost every replaceable part, including headlamps rims!

1958

It might be thought that with a 'free' year in which to consider the situation, the ACU and the British team management might have rethought its strategy for Garmisch in 1958. Unfortunately, this was not to be. 1958 was a year of almost unprecedented success for the Czechs, but it was an almost unmitigated disaster for Great Britain. The Czechs fielded 20 riders in the German event at Garmisch and all of them won gold

medals! This amazing performance won them both the trophy and the vase. In contrast, Great Britain lost men from both vase teams on the first day, and a trophy rider on the second. Notwithstanding this, the Ariel, Matchless and Royal Enfield teams won manufacturers' awards.

It seemed that the German organizers were determined to avoid the widespread retirements experienced in the very tough 1957 event. As is often the case, the result was an event that many considered to be the easiest since the war. The medal table is usually the best guide to this and, sure enough, contrasting the 25 gold medals from 246 starters in Czechoslovakia, the 213 starters in 1958 were awarded 109 gold medals, 18 silver (up to 25 marks lost) and 16 bronze (all other finishers).

The British trophy team produced no surprises at all. John Brittain (Royal Enfield) and Bob Manns (Matchless) were on 350s, Brian Martin (BSA) and Dave Curtis (Matchless) 500s and John Giles and Ken Heanes (Triumphs) on 650s. The vase A team was certainly not experimental either. Sid Wicken was on a 350 Matchless, Tim Gibbes and Ron Langston were on 500 Ariels

Start of the speed test in
Germany during the
latter stages of the 1956
event. Many observers
consider these special
tests ultimately ruined
the ISDT

and Roy Peplow was on a 500 Triumph. Thus, with the exception of the Triumphs, single-cylinder machines were the norm. It should not be thought that the winning nations put all their money on small capacity machines for the Czech trophy team included V. Sedia on a 350cc twin, two-stroke of course. Britain's only unusual team was vase B. In this Brian Stonebridge and J. Simpson were on 250cc Greeves, Peter Stirland on a 350cc Royal Enfield based largely on 250cc Crusader components, and Jim Sheehan a 500cc Velocette. Unhappily none of the teams was successful and mechanical problems, both old and new, were not uncommon.

The first day of the event was very wet but, by using the B time schedule and making alterations to the course, the organizers ensured that only 16 riders lost marks. However, disaster did not wait long to strike the British. Jim Sheehan's Velocette in the vase B team was using a bottom gear ratio of 14:1 and it proved to be too high. A succession of uphill hairpin bends proved to be too much for the Velocette clutch and he went out. Worse was to follow for vase A also lost Peplow, his Triumph suffering from gearbox problems. In additon to these retirements, Olga Kevelos (175 CZ), Brian Povey and Michael Martin (500 BSAs) also dropped out.

The second day was even worse for Britain. At the village of Kohlgrub, Brian Martin of the trophy team, with 15 minutes in hand, stopped the engine of his 500 BSA. It completely refused to start again despite all his efforts, and he was forced to retire. Most infuriating of all was the fact that later, back at base, it started perfectly normally. As far as Britain was concerned the team competitions were all over.

The event of course continued although it was not until Friday that reports suggest 'real' ISDT conditons were imposed. On that day the organizers used the 'A' time schedules and a climb of the 4900 ft Hochkopf, which proved very difficult. Indeed it should have formed part of the route on Monday and Thursday as well but they were anxious to avoid very difficult sections. On this day the Italians protested against the marshalling at the first time-check where one of their trophy men had lost a mark. This revealed a whole string of occasions on which the organizers had turned a blind eye to outside assistance on difficult parts of the course and made on the spot changes to the route to keep the event moving (and easy). The revised results reinstated the Italian trophy team.

The outcome of the easy nature of the event was inevitably that once more the speed test became a race to

Eric Chilton's 650 BSA being prepared for the 1958 event. Riding in the BSA works team Chilton's machine had a Road Rocket engine with reduced compression ratio in a Gold Star frame. He was destined to win a gold medal

The 248 Greeves of Brian Stonebridge at the British 1958 ISDT Preview. Five of these models were specially built for the ISDT and were notable for their light alloy cylinder barrel and head. A hard-chrome finish was applied to the barrel which obviated the need for a conventional liner

determine the winners. The trophy was fought out between Czechoslovakia, Germany and Italy. At last the Italians had the oportunity to demonstrate their speed. Their team was mounted exclusively on Gileras, two 125s, two 175s and two 250s. These overhead-valve four-stroke singles were simply not quick enough. Unfortunately for the Germans, although faster than the Italians, the team lost Richard Hessler's 250cc Zündapp and the trophy went, deservedly, to the Czechs. The vase was disputed by both Czech teams, Poland, Germany and Austria, and the Czech A team won it.

Although the event was disastrous for the British trophy and vase teams, 17 gold medals were won and many lessons should have been learned, not least by the manufacturers and riders from Francis Barnett, Greeves, James and DOT. The detailed list of British starters and results shown here indicates that all was certainly not lost. It should have been possible to produce trophy and vase winning teams for the future.

Rider	Marks lost	Award
J.M. Simpson (250 Greeves)	R	
E. Smith (250 Francis Barnett)	29	B
A.W. Glassbrook (250 Greeves)	R	
J. Harris (250 James)	R	
T.W. Cheshire (250 Royal Enfield)	61	B
J. Houghton (250 James)	0	G
P. Baldwin (250 Greeves)	63	B
A. Nicholson (250 DOT)	R	
D.J. Theobald (250 DOT)	R	
G.. Wheldon (250 James)	R	
B.G. Stonebridge (250 Greeves)	0	G
D.H. Brooker (250 Greeves)	103	B
B. Sharp (250 Francis Barnett)	0	B
T.J. Sharp (250 Francis Barnett)	0	G
P.N. Brittain (250 Greeves)	R	
J.V. Brittain (350 Royal Enfield)	0	G
S.B. Manns (350 Matchless)	0	G
P.T. Stirland (350 Royal Enfield)	0	G
S.R. Wicken (350 Matchless)	0	G
A.J. Lampkin (350 BSA)	0	G
P. Fletcher (350 Royal Enfield)	0	G
F.H. Carey (350 Royal Enfield)	R	
J.R. Giles (650 Triumph)	0	G
A.T. Gibbes (350 Arriel)	0	G
K. Heanes (650 Triumph)	0	G
E.D. Chilton (650 BSA)	0	G
B.W. Martin (500 BSA)	R	
R.J. Langston (500 Ariel)	0	G
D.G. Curtis (500 Matchless)	0	G
J.F. Sheehan (500 Velocette)	R	
B.F. Povey (500 BSA)	R	
G.S. Blakeway (500 Ariel)	0	G
R.S. Peplow (500 Triumph)	R	
S.H. Miller (Eire) (500 Ariel)	NS	
M. Martin (500 BSA)	R	

Key to awards: G = gold medal; S = silver medal; B = bronze medal; R = retired; NS = non-starter.

1959

1959 turned out to be one of the years which observers of the ISDT would rather forget. Throughout the decade the financial burden of the British contribution to the event had been borne by the manufacturers. They provided the machinery and back up, and the riders' salaries and expenses were frequently paid by the factories with which they were associated. Notwithstanding this it was the ACU which selected and entered the national teams and appointed the overall team manager. As Hugh Viney pointed out, this often meant that there appeared to be more than one manager as the manufacturers' representatives were very prominent. Indeed, with so many makes represented the situation was even more complicated.

Of course for the manufacturers the most important aspect of their participation was to ensure good publicity for their machines. In order for their investment to be cost effective, every entrant should win gold and the national effort should be successful in the trophy and vase contests. Of course, there were other benefits, for example the testing, modification and development of their machines, but these were secondary. Most important for the national effort was that faced with continuous failure, which was made worse by the fact that it was often due to the mechanical failure of their products, the manufacturers would not continue to support the event.

ABOVE **Brian Stonebridge won a gold medal for the tiny British Greeves factory in the 1958 event and in the process managed to shame many of the more fancied runners. He is shown here (right) with Jack Simpson at the 1958 ISDT Preview. Both are wearing the other's Barbour jacket, in a 'Little and Large' act**

RIGHT **Royal Enfield mounted Peter Stirland of the British Vase 'B' team, foots in leisurely style as he regains a main road near Krün, Bavaria, September 1958**

As yet no mention has been made of the state of the British motorcycle industry as a whole, for it was about to enter the period of terminal decline. What was worse at this particular time was its complacency and the failure to recognize the need for change. The increasing success of the products from European factories could hardly have been ignored but, by and large, it was. What the British manufacturers really wanted to do was to restructure the whole event, but the time for this was not right. Despite rumours of the inclusion in the event of a separate, shorter route for scooters and mopeds(!), rule changes in the winter of 1958/59 were limited mainly to the reduction of the 'starting' time from two minutes to one, the attachment of a numbered FIM seal to each machine in addition to the normal marking and the deletion of the numberplate seals. The overall

length of an event was reduced from approximately 1600 to 1400 miles. More significant for national interests was the new rule that no country would be allowed to stage the event more than twice in any five-year period. The last rule was necessary to prevent Gottwaldov and Garmisch from becoming semi-permanent ISDT centres!

The outcome of the British manufacturers' disillusionment was their decision not to suport the event at all in 1959. After a meeting of the manufcturers' committee the chairman stated that the Industries Association would not send a team, loan machines or allow their riders to take part. It was to these depths that the British effort had sunk by the end of the decade. Gallantly the ACU decided to raise the funds to send a 'privateer' trophy team. The Competition's Committee felt that £950 should be raised:- £175 from the ACU and the balance from the 800 member clubs. J.C. Lowe, the chairman, said he felt that it was possible to send a team of riders of reasonable calibre and H.P. Baughan, whistling in the wind, said the team would have a reasonable chance of success in the trophy competition. The £950 would, of course, only meet riders and team managers' expenses. It was hoped that dealers would provide suitable machinery. The result was a team comprising Eric Chilton (650 Triumph), Ken Heanes (650 Triumph), Ray King (500 BSA), Terry Cheshire (350 Royal Enfield), Colin Moram (500 AJS), Tim Gibbes (350 Matchless) and, as reserve, Roger Kearsey (250 Royal Enfield). Jack Stocker was team manager. In fact, this happy band whose courage and effort is beyond criticism, didn't stand a chance. Along with the team there was, as usual, a group of private individuals pitting themselves against the ultimate challenge for motorcycle and rider.

Johnny Giles and
Ken Heanes of the
1958 British Trophy
team scratching on the
final day's speed test –
both won 'golds' –
unfortunately other
members of the squad
did not do so well.
Giles and Heanes were
both riding 649cc
Triumph Trophy's

The event in 1959, based for the fourth time at Gott-waldov in Czechoslovakia, was less difficult than most. The Czechs chose this area because it was less likely to be badly affected by rain, but the summer had been long, hot and dry. So much so that the greatest hazard in Europe was forest fires.

No Six Days can be dismissed without comment but the mixture was very much of the same. The British were unlucky and suffered numerous mechanical problems. The Czechs, on the other hand, prepared as always to the highest degree, succeeded once again. Indeed, the trophy team lost only one mark as the result of a starting problem, and their vase teams, unpenalized, overpowered the opposition in the speed tests. As far as the Czech trophy men were concerned it was not as easy as all that. Until the fourth day the Soviet team was ahead, with the Italians close behind. The Russians, mounted on 175, 250 and 350cc 1Z and K two-strokes, put up a great performance, underdeveloped, underpowered and under-prepared machinery notwithstanding. Unhappily, the bone hard terrain took its toll and Victor Adajan (175 K) suffered a broken frame, which ended the Soviet team's chances. The Italians were hopping mad because, also on the fourth morning, their trophy man Tullio Masserini (175 Moto Guzzi) started the bike *before* the flag dropped and was penalized by five marks. In consequence, as all of the other trophy teams had lost men or more marks, the Czechs were home and dry.

The British trophy team fared badly. As was to be expected, their performance fell short of the normal efforts of British machines and riders. However, Terry Cheshire and Eric Chilton both won gold medals. Ken Heanes was on the gold standard until the sixth day when he lost one mark for failing to start the day within the one minute allowed. Ray King's BSA suffered front wheel damage on the first day and he was forced to retire. Tim Gibbes' Matchless broke its bottom fork yoke on the fourth day and Colin Moram was a non-starter on that day, having injured his foot quite badly on Wednesday. Roger Kearsey, team reserve rider, had problems with the gearbox of his Royal Enfield and failed to finish. The only other British riders to win medals were Albert Glassbrook (250 Greeves) and Ken Mills (498 AJS) with well-deserved bronzes.

With that the 1950s came to an ignominous end. What had gone wrong? In fact, this period does not show the British effort to have been in the hopeless state that is often suggested. In 1950 the win in both competitions was decisive, and in 1951 the trophy was secured again. The problems of 1952 could be regarded as bad luck, and in 1953 the British won the trophy. It might be argued that 1954 was a moral victory. 1955 was marred by mechanical problems and in 1956 only the failure of a single frame lug on John Brittain's Royal Enfield prevented the trophy team from entering the speed test without penalty. In 1957 there was no British presence and only 1958 was a chapter of disaster. Even this was mitigated by some fine individual performances. For any other nation it seems unlikely that such a record would have caused its manufacturers to withdraw support completely in 1959. The British effort might have been expected to recover. There were, however, factors which needed serious consideration. Despite the introduction of relatively small numbers of the smaller-engined two-strokes, notably from James, Francis Barnett and Greeves, the majority of British bikes remained in the category of large and heavy four-

LEFT **J Javurek 175 CZ (76) and G Raschig 174 Express (75) leaving the village of Bad Kohlgrub Bavaria during the 1958 ISDT**

RIGHT **After Moto Guzzi quit Grand Prix racing at the end of 1957 it switched its competition budget to long distance trials, including the ISDT. Here's one of their first efforts, the 1959 175 Lodola Regolarita (it was also produced in 235 and 250cc engine sizes)**

strokes based on roadgoing production machinery.

To return, however, to the beginning of this chapter, was this not the purpose of the event, i.e. a reliability test for production motorcycles and the skill of their riders? The Czechs did not seem to think so. It was, and for that matter still is, singularly difficult to buy an ISDT Jawa. It does not seem to have been the nature of the machinery itself which was the problem during this period. The British bikes were certainly heavy but they were also quite quick, strong and capable, in the right hands, of winning gold medals. There was concern about reliability but there seems to have been no obviously coherent pattern discernible and other nations suffered from similar problems. Engine failures, frame breakages and starting problems were widespread among all competitors. The only sort of problems which are difficult to excuse are those which were recurrent, e.g. waterlogged magnetos and leaking petrol tanks. Problems of this nature are quite different in kind from the failure of prototype components such as new frames. Nevertheless, with the right approach by manufacturers and first-class preparation for an event, most of these faults could have been eliminated.

The more serious problem lay with the engine size and the associated speed schedules. If these had been fairly assessed the British position would have been much stronger. Their teams were normally able to cope with the disparity in speed between time-checks during the first five days. Usually this was done by making up time on the tarmac sections of a day's route, but this was becoming very dangerous. Sometimes, as in the case of the German events, the tarmac surfaces were so slippery that this was impossible. As is quite clear, however, from the results of these events, it was possible to achieve gold standard on British machinery. Nevertheless, the advantage was shifting more and more to the smaller, lighter and more agile machines and, as always,

the various clerks of the courses produced more difficult routes.

What was always more difficult during this period was the differential speed schedules for the speed test. Recalling that the speed test was originally designed only to assess the mechanical conditon of machines at the end of the event and that its primary purpose was not to settle ties, it is noteworthy that Britain lost the trophy in 1954 and the vase in 1951, 1953 and 1956 on the test results. It seems only fair to surmise that even if their teams had been unpenalized in all the events during this period, if a tie with another nation had to be resolved it could not have won with 350, 500 and 650cc machines. The effect of the rules as they then stood, and the disparity in speed schedules, was effectively to prevent large capacity machinery from winning the trophy and vase competitions in anything less than very unusual circumstances. It was still possible for individual riders to win gold medals and many continued to do so.

Even so it may well be that, if the speed schedule situation had not existed, the British would still have been faced with a struggle of increasing severity. There was no substitute for a high degree of organization and single-minded, dedicated national effort. The Czechs epitomized this and their results reflected it. In terms of machinery the Jawas and CZs were purpose-built to win the ISDT and nothing was left to chance. Anyone who has had the opportunity to compare a 'cooking' Jawa with a works Six Days machine will understand this perfectly. Apparently hand-painted with a large brush they were mechanically superb and capable of tackling anything. Of course there were occasional failures but very rarely the same thing twice. Running a standardized set of machines naturally made service and support much more effective. The six British men and six different bikes was in the finest tradition of the amateur sportsman, but much less practical.

Approaching Cab on the 4th day of the 1959 event Horst Liebe (250 MZ) of East Germany leads Enrico Vanoncini (235 Moto Guzzi). Note deeply rutted trial through thick forest; typical Czech terrain for the Six Days

Of course it was not simply in terms of machinery and its preparation that the Czechs excelled, it was also in the support required by a team during the event itself. Support teams were drilled and prepared in the same manner as riders. Support vehicles were parked in their strategic positions 24 hours before the first rider was due, and every man received clean goggles and dry gloves at every check. Indeed, as in any military operation, everything was done by numbers. Moreover, in Eastern Eurrope it was always possible to run teams of full-time professionals who were nominally serving in the armed forces.

To sum up the Czech approach to the event, and it is only used as an example, for the German teams were also highly organized and meticulous, the experience of Olga Kevelos before the 1953 event is interesting. Having been offered a 125cc CZ for the event, Olga was invited to Prague six weeks before it started. After three days of sight-seeing she was despatched to the team training camp in the Tatra Mountains. The regime there every day was to rise at 6 am for physical training, followed by a tough 150-mile route on a bike similar to the event machine. This would be followed by maintenance instruction and practice. After 10 pm the riders could do what they liked!

It would be wrong to think that the lessons were not being learnt in Great Britain but the lack of overall coordination and the division of power between the ACU, the manufacturers and the riders was such that the necessary action was not taken. Neither were the British

able to produce the 'new' type of machinery successfully, for the tiny Greeves factory, courageous though their efforts were, could not sustain a European scrambling effort and produce Six Days' winning machinery as well.

In 1959, Hugh Viney, from his vast experience, suggested a recipe for British success. He believed that the machinery and the riders were available and that a standardized, national approach would make all the difference. The existing haphazard arrangements would have to be changed. Providing that the problem of financing the effort and coordinating the manufacturers' approach could be overcome, he felt that the most important factor was in the preparation of riders and machines.

The team should be selected by the team manager with the support of the manufacturers and it should be assembled at least six months before the event. Recognizing the problem of preparing for an event which was for British riders virtually a 'one off', with hardly any similar events in the United Kingdom, he suggested a regime of scrambles and road race experience backed by physical training and maintenance sessions. Alas, even this effort would have been part-time and, in hindsight, quite inadequate. At any rate it was 'pie in the sky' at the time.

The 1950s remain in the history of British participation in the ISDT as a decade of fading glory. Perhaps the manufacturers were right when they said that the British effort should have ended in 1959.

CHAPTER SIX

The swinging sixties

1960

The 35th International Six Days Trial, held at Bad Aus-see in the Austrian Niedere Tavern, included special tests sections for the first time. These sections – cross-country, hillclimb and brake tests – were attacked at the rate of two a day, and riders were awarded bonus points for their performance. The formula used to determine the actual points given was derived from the fastest time, divided by the rider's time, and then multiplied by 360. Special test points did not determine final placings for participants still had to keep clean sheets for timekeeping etc., and in order to gain a gold medal riders had to have zero marks lost on the course, and at least 1500 points gained on the special tests.

With these new rules in mind 275 riders from 17 nations set out from Bad Aussee on Monday 20 September to tackle the 265-mile run over the Grossglockner Pass. Of the seven trophy teams which cleaned the first day, Great Britain was the poorest placed in view of the number of bonus points gained. But by far the biggest disappointment was the failure of Sammy Miller to travel more than 40 miles before retirement. Sammy, who had originally been selected as a trophy team member, was relegated to the vase team, went out when one of the cylinder-head sleeve bolts of his Greeves sheared, a fate also encountered by Tiger Timms of the Greeves-mounted Army team, and the Dutchman, Frits Selling. The Streatham and District MCC mounted on a trio of Ariel Arrows, soon hit bad luck when Maurice Spurging was in collision with a car and had to retire. This was the team's second upset for they, and many other riders, initially failed scrutineering when the organizers indicated that their silencers pointed skywards, more than the permitted 10 degrees. Within a few miles of the start-line the 125cc Capriolo of the Italian trophy teamster Carlo Moscheni, came to a stop with electrical failure, thus dashing the hopes of the Italians. Together with the Polish trophy riders they were the only teams to lose marks on that first day.

Day 2 dawned with heavy rain and mist shrouding mountains which turned some of the softer going into mud baths. The churned-up morass spelt disaster to the small-wheeled scooters, and indeed to some of the smaller capacity machines, and many had to drop out as some of the stickier sections became impassable to them. At the end of the day six trophy teams and thir-

teen vase teams were still intact, West Germany having dropped marks when Erwin Schmider came into a control late. This lateness was caused by the collapse of a rickety wooden bridge over a stream. A protest was considered, but rejected by the organizers who said that this hazard was all part of the trial, a foretaste to the major organizational problems which were to follow.

After an easy third day all 265 starters were back home by 1 pm. Even though there were no retirements some riders would have gladly called it a day. Captain Taylor of the British Army, who broke two fingers the previous week, was having trouble with his BSA 250. An unwise choice of a high final drive ratio and seized up rear damper units, really slowed the bike's progress over the rough, but by now the much used kickstarter mechanism had failed. One consolation, after a frantic SOS to the BSA factory in Birmingham, a smaller gearbox sprocket finally arrived, but to no avail as he retired the following day with complete electrical failure.

At the start on a very wet begining to the fourth day, it was Zdenak Polanka who relegated the Czech trophy team to third place when he failed to get his 175 CZ going in the time allotted. This was to be the team's only lost mark, and Polanka was not pleased as he was responsible for his team's solitary lost mark in 1959, and for the very same reason.

The rain had made the surface of the morning's special test virtually impassable, and large queues of riders built up awaiting their turn. In the mud many riders stalled and had to be pulled out so that the event could continue. The organizers, as if to admit being at fault, extended the time schedule by one hour to cover the delay, and at the same time, actively encouraged *outside assistance* in retrieving bogged down bikes. The international jury fought long and hard that night, to iron out the problems. Italy wanted the special test scrubbed, on the principle that outside assistance broke the rules, but were out-voted. With this, Count Johnny Lurani, the Italian team manager, stormed out of the jury room.

Back on the road, riders were having a hard time for at 6000 ft the snow lay three feet deep and visibility was down to 200 yards. Further down in the valley spectator traffic became a major headache, causing a few spills. Volker Von Zitzewitz, the West German trophy team captain, was seriously hurt when he firmly embedded his Maico into the front of a tourist VW minibus. British trophy team member, Triss Sharp, was in collision

with a private motorcyclist, although unhurt the local police decided action should be taken, and impounded the Greeves rider's passport pending prosecution. Triss was finally given his freedom some time later after the trial had finished, ending up with a suspended sentence for endangering human life.

Friday morning dawned clear and bright which was a bonus to the riders, still numbering over 200, all of whom started the day's trek. The contest for the Silver Trophy had been resolved into a conflict between Austria and Sweden, each with zero marks lost. In the vase contest ten teams were still on zero, but the Italian B team held a slender margin of 12 bonus points over the Czechoslovakian B team. This was still the case at the end of the day which saw a further six riders go into retirement.

Many riders and team officials were not happy with the way in which the trial had been run, accusing the organizers of inexperience and lack of flexibility, and it was the events of the final day which backed up their accusations. On the 80-mile run to the Zeltweg circuit for the one-hour speed test, the course crossed the land of an irate farmer who had initially refused permission for its use. An alternative track was chosen, but this did not agree with the farmer either who then altered the route marking. Needless to say, many riders got lost and arrived late at the Zeltweg circuit, to the detriment of their score sheets. By clever guessing or good reconnaissance the Czech trophy team managed to find a way through and retain their clean sheets, but the Austrians and other contenders dropped marks. During the speed test, the results of which would not affect the overall result, the jury met and decided to use a differential time schedule for that part of the course in dispute.

When the new scores were worked out, Czechoslovakia was placed first, followed by Great Britain and then Sweden in the trophy contest. The jury met again on Sunday morning, and after much debating and a secret vote, it was decided to omit the disputed section altogether. This decision caused further uproar as it gave the trophy to the home team. The Czech team protested the loudest and lodged a complaint at the FIM autumn congress for they had had the trophy in their grasp all week, only to have it taken away from them on a technicality at the eleventh hour. How disappointing it must have been for them.

1961

After the problems of the Austrian event, the honour of staging the 36th trial in the series was given to Great Britain. Held once again in mid Wales, and centred on

LEFT **A breathtaking panorama beside the placid waters of the Stausee. With its base at Bad Aussee, the Austrian ISDT of 1960 was staged in an area of outstanding natural beauty**

The Polish team finished 8th in the Trophy contest in 1960. Two of their squad were mounted on 349 Junaks; a unit construction ohv four-stroke single with four-speed 'box

the town of Llandrindod Wells for the seventh time. This event should have been a walkover for the British team. Hopes in the British camp were running high, for they considered it to be their event, held on their territory, and local knowledge of the terrain was manifest. Since winning the trophy in Czechoslovakia in 1953, the British have never won it again, although getting very close. Now it was viewed that this could be the chance for which they had been waiting. But, as we have seen before, anything can happen during the trial, and it did, relegating the British team to the bottom position of the eight trophy teams who competed.

Competitors began to arrive at Llandrindod nearly a fortnight prior to the start and found the town filled with vicars and parsons who were holding a Church conference. Once the clergy had departed the town took on the air of being host to the International when the flags of the competing countries were hoisted, together with the banners of the Daily Herald newspaper, who sponsored the event. Organized by the *Auto Cycle Union*, the trial used many familiar tracks, last employed in 1954, but others had been lost for the march of progress had led to some lanes being paved, making them unsuitable for this type of event. These deficiencies were made up by the increased use of Forestry Commission land, which abounded in the area.

On the first day it was the British trophy team of Brittain, Chilton, Gibbes, Giles, Heanes and Moram, who started hot favourites. On the first acceleration and braking test, Johnny Giles scored the maximum of 60 points on his 500 Triumph, when he equalled standard time. Other riders on maximum points were the Italian trophy man Strenghetto on his Capriolo 75 and West German vase B rider, Ancheidt, on his Kreidler 50. The second special test of the day, a cross-country dash, saw Nachtmann of the West German trophy team, equal standard time on his 600cc BMW, together with Colin Moram on his 500 AJS. It was shortly after this test that Colin was found lying unconscious beside his bent machine, a victim of over exuberance on the narrow tracks. Bystanders rendered first aid and an ambulance was called, but Colin, on coming round, would have nothing of it, straightened his AJS and rode away to finish the day with 58 marks lost for late arrival.

During the afternoon the fate of the British trophy team was sealed when the gearbox of Eric Chilton's 650 Triumph seized, putting him out of the event and saddling his team with 100 marks lost per day. Eric reflected bitterly that the gearbox internals were the only items of this immaculately prepared Triumph that he had not overhauled personally.

Of the 271 starters, who had to cross the line under power within one minute of start up or lose 20 bonus points, 15 riders failed to finish the day's run. Of the three lady riders entered, Olga Kevelos, riding a 174 Maico, was one of the retirements. Olga's reasons for retirement were tiredness and fibrositis, little wonder for the Maico weighed in at 380 lb, the end coming when the battery fell off after a minor spill. Mary Driver, who had trouble getting away at the start up – she had switched to emergency rather than normal ignition on her BSA 250 – was on schedule and even had time in hand at checks. But Jill Savage was having trouble at keeping up, riding hard she was only just managing to stay on time.

Colin Moram bravely started on the second morning, but gave up shortly afterwards when he realized that he was not as fit as he initially thought, and his retirement cost the British team a further 100 marks lost per day. The British vase A team, lying in fourth position after

RIGHT **One of the Puch mounted Austrian Trophy team at the 1960 event. They won, but only in controversial circumstances, this was after Czechoslovakia had originally been declared the winners**

BELOW **A Puch 248cc split-single two-stroke of the type used by the victorious Austrian Trophy team in the 1960 Six Days**

Monday's leg, were suddenly out of the running when Triss Sharp sheared the gearbox mainshaft of his Greeves 250, and went into retirement. The sole Danish rider, P. Bogehoj, who led the field away at 6.30 am on the first morning, fell off and hurt his back, his subsequent retirement was a merciful release, for he had suffered five punctures and lost 62 marks on the first day alone. Interest was now switching to the needle match between the Italian and West German trophy teams, with Nachtmann and Schmider for Germany, and Strenghetto and Bertotti of Italy all gaining near maximum bonus points. But it was the ex European motocross champion, Rolf Tibblin, who gained maximum points on both tests, riding his special Husqvarna 250 for the Swedish trophy team.

When the battle commenced on the Wednesday morning, five trophy teams remained clean, with West Germany leading Italy by half a bonus point. The day's run was unspectacular until riders reached the second special test, a ¾-mile hillclimb where the going was very soggy and a huge queue built up as riders got bogged down. As luck would have it, the Austrian juryman,

Karl Basch, was at hand to witness the incident. As he was cruelly criticized for the same problem the previous year in Austria, he protested long and loud at that evening's meeting which resulted in a sliding scale of time allowances being used to determine placings. This scale resulted in Italy dropping two marks which took them down to fourth place overall, and lost them the (already freely expressed) right of organizing the 1962 International. Some riders not caught up in the delays actually made up time and stopped to do routine maintenance. The remaining Russian trophy team, for Pylajer had retired when he crashed his 350 IZM, changed and greased chains, while the Swiss vase riders, Haller and Steiner, changed brake shoes on their Kreidler 50s. Sammy Miller, Johnny Giles and Ken Heanes even had time to change rear tyres back at Llandrindod.

Thursday saw yet another British trophy man drop out, leaving only three riders to fly the flag. The gearbox of Ken Heanes' Triumph cried enough and shed a tooth, in retaliation to Ken's enthusiastic riding, for he had gained 357 bonus points out of a maximum of 360 for the last three days. Sweden also suffered when the back wheel of Bo Sjosvard's 125 Husqvarna collapsed, taking them from second to fifth place in the trophy contest.

The 125 Capriolos of the Italian Trophy team members C Moscheni and J Strenghetto after the Six Days, on show at Earls Court, London; November 1960

More marks were lost for the British trophy team on Friday when Tim Gibbs lost his way, due to a crowd of onlookers standing on the course markings painted on the road. The final special test of the day involved the climbing of a steep muddy hill. It was on this hill, which would have done justice to a one-day trial, that Sammy Miller fell off – much to the astonishment of the crowd. He remounted and carried on. Even with this unfortunate hiccup he still managed to amass 119 bonus points out of a possible 120.

On the very last day the hopes that the Czechoslovakian Trophy team would overhaul the West Germans were dashed when Sedina failed to arrive at the final speed-test venue. The chain of his 350 Jawa had snapped and damaged the gearbox. From being 28 bonus points down on the Germans the Czech team then went to fourth place with 100 marks lost.

When the riders assembled at the 1.74-mile Shobdon circuit for the final speed test the outcome was a foregone conclusion as the test only counted for bonus points. Before the test could start the jury had to hear a protest by the Russians as to the state, and therefore safety, of the circuit. The Russians wanted the test cancelled but were out-voted. Instead, a compromise was reached and the test reduced to 30 minutes. Although not a race, some spirited dicing was noted. Italian Tossi on a 250 Guzzi and Austrian trophy man, Leitner, on a 350 Puch, stayed neck and neck for the whole 30 minutes. Rolf Tibblin set a cracking pace until forced out

LEFT **A narrow forest track near Plynlimmon, during the 1961 event. The going is typical of the Welsh terrain used that year. Swedish Trophy man B Ekeburg (175 Husqvarna) is the rider**

RIGHT **Often called the greatest trials rider of all time, the Irishman Sammy Miller with the 500 Ariel single he rode to score gold in the 1961 Six Days'**

with a holed piston, and Nachtmann left the field standing on his 600 BMW.

The week finally ended in the best Welsh tradition, with music and singing at the Grand Pavilion, when the victorious West German team received the trophy. The Czechoslovakian B team won the vase by the slenderist of margins over their A team, with Great Britain B coming third. The manufacturer's prize went to the Italian Capriolo Aeromere team, with the CZ team in second place, and the Czech Dukla Praha team beat the German ADAC team to take the club prize.

One distinguished visitor to the International was Bud Ekins, three times winner of the Big Bear Run, America's toughest offroad event. Bud, who formed one third of the U.S.A. contingent, was running clean until the last day when the gear-selector mechanism of his 650 Triumph locked up. Repairs took time and lost him 12 marks, but this was enough for him to take home a silver medal for his efforts. The big American promised he would be back for another try, as did the vast majority of the entrants. His name and many others, would reappear time and time again in the entry lists for future events.

1962

With resumption of trade support, after a meeting of trade barons as early as February, for the 1962 event it looked as if the British trophy team were in with a chance of winning again. The team, comprising Billot and Blakeway, mounted respectively on a 350 AJS and 350 Triumph, Giles on a 500 Triumph, Harris on a 500 BSA, Gibbes on a 600 AJS and team captain, Ken Heanes on a 650 Triumph, were selected when the

The American star Bud Ekins taking his 649cc Triumph through muddy going during the 1961 event in Wales. On the final day he suffered the cruellest luck when he was forced to remove the gearbox cover to free a sticking selector which cost him 12 marks and his gold medal

tain stood a very good chance, but it was the Jawa/CZ factory sponsored Czechoslovakian team who rode faultlessly to win the trophy for the seventh time.

The Bavarian Alps town of Garmisch-Partenkirchen was host to the International for the fourth time since its conception, and riders knew the difficulties that this alpine terrain could offer. In previous years, snow, mist and heavy rain had taken its toll, together with mud on the steep slopes within this predominantly forested

LEFT **Programme cover for the 36th International Six Days' Trial staged between 2-7 October 1961**

ABOVE **1961 ISDT speed test, Mrs Mary Driver 250 BSA C15**

BELOW **Unusual sight at the 1961 event was this 175 Lambretta TV scooter piloted by Alan Kimber – the UK sales manager for the Italian marque. Alan finished the week with a bronze medal for his heroic efforts**

ACU met at Stroud in late May. Also selected for the vase A team were Brittain, Fletcher, Miller and Sandiford, with Lampkin, Peplow and the Sharp brothers as the B team.

Disaster struck early when Sammy Miller, who had been offered the use of a Jawa for the forthcoming International, was involved in an accident whilst scrambling at the Bassenthwaite Whitsun Bank Holiday meeting. Sam sustained a broken pelvis, shoulder blade and four ribs when he was bulldozed by a Gold Star, after coming off his James 250. The ACU selectors, not counting on the tenacity of the Ulsterman, dropped him from the team, his place being taken by Roy Peplow, promoted from the B team. Reservist Vic Eastwood was then upgraded to Roy's place to complete the line-up.

Miller did not take kindly to his infirmity and vowed to be fit in time for the International. His critics, both motorcycle and medical, were confounded when Sam won the Manx two-day trial in early September, but the ACU selectors would not reinstate his vase A place. Instead, he entered as a privateer, gaining a gold medal on his Ariel, which many critics considered to be out-of-date.

Favourites to win the trophy in 1962 must have been the West German team – for they were on home ground – after their win in Wales the previous year. Great Bri-

Three stalwart 'Brits' after surviving six gruelling days in the Welsh countryside and gaining a gold medal apiece. Left to right: Gordon Blakeway, Roy Peplow and Johnny Giles. All rode works prepared 490 Triumph T100SS models

area. As an insurance against hold-ups caused by riders becoming bogged down, the organizers sought approval from the FIM for the use of sports tyres. In previous years the boldest tread pattern approved was that of the trials tyre, but with fears of sudden weather changes and loss of wheel grip, the swap was made. As luck would have it, the tyre insurance guess was correct, and it paid off in that delays were minimal. The FIM, in giving the approval, voiced the opinion that they did not want the event being turned into a six-day scramble. If only they could see the event as it is today, that approval would never have been given.

On the first day of the trial all teams, with the exception of the Russian trophy squad who dropped 10 marks, were clean. Czechoslovakia led the trophy contest and West Germany B the vase competition. This was to be the final outcome of the event, but the other teams on the leaderboard did chop and change, due to the various misfortunes encountered by the riders.

Tuesday morning saw Sebastian Nachtmann bravely start on his 600 BMW but retire shortly afterwards. Having had a sleepless night and being in great pain with a cracked bone in his arm he retired, putting the German trophy team at the bottom of the list with a 100 mark deficit. Great Britain dropped from second to fourth position when Fred Billot got a double puncture in the rear tyre of his AJS. The first nail in his tyre was seen and the tube replaced, but the second undetected nail then began to work, and the tyre deflated within minutes. This delay cost Fred and the British team three marks.

Fred Billot dropped a further two marks for late arrival on Wednesday when he lost his rear brake after colliding with a rock. The clutch on Gordon Blakeway's purposely overgeared Triumph started to slip and he lost the team a further three marks for timekeeping. The British team had now lost eight marks, but other teams had lost a lot more, including Italy and Sweden who had remained clear until the third day. At the half-way stage the British team were now elevated to second position in the trophy contest, behind the Czech team, but eight marks adrift and 55 bonus points down.

In the vase contest, the West German B team, mounted on Kreidler and Zündapp 50s, plus a Victoria 75 and a 100cc Zündapp, were forging ahead, taking full advantage of the slower speed schedules in force for the tiddler classes. Seven vase teams were still clean, including both British squads with the B team of Eastwood, Lampkin and the Sharp brothers, lying second, 61 bonus points behind. This state of affairs continued for a further two days with only minor upsets. Tim Gibbes had trouble with a sticking kickstart, Bryan Sharp's speedo drive tightened up and Johnny Giles was having trouble with sprocket wear. The only change to the leaderboard came when the Italian vase B team lost a man thus putting them out of the running.

On the final run in to the Ettal circuit for the half-hour speed test, fortunes fluctuated. When Gordon Blakeway's clutch finally gave out, it put the British team down to third place. A Russian trophy rider then got into serious trouble when his machine began to disintegrate around him, losing his team 51 marks, and relegating them to third position, and putting the British team back into second place.

Italians getting down to it on Shobdon Airfield during the final day's speed tests. Number 27 is F Vergani (100 Capriolo) who put up the best individual performance of the 1961 Six Days. Vergani gained no fewer than 658.71 points out of a possible maximum of 660

Before the speed test the outcome of the event was known, for the Czech trophy team, completely reshuffled since the last trial, was unbeatable, as were the West German vase B team. Great Britain lay second in both contests, and the Russians took third place in the trophy. One facet of the scoring system which was noted by many riders and managers, was the apparent favouring of the tiddler class, with three members of the German team gaining 599 bonus points from a maximum of 600 available during the week. This advantage was realized by the FIM and before the event finished it was decided to make the trial stiffer on the under 100cc class the following year.

Of the overseas entrants, it was Bud Ekins who won the hearts of the locals. His performance during the week, and especially in the speed test, was impeccable, for this feat he gained his first well deserved gold and set a trend for further American participation.

1963

Winning the coveted International Trophy in Germany the previous year gave the Czechoslovakians the privilege of holding the 1963 event. Again centred on the town of Spindleruv Mlyn, the course ran through the Giant Mountains, which form part of the border with Poland to the north. The trial took place from 2–7 September, and it was, by prior event standards, a pretty strenuous affair. Brilliant course plotting by the Czech organizers over the superb territory available produced an event which tested riders and their machines to the full. The predominantly rocky going, which was unaffected by the heavy rain that fell on most days, had a marked effect on the transmissions of the participating machines – judging from the retirements due to gearbox failures. Riders also faced difficulty as the paved sections, which should have offered a breathing space, were in poor condition and bumpy, not giving riders time to relax between the more difficult parts of the course. Many riders did comment on the severity of the event, the most arduous for years, with Sammy Miller saying that parts of the course would do justice to a national one-day trial. Other problems encountered were mainly carburation, due to the poor quality of the petrol on issue to riders. Once carburettors had been tuned, during the practice and recce sessions, these problems were eased. Was it the low-grade petrol, or an undetected lack of oil in the mix, which caused Triss Sharp, of the British vase B team, to retire after five miles when the big-end of his Greeves locked up on the first day?

On home ground, it was the Czech trophy team of Polanka, Zemen, Miarka, Hoffer, Klimt and Stepan who were feared most, but the West Germans and the meticulous Italians also figured highly in the forecasts. Initial prophecies were all deemed to be wrong when at the end of the event it was the relatively unknown East German team which emerged as the overall winner.

British hopes of a success were running high, but trouble beset the team even before arrival in Czechoslovakia. The transporter carrying many of the trophy and vase riders, with their machines, ran a big-end whilst travelling through Germany. Undaunted, the British riders stripped the engine while Henry Vale of Triumph dashed back to Frankfurt for spares. Once rebuilt, the engine only lasted a few miles and was restripped. This time, the offending rod and piston were removed, and the wagon continued its journey on five cylinders, arriving at the start dead on schedule.

On the first morning of the trial riders revelled in unexpected warmth and dryness, as there had been unrelenting rain till that point. Two riders had cause to be gloomy at the start as their machines would not respond to the kickstarter. Both Polanka and Triss Sharp

During the early 1960s the West German Maico concern emerged as a serious threat to the established off-road marques both in moto cross, and more importantly, long distance trials. One of their ISDT bikes of the era is shown here

had to bump start their machines over the line, incurring a deduction of 20 bonus points from any they may have made on the first special test. A cross-country run which included a long rocky climb, was used as the morning's special test, and it was in this section that Arthur Lampkin was recorded as setting the fastest time overall. Second fastest was Miarka on his CZ, with Sebastian Nachtmann setting the fastest time for the 750 class on his 600 BMW. Nachtmann went on to record fastest time in his class for every succeeding test and gain absolute maximum in bonus points, for himself and the West German trophy team. All the bonus points in the world could not make up for the loss of marks incurred by a team member retiring, and this was the case for the West German trophy team when Lorenz Specht retired after blowing a head gasket on his 175 Zündapp. The British trophy team suffered a double blow on the first day when the oil pump on John Harris's BSA packed up and Gordon Blakeway smashed the rear brake anchorage on his AJS. Sweden also lost any chance of the laurels when Hans Hanson came off his Husqvarna. Vase teams out on the first day were the West Germans when the gearbox of Rotermundt's Kreidler gave up, the same fate befalling Petr Valek of the Czech B team.

The major talking point after the first day's run, was the riding of the MZ-mounted East German team, who were top of the leaderboard. The regimented and professional way in which the team attacked the day's run was an example for all other teams to follow, their riding setting a precedent which was maintained until the end, gaining them the trophy for the first time. Another talking point was the Jawa-mounted vase team from Finland who topped the leaderboard for the first three days. Had it not been for Pertti Karha retiring on Thursday when his gearbox gave up after hitting a rock, the team could have carried on to an eventual second place.

Horst Liebe, MZ's star Six Days' rider of the late 1950s and early 1960s; he won a host of medals in long distance events including the ISDT

LEFT **A 348cc Jawa 575 twin of the type used by F Hoffer and V Stepan of the Czech Trophy team which won the 1962 event at Garmisch-Partenkirchen, Bavaria**

BELOW RIGHT **Franco Dall'Ara and Nino Tagli on Moto Guzzi's lead a bunch of riders during the speed tests at the ISDT in September 1963. Tagli was a member of the victorious Italian Silver Vase team**

By Thursday evening the British vase A team was holding second place, but Peter Fletcher was having trouble with the gearbox of his 250 Royal Enfield. Fletcher, running on trials tyres, for the use of sports tyres had once again been sanctioned, had lost second gear earlier on, but on Friday the box gave up altogether. This retirement saddled the team with two days' worth of lost marks, putting them into third position. Friday was also the day that the hitherto clean Czech trophy team dropped their first marks. Frantisek Hoffer, anxious to stay on time, was in collision with an unnamed British rider, later reported by the Czechs to be none other than Sammy Miller. Hoffer's Jawa was damaged, repairs costing time and two marks, but Miller carried on unpenalized to the end. Alan Lampkin (brother of Arthur), was another of Friday's retirements, riding his first International, he was clean until he pranged heavily during the morning, he rode on to the next time-check where he was examined by the very efficient medical back-up team. It was only then, after medical advice, that he gave up, suffering from concussion.

The short run in to the 4.6-mile Jilemnice circuit for the final speed test saw the retirement of Bob Sharp when he holed the piston of his CZ. Bob, together with Eddie Crooks and Tony Sharp on Jawas, were representing the Barrow and District MC. The machines they rode were genuine works bikes loaned by the factories, a move made possible by Eddie's contacts, for by then he was a Jawa dealer. The speed test had no major issues to decide but, nevertheless, some riders took it seriously – none more so than Sebastian Nachtmann and Bud Ekins, both of whom received gold medals for their efforts.

Of the 280 starters, 102 gold medals were awarded, 40 silver and 27 bronze also going to riders who had incurred penalty marks. East Germany won the trophy, with the immaculately turned out Italians, who also lost zero marks, taking second place and the silver vase. The Italians have always been so close to winning the trophy but have always lost out by the merest of margins. Their Moto Guzzi A, B and C teams took second, third and fourth places in the manufacturer's contest, and of ten Italians entered, they took home 10 gold medals, which was their only consolation for getting so near once again.

1964

In honour of the East German win in Czechoslovakia, the 1964 event was run for the first time in the eastern part of the then divided German republic. Centred on the town of Erfurt in the province of Thuringia, the trial was run through the mainly forested Thuringia Wald mountains which lay just over the border with the west. Politically, the venue caused a few problems, for the issue of entry visas became a long and lengthening task for the participating teams. It was not the problems with visas that stirred the Italians and West Germans into boycotting the event, but the organizing country itself because they had not seen eye to eye for some time. For this reason, as well as the financial aspects involved in organizing an event of this nature, the East Germans hosted the trial only once, even though they went on to win the trophy six times during the decade. With the non participation of the Italian and West German teams (for they were both highly rated), the event was expected to be a scrap between the up and coming East Germans, the dominant Czechs, and the ever present British teams. When the final results were announced, two trophy teams remained clean – Britain and East Germany – the English team gaining second place with over 100 bonus points behind the MZ-mounted home team. It was indeed surprising to see that the Czechs only gained fifth place, as they were beaten by the Russian and Swedish teams.

The East German event was notable in that it saw the participation, for the first time, of two United States vase teams. The Americans had gained much experience in long-distance desert races like the Baja and the Big Bear, and now considered it time to attack the damp forested events of Europe. Led by Bud Ekins, the A team also consisted of his brother Dave, Cliff Coleman and the legendary Steve McQueen, all mounted on 500/650 Triumphs. Their team manager – well known accessory manufacturer Ted Wassell – encountered problems when the transport booked to take the team across Europe failed to materialize. After frantic searching alternative transport was found, and the A team taken to Erfurt. It was there that Ted, unknown to him at the time, found a second team of expatriate Americans waiting for him. The Americans did not disgrace themselves, returning home with two golds, two silvers and a bronze medal.

After a hot and dusty weekend, 226 riders set off on a dampened 253-mile first day run for rain had fallen during the evening. Prompt at 5.30 am the riders departed in groups of three, seen off by a German chimney-sweep in full top hat regalia. It was to the sweep that several East German riders made their way, touching him for luck – a tactic which paid off according to the final result. The first special test of the day was a 3.2-mile cross-country run, the fastest time being set by Arnost Zemen of the Czech vase B team on his new red and white 250 CZ, the drab black of previous years was now gone. Two seconds behind the Czech came Werner Salevsky of the East German trophy team on his 250 MZ, with Sammy Miller sixth fastest and Ken Heanes setting the 750 class standard time. Despite the relative easiness of the first morning's run, it saw the retirement of both British lady riders. Olga Kevelos stopped after only 18 miles when her Honda 50 lost power, and Mary Driver ran out of time at the lunch break after a spate of punctures. Roy Peplow had a hectic moment when the throttle of his 350 Triumph stuck open on the timed hillclimb, which was the afternoon's special test, but he held on and finished the climb in style.

The USA vase A team was forging on in great style, attracting much attention on both the course and the

parc fermé, for the locals wanted to see if Steve McQueen could indeed ride a motorcycle the way he did in films. The spectators were not disappointed, for his style was rather aggressive and hair-raising. It was this style which caused him to cast away his Triumph in spectacular fashion on more than one occasion. By the end of the first day it was Dave Ekin's distinction to be the only member of the team to stay on board, but nevertheless, the whole team finished the day with no marks lost.

By the end of the second day's run the home team had increased its lead over the Czechs and the British teams who were still clean, but on Wednesday the Czechs were relegated to fourth place when both Valek and Miarka experienced trouble with the new five-speed gearboxes of their CZs. From the success the Czechoslovakian teams had gained during the previous decade, it was hard to see why they were now failing to achieve the desired results. As the Czechs themselves put it, the teams were in the slow process of change, which marked the gradual exit of one generation and the arrival of a new one, both in machines and riders. One rider to call it a day on the closing stages of the trial, was Sasa Klimt. Having crashed his 350 Jawa on the run to the speed test, he retired not only from the 1964 event, but for good. This was a sad end to his fourteenth International and his career for he had been so closely associated with the brilliant victories of his team in previous years.

East Germany continued to dominate the trophy contest by the brilliant riding of its team members, ending the trial with 119 bonus points clear of the British team, once again showing the advantage of using lower capacity machines. The MZs used by the team comprised 173, 242 and 282cc models. The 292cc MZs ruled the 350 class, establishing many standard times on the special stages, a capacity class once regarded as the domain of the British rider. In the 500 class two-strokes again ruled, with the 352cc MZ of East German moto-cross champion, Fred Williamowski, taking top honours, putting top British 500 riders like Sammy Miller and Dave Nicoll well below him.

The fate of the United States vase A team was sealed on the Wednesday when Bud Ekins hit a bridge. He finished the day but a trip to hospital revealed a broken bone in his leg. Steve McQueen also retired on the same day after falling off his Triumph on several occasions, managing to flatten an exhaust pipe which he duly rectified with a woodman's axe, in the best Hollywood style. He finally called it a day after another prang which rendered the machine beyond repair.

D J Müller (175 CZ) has come to grief in a sea of mud during the second day of the 1963 Six Days. This picture gives a good idea of the difficult conditions which confronted competitors in this gruelling event

Many riders of experienced status even considered the event to have been far too leisurely, with Sammy Miller quoted as saying 'it was too easy', Roy Peplow called it 'monotonous', and Ken Heanes could only call it 'boring'. This relaxed attitude of the seasoned riders also showed up in the evenings when participants gathered at the Trade Support Encampment, to swop yarns and drink British tea, dispensed by the Renold chain representative, Vic Doyle and his wife. The gatherings enabled the riders to relax and compare notes, or just listen to the hilarious stories which Steve McQueen had to tell about his exploits.

All participants considered the East German event to have been a success, apart from the delay in issuing the results, for the organizers had not geared up to meet the sheer weight of paperwork involved. Catering by local standards was good, but the staid British rider, when faced with such culinary offerings as chocolate soup and liver pudding tended not to appreciate it. Much of the food had been brought in specially to cater for the needs of the foreign riders as the hard pushed local economy had nothing like it. Olga Kevelos remembers offering a banana to the local children only to find that they did not know how to peel it, and being pounced upon by the local police who said that offering fruit to children was forbidden.

Once again the final special test of the event – the speed test – became a mere formality, as the result had

LEFT **British Trophy teamster Ken Heanes during the 1963 ISDT at Spindeler Mlyn, Czechoslovakia. Ken was Britain's leading Six Days' rider for many years**

BELOW LEFT **Russian 250 IZ two-stroke single ridden by Alexander Jegorov in Czechoslovakia, 1963**

BELOW **The East Germany team who won the 1963 Trophy. Left to right: Werner Salevsky, Peter Uhlig, Bernd Uhlmann, Horst Liebe, Hans Weber, Günther Baumann and mechanic Walter Winkler. All rode MZ two-strokes**

been decided in the forests. Nevertheless, many riders attacked the 2½-mile course, set out on the runway of Erfurt airport, with as much effort as they could muster. The highlight of the test was the Sharp brothers on their Greeves Challengers as they diced neck and neck for the whole 30 minutes. Their spirited riding earned them the appreciation of the crowd, and a manufacturer's team prize.

As the riders packed up to return home, the question being asked was, where will we meet next year? It was Great Britain's privilege to stage the next event, but rumour had it that Spain and Poland were angling to get in and promote their countries. That decision had to wait until the next FIM congress which was held in Prague the following month.

1965

Speculation as to the venue of the 1965 event ended when it was announced that Great Britain would once again be host nation, but it was the chosen location which worried many officials. The British ACU, as organizing body, came up with an entirely new format, forsaking the traditional mid Wales area in favour of a course set on the Isle of Man. The island, measuring some 30 miles by 10, and home of the TT road races, was considered by many to be too small to hold an event of this magnitude, but the organizers made use of every square inch, which resulted in a course length of some 1122 miles. Clerk of the course – Geoff Duke – and his team, plotted out two runs per day. Fanning out from the headquarters, centred on the TT grandstand at Douglas, these runs never crossed or duplicated themselves and took in some of the most varied terrain ever seen in an International, from mountain passes to sandy beaches and peat bogs.

In past years since the introduction of the bonus points system, no International had been decided on marks lost for timekeeping alone. The ACU decided to alter this state of affairs by making the going tougher, and the time schedules tighter. This they would have achieved admirably, but there was no taking into account the weather conditions which prevailed that year. By the time of the start on 20 September, the island was being lashed by the tail end of hurricane Betsy, and the

high winds and torrential rain made the conditions the hardest experienced for a long time. So hard in fact, that only 82 of the original 299 starters stayed the course, and of these, only 18 riders gained a gold medal for a faultless performance. Top of the league, was West Germany whose riders gained no less than nine golds from its contingent of 61 participants. As expected, the largest entry came from the United Kingdom, fielding 71 riders, with a further 60 on the reserve list waiting for someone to drop out. The reason for such a high number of British reserves, lay in the fact that the ACU could only accept 50 per cent more entrants than the largest entry from a foreign country, after the trophy, vase and manufacturers' teams had been subtracted.

The local inhabitants of the Glencrutchery road were awakened at 6.30 am, not to the sound of racing machines on early Monday morning practice, but to the buzz of trials machines making their way north on the first leg of the first day's run. The course took riders up the eastern side of the island to Point of Ayre, then back across the mountain of Douglas, and was covered twice during the day. The morning's special test was a timed ascent up Glen Auldyn to join the TT course near the Guthrie Memorial, but this climb was baulked by fallen riders, and resulted in more than 80 riders going over time caused by the delays. Protests would have flooded in had it not been discovered that the control clock at the next checkpoint was three minutes slow, and to save

the day, the organizers scrubbed the test and reinstated any marks lost at the subsequent time-check. In the afternoon on the second lap of the day riders tackled a four-mile run through the sand dunes from Point of Ayre to Blue Point. The sandy going caused problems for some riders in finding grip with the trials tyres which the ACU had specified for the event, for out now was the use of knobblies seen in previous Internationals. Dutchman, Frits Selling, on his 260 Greeves, and Rolf Tibblin on his 360 CZ, were in their element as they regularly competed in this sort of environment in their home countries. The test itself was not without disaster as the cylinder-head blew off Don Barret's 125 Suzuki and John Catchpole holed a piston on his Velocette/ Villiers special. At the end of the day five trophy teams were still clean, with Great Britain top of the leader-board, the Spanish team losing Gomez when the crank-shaft of his 175 Bultaco broke, and Poland losing Kopiel when the front wheel of his 125 WSK collapsed.

Tuesday's run was a repeat of the pevious day, but run in the opposite direction with the Glen Auldyn hill-climb deleted. The going by this stage was relatively easy but, nevertheless, riders still came to grief with Swedish trophy rider Johansson suffering a broken shoulder when he crashed his 175 Husqvarna, and Rolf Tibblin putting his CZ into a wall in Old Laxey village.

By Wednesday the weather had deteriorated, which put an extra strain on riders attacking the third day's run that took in the slopes of Snaefell and the Greeba forest. The conditons were so severe that every team lost marks for timekeeping, but it was the East Germans who lost the least and took the lead, putting the British team into second place in the trophy competition. The West Germans gained the lead in the vase conflict, at the expense of the other teams who were going down like flies. On the high ground the visibility was down to a few yards with rain and swirling mist. Riders, by now soaked and cold, were becoming very dispirited. After manhandling their machines through bogs and mud-holes the retirements began to mount. Of the 14 starters

in the over 500cc class, only Ken Heanes survived the day with one mark lost, the conditions finally overpowering even the great Sebastian Nachtmann on his 600cc BMW.

The fourth day saw riders again battling against the elements, with many more retiring from the one-sided fight. By the end of the day's run all the works-entered 350 and 440 BSAs, which formed parts of the British trophy and vase teams, had gone out with electrical problems. It was at this juncture that the remaining British riders started to look at the facilities enjoyed by their European rivals. Hot drinks, dry clothing, and spares

LEFT **Big cheer from race fans during the 1963 Italian GP at Monza for Italy's winning Vase team**

RIGHT **BSA's unit construction ohv single saw frequent use in the Six Days during the 1960s. It was eventually built in a variety of engine sizes from 247 to 499cc. A 1964 343cc B40 is shown here**

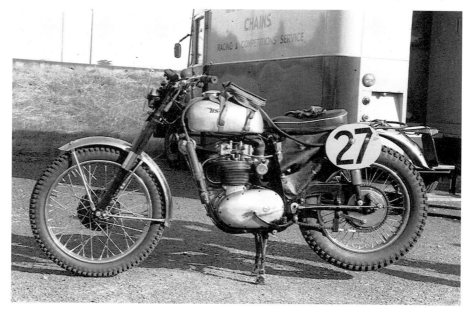

RIGHT **Another British bike which was very much a part of the 1960s ISDT scene, the Greeves. This 246cc MXI Challenger (first built in 1964) was typical of the tiny Essex factory's products**

The American Greeves team which crossed the Atlantic to contest the 1965 Six Days on the Isle of Man. It comprised Nicholson, Switzer and Lingelbach. The latter was destined to go down with a dose of flu which put him out of the event. Also in the picture is Greeves' competition manager Bill Brooker

seemed to be available at every check, supplied by the very well-organized continental back-up crews. The British riders were looked after by a support team, but by the standards set by the East Germans and the Czechoslovakians, it was of a poor quality. Voices began to be raised against the ACU for not looking after the British riders and this dissent turned to revolt when Triss Sharp refused to turn out the following morning.

The last two days saw the East Germans increase their lead over the Czech teams in both the trophy and Vase contests. Because the lead was so clear cut the final speed test did not turn into the usual race of previous years and the remaining riders toured round to save their machines. During the speed test the rains ceased and by the evening the island was once again bathed in sunshine, a fitting ending to the trial run in the worst weather conditions encountered for a long while. Local folklore summed up the week's climatic conditions, by saying the fairies had been at work – as there had been too many foreigners on the island, the fairies had brought down the mist and rain to hide it from their curious stares.

1966

East Germany did not take up the offer of running the 1966 International, which was their right for winning the Isle of Man event, on political as well as financial grounds – a lesson which had been learnt back in 1963. In the end it was the Swedes who gained third place the previous year, who hosted the 41st International Six Days, after second-place Czechoslovakia also declined the offer. This was Sweden's second effort at organizing the trial, after a joint attempt with Norway in 1923, and was staged between the towns of Orebro and Karlskoga.

Sited on an artillery training area, with the headquarters set up in the army camp at Villingsberg, the course was plotted in heavily wooded but not mountainous terrain. The military were also pressed into use, to act as marshals and to provide communications and back-up, with military policemen supervising every junction and hazard. Because of the isolated location, away from built-up areas and main roads, spectators were few, apart from the enthusiasts who had travelled to watch their countrymen compete.

Traditionally staged during the month of September, the Swedish organizers brought the starting date forward to 30 August, and were blessed with fine weather for the first two days. The wet weather made little difference to the sheltered wooded terrain but laid the dust on the earth roads which were used in the easier parts. The course, which used a variety of tight winding forest paths interlinked by earth and stone tracks, was reminiscent of the Isle of Man, not in its severity, but because at no time was a rider any more than 20 miles from the start and finish area.

Top of the trophy leaderboard on the first day was West Germany whose six-man team rode nothing larger than a 125, gone was the legendary Nachtmann on the big BMW, the selectors having seen fit to benefit from the advantage offered by the smaller capacity machines. Four other teams remained unpenalized, including the East Germans, Sweden, Great Britain and the Czechs, both the Russian and Spanish teams having lost marks. In the vase contest, East Germany ruled, with their A and B teams taking first and second places in a field of 15 clean sheets. At the start, oldest rider Frank Carey failed to get his 125 Suzuki going in the prescribed time, and was retired, as were 22 other riders who disappeared during the day, amongst them Olga Kevelos on her 75cc Suzuki. The luckiest rider of the day must have been new boy to the British vase A team, Gordon Farley, who hit a rock and holed his primary chaincase. A temporary repair was effected with a rubber tyre patch to get him back to base where a metal patch was glued on. This patch lasted out the week.

On the second day riders tackled two laps of a 90-mile course to the south of Villingsberg, again in fine conditions. The route was easy and many riders arrived at controls with time to spare, but it was the unexpected rock or loose surface which unseated some riders. One such casualty was Scott Ellis whose machine was too badly damaged to carry on, putting his BSA team out of the manufacturer's awards. Ignition failure put out Russian trophy man, Georgei Tchatchipov, who was riding a 350 IZH, and engine failure of the Bultaco ended Ferrer's chances of a Spanish win. Drahuslav Miarka of the Czech team also retired when the piston rings of his Jawa 350 disintegrated, but not until after he had gained the best class times in both the day's special tests.

Rain on the third day ended the hopes of a West German trophy win, for it got into the magneto of Loni Specht's 125 Zündapp, losing him and his team four marks for late arrival. Rain hampered the efforts of René Bennett to mend a puncture on her Greeves 250, also putting her over time. With the demise of the West Germans, Sweden should have taken the lead, but Torsten Andersson had been seen trying to fix a leaking petrol tank in the *parc fermé* prior to the start up. He was excluded from the event, losing 100 marks per day, but allowed to continue pending an appeal which was rejected. With Sweden out of the running East Germany now led, with Great Britain in second place, the only teams to retain their clean sheets.

The fourth day dawned dull with occasional rainfall, but did not change any positions on the leaderboard. The number of unpenalized vase teams dropped by two when both Austria A and the Russian B teams each lost a rider through retirement. The morning's special test was a long and hard climb up a rocky path through the woods, and was one of the toughest tests of the week. It

A great favourite with the British crowd at the 1965 event, the legendary West German Sebastian Nachtmann (590 BMW). He earned the nickname 'Gentle Giant' for his Six Days' exploits

Geoff Duke (left), Clerk of the course, with Lew Ellis of Shell and Malcolm Edgar of Castrol discussing refuelling points, 1965 ISDT

was on this test that two West Germans BMW 600 riders took heavy falls which led to their eventual retirement.

The special test on day five was the highlight of the whole event, for the organizers had bulldozed a zigzag course up the side of an enormous slag heap near the town of Kulma. The heap was part of a petrol and gas complex which was usually enveloped by clouds of evil smelling and choking vapour. Despite the smell, more of the local populace were in evidence than on any other part of the course. Riders' times for the test were naturally quicker in an effort to reach fresh air at the top of the heap.

The last day started with the MZ-mounted East German team still in the lead over the still clean British team, with West Germany B leading East Germany A in the vase contest. The situation did not alter even though Mick Andrews of the British vase A team lost a sump plug, all his engine oil, and eventually seized his AJS. All the leaders cleared the 72-mile run to Karlskoga, for the speed test on a 3-km circuit near the town. The test results had no effect on the leaderboad, thus giving the East Germans their fourth trophy win in a row. In second place came the British team only 150 bonus points behind, the nearest they had been for many years.

The British team nevertheless were happy at getting so near after the fiasco in the Isle of Man, for it was noted that organization and back-up for the team had improved enormously under the guidance of Jack Stocker. Many British riders revelled in the effortlessness of the event, with Sammy Miller being quoted as saying 'it's too easy, when is the trial going to start?'. All was not straightforward though for the British contingent faced a ferry trip in the teeth of a gale to get to the event, and then to find that they were billeted some 20 miles away from the *parc fermé*, necessitating an early start every morning. The return journey home for the British team was without incident, apart from the party

A close up view of a 246cc Russian IZH two-stroke at the Isle of Man Six Days'

in the ferry bar, but some six weeks later a plea appeared in the pages of *Motor Cycle* entitled 'ISDT Model Lost'. It called for all British railway employees to look into parked wagons, for somewhere on the railway network was an errant Triumph motorcycle, en route back to Meriden. The bike in question was Ken Heanes' 540cc, gold medal winning mount, still bearing the 111T racing plates, and the mud and scars of the event.

1967

As in previous years the East Germans demonstrated their reluctance to stage the next International, after their convincing win in Sweden in 1965, and this time the FIM offered the venue to any country who was willing to take up the challenge. It had been made plain for some time that both Spain and Poland wanted to stage the event, in order to show off their country's products, the justification being that they both had been fielding trophy teams for the past few years. Rumours stopped once the FIM announced that Poland would be granted the privilege of putting on the 1967 event, centred on the ski resort of Zakopane, 65 miles south of Krakow in the Tatra mountains – home of the famous Tatra Three Day Trial.

Firm favourites for another trophy win were again the East Germans, followed by the Czechs and Great Britain, after the masterly second place gained by the

British team in Sweden. Long before the trial started the British hopes were high, but apathy set in when the ACU announced that they would be looking after the team, as the manufacturing giants had axed their support saying that the trial no longer represented a fair test of their road machines and had therefore outlived its usefulness. Jack Stocker once again managed the British team which for once did not include Sammy Miller, who had voiced his disapproval of the organizers and the futility of competing against the overwhelming odds stacked against the British contingent using overweight and underpowered four-strokes.

Once the selection tests and final briefings were over the British team headed east towards Poland, but this trip was not without incident. The Ford Transit carrying Roy Peplow, John Giles, Gordon Farley and Jim Sandiford ran out of road and got straddled across some tram lines. After extracting the van the team got away only to be slowed by a defective fuel pump which they fixed by strapping a bike tank to the roof. Once in Zakopane the quartet got into further trouble by disputing an extortionate bar bill, which was settled only after they were marched off to the local police station. Members of the Finnish vase team also had trouble getting to the event, their Saab tow car blowing up en route. The trip was completed by train and they managed to arrive just in time.

Before the start West Germany lost two of its vase B team riders, both Brandl and Augustin being injured in practice crashes. When riders presented themselves for a newly-introduced mandatory medical check prior to the start, doctors excluded at least two entrants for high blood pressure and a fractured collarbone – the Poles were taking no chances on their first event. The army was once again used to good effect, with paratroopers running all the check-points to help riders on their way. Even the local police force helped by giving participants right of way at junctions on the road sections.

At 7 am on the first morning 315 riders got away in threes at one-minute intervals, to tackle the 25-mile run to Nowy Targ. This leg was used each day to get riders into the mountains, before embarking on daily circuits through the forests. These daily runs contained only one special test, a tactic devised by the organizers to make the scores much closer. At the end of the day, as expected, it was East German MZ team leading the trophy contest with Austria in second place. Italy, who had been absent from the contest since 1962, lost Gritti when he fell from his 175 Morini and broke his collarbone. Great Britain's hopes faded when the ignition system failed on the Scott Ellis BSA – an all too familiar story first seen in the Isle of Man – saddling his team with 100 marks per day. This premature ending to Scott's participation must have been a bitter blow for he was originally a reserve, taking Jim Sandiford's place when his Greeves failed to come up to expectation. The home team was another to lose a man on the first day,

RIGHT **Olga Kevelos (73 Suzuki) crosses the tram track above Laxey watched intently by a small band of enthusiasts**

BELOW **American Leroy Winters investigates his waterlogged Honda 90 during the 1965 event**

when the gearbox gave out on Jerzy Warchol's 125 SHL.

The special test on day two was a hillclimb on a metalled main road, which included plenty of twists and turns. Roy Peplow, on his 504cc Triumph, gained maximum points for his effortless run up the hill, closely followed by Ken Heanes, also on an overbored Triumph, for these were the only runners in the over 500cc class: a sure sign that participants were now favouring the smaller machines and their inherent advantages. But it was the small machine of Norbert Gabler that spoilt the chances of the West German trophy team when he retired after his Hercules 75 shattered its piston rings.

A double disaster hit the British team on the third day when both John Lewis and Ken Heanes both retired, John with ignition problems and Ken with a seizing engine, thought to be caused by the local petrol – a problem not experienced by the Czechoslovakian team for they had seen fit to bring their own supplies. At the half-way point it was still the East Germans in the lead, but the Austrian team were only three bonus points behind and the Czech team another 15 behind them, and all clean. Nine vase teams still had clean sheets, with Czechoslovakia A leading West Germany B by eight points.

The British vase A team, being made up of army riders – disguised as civilians in order to ride in a Warsaw Pact country – finally ended their efforts on the fourth day. Mick Soames dislocated his shoulder in a fall, Ted Johns' 500 AJS developed a big-end death rattle and Mick Noyce lost the sparks on his BSA. Peter Lasota

Another American Nick Nicholson (246 Greeves) travelling along one of the Isle of Man's beaches. The island measuring only some 30 miles by 10, presented the Clerk of the course, Geoff Duke, and his team, with a real challenge for an event which had a course length of some 1,122 miles

having retired on the first day when the flywheel key on his Greeves sheared. The sensation of the day was the announcement that the Puch-mounted Austrian Trophy team had gone into the lead overtaking the East Germans by 8 points, a truly great feat in view of the fact that the team had only two professional riders, the rest being enthusiastic amateurs. Another sensation on the fourth day was a jury ruling a ban on the use of walkie-talkie radio sets, deemed to constitute outside assistance and, therefore, not allowed by the event rules. Both the German teams as well as the Russians and Czechs had been using them to assist riders with time-keeping and navigation, much to the disgust of countries who were not.

On the issue of the instruction, teams ceased using these unfair electronic aids, except the Russian team. This practice soon ended when the Polish army radio unit found the frequency and jammed it.

On the fifth day the British trophy team were down to only two riders, for Roy Peplow had retired the previous afternoon when the clutch of his Triumph gave up. But by far the biggest upset of the day was the retirement of Johann Sommerauer, when the frame of his 166cc Puch broke, putting the Austrians back down to third place. After the evening's jury meeting the Austrians were moved up to second position when it was revealed that Zdenek Cespiva had been spotted changing a suspension unit on his 250 Jawa. The unit, a marked and therefore non changeable part, earned Cespiva an exclusion and the Czech trophy team a 100-mark deficit.

The final day's speed test run over a 2½-mile road circuit on the outskirts of Zakopane did not change the outcome of the trial. East Germany took the trophy for the fifth time in a row, with second place going to the gallant Austrian Puch team. Czechoslovakia A won the Silver Vase, with their all Jawa-mounted team beating the East German A team into second place.

The Polish event was praised for its organization which was free from any major upsets, but it will be best remembered for the meteoric ride of the courageous Austrians riding their 50, 125 and 166cc Puch machines.

1968

Italy hosted the 1968 International which was based at the resort of San Pellegrino in the Italian Alps, the home of the Vali Bergamo three-day event, this time with a reduced distance of 788 miles due to heavy rainfall making parts of the original course impassable. The reduction in overall mileage may have given the 298 starters a false impression of the Italian organizers, but as soon as the trial started the true severity of the event became apparent. Battling over narrow rock-strewn mountain tracks, against an extremely tight time schedule, soon had riders practically on their knees and accounted for many retirements, with the usual loss of marks. The Italians, with a view to making scoring easier, had come up with a new marking system, which unlike previous years now gave deficit marks for special test performances. The fastest man in each capacity class scored zero, while other riders were penalized one mark for every second over the leader. These marks were then added to any marks lost for bad timekeeping or any other default such as failure to start in the time allowance given.

Favourites at the start were again the East Germans looking for their sixth trophy win in a row, closely followed by the Czechs and the Austrians. Great Britain again put in a team, managed this time by Alan Kimber, but without Roy Peplow who had voiced his disapproval of the lack of official support. Roy did ride in the trial, but only as a private entrant on his 504cc Triumph and won a silver medal.

Once again, the British motorcycle industry refused to back a team, which was this time funded by a sports council grant and money raised by donations from enthusiastic motorcycle dealers and suppliers. A sad state of affairs for a once formidable force.

The Italian event was not without problems as many riders turned up without green card insurance cover, due to an oversight in the compilation of the joining instructions. The British and American teams managed to arrange the necessary cover at £15 per head, but the East Germans at first refused claiming that they had block cover at home, and no money anyway. The next problem arose when riders discovered that they had to pay for their petrol at the full Italian rate. Angry protestations were made to the Agip company who had purchased the petrol rights for the event – who relented – and offered to let the foreign riders have their fuel at the 30 per cent tourist rate. Walter Kaaden, the East German MZ engineer, was not happy at the thought of using the heavily leaded Agip fuel, preferring the Shell variety, and to prove his point his MZs suffered many

Competitors travelling over a bleak, boggy section in the Isle of Man; note the wooden fencing laid down to prevent riders sinking into the mire

seizures during the six days. During the weigh-in, while the East German machines were being checked, Jon Tye and two other Royal Air Force riders saw an East German official slip a tin of special marking paint into his pocket. This incident was reported, but no action was taken as the next day it was found that all the marking paint had disappeared, necessitating the authorities to change the paint colour and remark all the entries. Because it was hurriedly done, some items were missed, and did not come to light until later checks. Fiddling was suspected when British Army rider, Bryan Cowshall, was found to have an unmarked rear hub, and East German rider, Rolf Uhlig, an unmarked cylinder head, but the jury gave them the benefit of the doubt after a vote.

After a hectic first day, the East Germans were at last relegated to second position in the trophy by their old political and sporting adversaries, the West Germans, who retained a clean sheet to the bitter end. The East Germans' downfall came during the first tight section, when Hans Weber suffered ignition problems on his 250 MZ, and lost three marks. Italian trophy man, Carlo

West German Vase teamster S Giegnger (98 Zündapp) screaming his tiny mount to a gold winning performance in the 1965 Six Days'. This is a typical 'all-action' photograph from master craftsman, Nick Nicholls

Moscheni, riding a 175 Gilera, lost four marks on the same section putting the home team into third position. Great Britain's hopes faded when John Lewis lost compression on one cylinder of his Cheney Triumph, and Jock Wilson broke a gear selector spring on his 250 Greeves, their retirements putting the team at the bottom of the table. In all, 13 British riders retired that day, amongst them ACU competition's manager, Mary Driver, when the ignition system of her Greeves gave up.

Less than ten miles from the start on the second day, Ken Heanes – the British trophy team captain – lost all the gears of his Triumph, leaving his team down to three men. This tally became two shortly afterwards when Dennis Jones retired after shattering the rear chain of his 256cc Greeves.

Day 3 saw the organizers bring in a slower schedule, probably as a direct result of the number of casualties inflicted on men and machines during the first two days. As a result of this slower speed, all five teams in both the trophy and vase contests dropped no marks at all, leaving the West Germans top in both competitions. During the third day it became evident that there were a number of spectators from several countries riding machines identical to the competitors, and even dressed like them. This, said the jury, must have been a mobile source of spares, and illegal under the

ABOVE An unfamiliar Governors Bridge scene on the world famous TT course, taken during the speed tests of the 1965 ISDT. Riders are: H Trinkler 49 Hercules (19), A Brandl 50 Zündapp (4) and A Lehner 50 Zündapp (15), Trinkler and Lehner won golds, Brandl a silver medal

BELOW East German Simson GS was built in either 50 or 75cc engine sizes. Both proved gold medal winners in the ISDT during the late 1960s

outside assistance rule. To stop the practice the local traffic police were called in to keep an eye on things, and the organizers marked all machines with special stickers to stop any bike swapping. These proved worthless for riders soon found a way of removing them.

West Germany's chances of a double were dashed on the fourth day when Rolf Witthoft broke the fork yolks of his 125 Puch, allowing the Italian A team to take the top position in the vase contest. At the jury meeting that evening Giuseppe Rottigni of the Italian trophy team was excluded because the cylinder-head seal was found to be missing on his Morini 100. Rolf Uhlig of the East German vase B team was also excluded for missing a stamp check on his 75cc Simson.

The sensation of the fifth day was the spectacular retirement of the East German trophy ace, Salevsky. Running out of road on a bend, his 360 MZ plunged 300

simson **GS 50/75**

feet down into a valley, but with outstretched arms he managed to grab a tree before going over the edge.

After an uneventful run to the Monza Autodrome for the last day's speed test, riders had to lap for 30 minutes on the 1½-mile junior circuit, but this again had no effect on the final outcome for the West German Zündapp-mounted team were well and truly in the lead, with the Italian A team taking the vase.

The week will be remembered for the dismal showing of the British teams, saved only by a meritorious performance by the vase A team, comprising members of the British armed services. Mounted on totally inadequate army issue BSA 441s, Mick Soames, Mick Noyce and Bryan Cowshall were backed up by RAF Pilot, Jon Tye, on a 360 AJS. At the finish their machines were in a sorry state – only fit for the junk yard – but they did manage to get two silver and two bronze medals between them.

1969

Honouring the West German win in Italy the previous year, the venue for the 1969 International returned once more to Garmisch-Partenkirchen in the Bavarian Alps. This setting, liked by many riders, was hoped by the Germans to provide a home advantage for their trophy team, again all mounted on small-capacity – but far from low powered – Zündapps. But the locals who turned out in force to see their heroes had not reckoned on the tenacity of the MZ-mounted East Germans and the Czechs on their Jawa/CZs.

Before the trial started the ACU-entered British teams found themselves in trouble because the entry fee cheque had still not been cleared by the Bank of England. The German organizing body, ADAC, was all for excluding the team, until Cliff King – the British jury member – guaranteed the necessary £1500. As noise was now becoming a problem, especially with some of the motocross-engined machines, ADAC had put a limit on it, with penalty points for failure. This did not bother the riders of standard machines too much, but competitors using the over 350 two-stroke moto-

BELOW In 1966 the Six Days' was held in Sweden. Here Russian Victor Pylaev (246 IZH) is about to leave one of the checkpoints

RIGHT Klaus Teuchert (350 MZ) from the East German Trophy team who helped his team to a fourth consecutive win the Trophy contest in Sweden

Poland was the setting for the 1967 ISDT. The British rider Roy Peplow (490 Triumph) leads the American Bud Ekins (HVA) over some Polish cobblestones

cross engines had to do something about it, for there were more now than ever before. To abide by the rules many teams fitted extra large silencers to their expansion chamber systems in the hope of avoiding penalties.

Day one saw the noise meter in action on the acceleration special test. Small machines of 50 to 75cc were allowed 90 decibels, and above 350cc 95 decibels. Despite precautions, over 80 riders failed the test and were awarded 20 penalty points, the 250cc class two-strokes being the main offenders. Another ruling, but this time being enforced by the local police, was the compulsory use of lights in tunnels. This edict required the cutting of holes in the front numberplates of many machines, because they obscured the head lamp and could not be swivelled up out of the way.

Apart from the Soviet Union, when Victor Pylaev retired with a seized piston, all trophy teams finished the first day with clean sheets. East Germany led with fewer penalty points followed by Czechoslovakia. Biggest upset of the day was the total collapse of the Scot-

tish ACU's first attempt, putting every one of their teams out of the running. Scottish ACU Club team rider, Jimmy Ballantyne, hit a lorry and broke both his legs, and team mate, Jackie Williamson, broke the gearbox of his 250 Montesa. Private entrant, Jimmie McCall, lost the ignition on his 250 Bultaco, but the major crisis was when Ian Miller retired with a broken chain adjuster on his 125 Dalesman, which meant 100 marks lost per day to the Scottish ACU-entered British vase B team.

The weather had been kind to the riders, the rain, what little there was fell during the night, resulting in a few greasy patches under trees. But now the organizers sought to hot up the pace by introducing the higher speed schedule for the second afternoon's run. This resulted in the retirement of a further 67 riders and the loss of marks for four trophy teams and various vase teams. The Austrians lost Pachernegg, Stuhlberger and Leitgeb, all with mechanical problems. Swedish Husqvarna rider, Lars Johansson, bashed his ankle, and Italy's Fausto Vergani sheared a cylinder-head stud on his Morini 100, both retiring as a result. John Pease lost one mark when the rear brake rod came adrift on his Greeves, putting the British trophy team in fourth place behind East and West Germany and the Czechs. The British vase A team – again using a mixture of Army and Air Force riders – lost Jon Tye when he broke a rear suspension unit on his 125 Dalesman. Mick Noyce dropped 17 marks during the day and Tom Fayers a further 6, putting the team at the bottom of the list with the B team.

West Germany lost all chance of a repeat performance when the gearbox of Heinz Brinkmann's Zündapp 50 gave up on the third day. The Austrians lost yet another rider when Franz Dworak dropped out with ignition failure on his 125 Puch, leaving only two riders to fly the flag. The following day the West Germans had to suffer the ignominy of trophy rider Andreas Brandl being excluded for outside assistance. The unfortunate Brandl blew up the gearbox of his 50cc Zündapp and was towed in by team mates, and efforts were made to fit new parts to the ailing machine. Two further West Germans were also excluded for carrying out illegal repairs, Kurt Distler swapped a rear suspension unit on his 750 BMW, and Kurt Rentschler tried to repair the forks and front wheel of his 420 Jawa, but both were caught. Ignition problems sidelined British trophy rider Colin Dommett and vase A man, Tom Fayers.

Day 5 saw the East Germans and the Czechs still both with clean sheets, the MZ riders increasing their advantage on the special test points. In the vase contest six teams were yet unpenalized with both West German teams at the top. The day, run on the slower schedule, was quite uneventful, until the jury meeting in the evening when an Italian juryman alleged that one of the East German Simsons had been swapped out on the course. No name or number was given, but the Italian said it was on cine film, which would be forthcoming in the morning. The jury inspected all the Simson machines under infra-red light to check the paint markings, but nothing was found and the following morning the promised film also failed to appear. The jury were not amused and the Italian faded away into obscurity, the incident forgotten.

The final day saw riders assemble at the 4.3-mile Ettal circuit for the speed test, the East Germans still had a commanding lead and barring accidents could not fail to win. Their luck held, for it was the second place team which hit disaster. The contact breaker arm of Jaroslav Briza's 420 Jawa snapped after only three laps and cost the Czechs their clean sheet. So the decade came to an end with the East Germans the decisive winners, having taken home the coveted trophy for the sixth time, a feat only bettered by the Czechs ten years previously, and the British teams in their heyday many years before that.

Italy hosted the 1968 International which was based at the resort of San Pellegrino in the Italian Alps. But it was the West Germans who won the all-important Trophy contest. Their entire six man squad was mounted on small capacity Zündapp two-strokes

CHAPTER SEVEN

Czech-mate

1970

The initial event that heralded the dawn of a new decade, saw quite a few changes over the original trial format. After much prompting from participating countries, who themselves were not motorcycle manufacturers of a sporting nature, the FIM decided to open the trophy competition to all members of the Federation, enabling them to field a trophy team mounted on foreign machinery. One of the major forces in this decision was the USA, who had been entering vase teams mounted on other country's machines for some time. As long-distance offroad racing was a fast growing sport and, therefore, a big money earner, the Americans wanted to play a bigger part on the International scene to boost the home events. With this new ruling many countries took the opportunity to re-equip their trophy teams with new machinery, much of it Japanese as at this time they were beginning to prove themselves in competition. Other non-producing countries stayed with the proven offroad machines, like Jawa and Husqvarna, but then simply entered as a trophy team rather than a vase team. The major motorcycle manufacturing countries continued to use their home products, but now an International win had added prestige for the Silver Trophy was renamed the World Trophy and the winners were entitled to call themselves the World Champions.

The first contest to decide the World Championship was held in an entirely different location to the more usual ones that riders were familiar with. After much trying, Spain was finally granted the privilege of hosting the 1970 event, another first in the everchanging event format. Centred on the small town of El Escorial, 50 km north of Madrid, the days' runs led riders over the barren and rocky hills of the Guadarrama range, returning each evening to El Escorial, famous for its historical royal monastery. Used mainly to the damp, soggy forests of northern Europe, riders revelled in the warmth and dryness of this arid region but at times this hampered progress due to the blinding and clogging dust which was kicked up by the riders' hurried passage.

Firm favourites again were the East Germans, after their win at Garmisch, but the unexpected retirement of Uhlig on the third day due to ring failure, and the loss of a further three riders the following day due to magneto failures, ended their efforts, leaving Czechoslovakia to slog it out to the end with the powerful West German team mounted again on small-capacity Zündapps. Great Britain dropped 21 marks on the first day after John Pease was plagued by punctures and John Giles split the fuel tank of his Cheney Triumph. The team lost no more marks and ended up sixth in the rankings at the end of the week. The Kawasaki-mounted Canadian trophy team, in its first attempt at the premier award, lost four riders on the first day, the main problem being the vulnerable side-mounted carburettors of their machines being attacked by the rock-strewn terrain in the Valley of the Fallen, an aptly named place which lost marks for a quarter of the 323 starters.

Old hands at the International began to feel at home when the rains came on the third day, but this turned to snow and hail up in the mountains, causing much discomfort to the less wary participants who were riding in sweatshirts and leather jeans. Regular entrants knew the score and were suitably kitted out right from the start. Czechoslovakia maintained its lead over the Zündapp-mounted West German team, with Italy and Sweden close behind, all with clean sheets. Jim Sandiford, Bill Wilkinson and British team captain, Ken Heanes, put up some memorable performances on the motocross track, which was used as a daily special test to decide evaluation points. The trio led the above half-litre class to the end, mounted on their 504cc Cheney Triumphs, beating the much favoured West German-entered 750 BMW monsters.

The Czechs stayed in front by sheer hard work, dropping just enough evaluation points to outwit the West Germans who were catching up fast, only seven points behind at the start of the final speed test. As every rider knows, anything can happen during the event, and on the last day, it was the unexpected stopping of Jaroslav Briza to replace a carburettor jet, that nearly spelt disaster for the Czechs. When the repair was completed, Briza's Jawa refused to restart and he lost many precious minutes before the machine eventually fired up. He completed the final stage on full throttle, to arrive at the control with only 20 seconds left, before losing marks for himself and the trophy for his team. The Czechs were safe, and all that remained was to ensure that they lost less evaluation points than the West Germans during the five laps of the Jarama 2.1-mile circuit. Ably directed from the pits by Jan Krivka – the Jawa chief designer – the Czech team stayed in front just enough to beat the West Germans by 47 points to

ABOVE **As the 1970s dawned the East Germans entered the new decade having won six of the previous seven years ISDT Trophy contests. Much of the credit went to their two-stroke MZ machines. Their record of reliability was almost without blemish. But could they maintain this success?**

LEFT **West Germany was also a strong contender for Trophy honours, and none more so than Erwin Schmider the former NSU works rider who rode for Zündapp in the late 1960s and early 1970s**

become the first World Champions. Not only did they take the Trophy home but also the Silver Vase and a manufacturer's team prize, all with no marks lost at all. This was a truly magnificent feat by a team who had been relegated to the also-ran class for the past decade by the all-conquering MZs.

1971

The venue for the 46th International saw a return to the Isle of Man for the second time. With memories still vivid in the minds of riders who competed in the atrocious weather conditions of 1965, it is not surprising

Zündapp star Erwin Schmider during German selection trials for the 1970 ISDT

that they viewed the 1971 event with some trepidation. As luck would have it, the sun shone all week long with above average temperatures for the time of year, a sure sign that the Manx fairies welcomed the return of the International and its many foreign riders. Of the 297 starters, the largest contingent naturally came from Great Britain, with 58 riders, followed by West Germany and the USA. American trophy team captain, John Penton, was recognized as the competitor who travelled the furthest, released from his army duties at Da Nang in Vietnam, to take charge of the KTM-engined Pentons of the USA team.

After a four-year break Sammy Miller once again returned to the Six Days, but this time with a purposeful task in hand. Riding a Comerfords-entered Bultaco 250 he intended to have a crack at winning the Maudes Trophy for the Spanish firm, by riding the same bike in the production TT and then in the ISDT. On checking with the ACU it was found that his International Road Racing Licence had expired and a replacement could not be issued in time for the TT. Plans were amended to take in the following year's Thruxton 500-mile race, but Bultaco stepped in and cancelled the whole attempt. Nevertheless, Sam went on to ride in the ISDT gaining another gold medal for his collection.

Fresh from their Spanish victory Czechoslovakia fielded 18 riders, but not all of them got as far as the starting-line. During practice, vase rider, Josef Rabas, was seriously injured and was hospitalized for the week, his place in the A team being taken by newcomer, Petermann. Mounted entirely on Jawas, the Czech trophy team used the same riders as the previous year, but this time using a mixture of 250, 350 and 360cc machines,

which best suited the expected conditions on the island.

Even before the half-way stage the event had become a three-horse race between the traditional rivals, East Germany, West Germany and Czechoslovakia, Great Britain having gone out on the first day when Mick Wilkinson ran into oil pump troubles on his 504cc Cheney Triumph. High hopes were expected of the Ducati-mounted Italian trophy team until Dall'ara retired on the third day. On the fifth day Dossena's wheels were checked and found to have the number 285 scratched in the marker paint. On Closer inspection this was found to be originally 275 modified to look like 285, and were in fact Dall'ara's original wheels. Dossena retired in disgrace. Other teams were up to the same tricks, which were confirmed when the Chief Marshal spotted two Maicos, each bearing the number 244, in the camping

ABOVE **Another contender for national honours in the early 1970s were the Spanish; headed by the Bultaco marque. One of their 246cc Madators is shown. Spain hosted the event in 1970, the first time ever**

LEFT **American Trophy team captain, John Penton, travelled from his army duties in Vietnam, to take charge of the KTM engined USA team in 1971**

area. The number belonged to Horst Lampe who was supposed to be out on the course, word must have reached him for he did not clock in that afternoon and he disappeared.

In contrast to the Spanish event, West Germany took the lead from day one and managed to retain it until the very last day, largely thanks to the domination of the lower capacity classes by the diminutive Zündapps. Czechoslovakia and East Germany held on, but mixed with other machinery in the larger capacity classes they amassed too many evaluation points on the daily 3½-mile cross-country special tests on the Douglas Head scrambles course. The evaluation points scoring system, devised by CSI president, Otto Sensburg, gave one point per second for the cross-country tests and five points per second for the daily acceleration tests, added to which were the set penalties for noisy exhausts and failure to start on time. From this figure the growing total of the top man in each capacity class was deducted to decide the order in that class. Team totals were then added together to give team placings. It was a complicated business which no one liked for it was open to abuse. Like it or not, teams were stuck with it, and it was this system which put West Germany in the lead and then toppled them in the final speed test.

The final decision once more hinged on the outcome of the speed test. Gold standard was to be an average of 41.6 mph for the over 75cc machines around the Parkfield circuit, with evaluation points depending on lap times. Jan Krivka once again took charge of Czech tactics, he had given each of his riders one East German to beat to top their class, and even told them by how much to do it. By now the West German tiddlers had gone beyond their best, not being able to render anything like their top performance, and in two of the capacity classes, actually failed to stay in front. With the resultant loss of points the Czechs came out on top and were crowned World Champions for the second year running. In the vase contest the Czechoslovakia B team came out on top, narrowly beating the A team, but it had been the other way round during the week, with the A team leading until the final speed test.

Everyone breathed a sigh of relief when the trial was over, as each and every rider expected a repeat of the storms of 1965, but it never came, and the event was graced by pleasant motorcycling weather for a change.

Sammy Miller (246 Bultaco) in action during the 1971 ISDT staged in the Isle of Man. An American competitor who has got into difficulties is behind the Irishman and going in the opposite direction!

The 504cc Cheney Triumph of John Pease, Isle of Man 1971. Although soundly built these machines were simply not in the same class as the purpose built machinery from Eastern Europe

As entrants departed by the island ferry their thoughts were on the next event – hosted by the Czechs on their own ground. It would potentially be a massacre as the Czechs were going for a Grand Slam.

1972

The Bohemian ski resort of Spindleruv Mlyn, in the Great Mountains, part of the northern territory of Czechoslovakia, hosted the 1972 International and attracted a record entry of 382 starters. The town and its surrounding area was bedecked with banners on every lamp-post and telephone pole, advertising the ISDT and calling for International friendship. But the treatment of machines was exactly the opposite. At the weigh-in all stickers and logos were taped over or removed from the participating machines, except for the manufacturers' tank badges, in an effort to clamp down on advertising. Even the national flags, denoting the rider's country of origin were removed, together with the ACU approval transfers on helmets, for these too, had to be bare. The Czech organizers, being inflexible over scrutineering, pledged to be even harder on

offenders during the event, and promised that this the 47th in the series, would be the toughest yet.

Before the trial began, the Czechs appeared to be in trouble with the loss of Kvetoslav Masita due to practice injury, his place being taken by Jaroslav Briza. This substitution heightened the fortunes of both the East and West Germans who considered themselves to be in with a chance. The luck of the East Germans was dashed on the first morning when Werner Salevsky did not start. Salevsky had been declared medically unfit due to an eye injury and his place was taken by moto-cross specialist, Rolf Fisher. The British trophy team, which included foreign-made machinery for the first time, was in a panic even before the weigh-in. The 250 Ossa which Mick Andrews planned to ride was stuck in a customs-sealed van, and took three days before a local customs man would release it. Gordon Farley's Montesa was in transit from Spain and did not arrive until late Saturday night, just in time for the Sunday weigh-in. Both the Swedish and American teams nearly withdrew, due to the non delivery of their riding suits. The British firm of T.T. Leathers had promised to send out the suits with an English rider, but this fell through and they had to be finally air-freighted, arriving with less than 12 hours to go before the start.

Day one saw the end of any hope for a British success when Arthur Browning failed to start his 504 Triumph in the time allowed, and Gordon Farley got the gearbox

Another of the Cheney Triumphs having its rear tyre attended to by its rider, Jim Sandiford during the 1971 event

A 125 Morini four-stroke single being sealed by an ACU official. The 'V' on the number plate denotes this machine to be a member of the Vase team

of his Montessa stuck in fourth during the cross-country special test. When the day's results were announced it was the West Germans who were in the lead over Czechoslovakia, East Germany, America, Italy and Russia, all with clean sheets. The following day Brinkmann lost his way, and screamed his Zündapp into a time control seven minutes late, dropping the West Germans down to sixth position. Gordon Farley started on the second day after changing his gearbox selector mechanism in the ten minutes maintenance period. This feat being carried out after practising on a spectator's Montesa throughout the previous evening. After the change the gearbox worked perfectly but the following day the piston failed and he retired.

By mid week the Czechs were once gain firmly in the lead, but the East Germans hung on hoping for a retirement, even though Paul Friedrichs and Jan Kempter were both in pain due to earlier crashes. Both riders were watched intently by rival team managers, cameras in hand, ready to record any outside assistance the injured riders might have received. The remaining British trophy riders were also having medical problems, both Arthur Browning and Dave Jeremiah had caught a local stomach bug and were feeling very low. Mick Andrews visited the local hospital for some cream to ease a wrenched shoulder, and ended up with an injection of gargantuan proportions which did not ease the pain. The subsequent use of strong painkilling tablets had Mick flying in more ways than one, but whatever it was worked and Mick ended up with a gold medal.

The Czechs carried on in the lead, going just quick enough to avoid penalties, but slow enough to avoid trouble, and the final speed test on the sixth day only confirmed their supremacy. They took the World Trophy and the World Championship for the third time. Three other teams were still clean at the end – East Germany, Italy and Russia. The Italians were using KTM machines, while the Russians had chosen to use Jawas. The Silver Vase also went to Czechoslovakia with the A team just beating the B team. In the manufacturer's contest the first place was taken by the Zündapp A team, closely followed by four Jawa teams. Jawa and Zündapp also cleaned up in the capacity classes with Zündapp taking the 50, 75, 100, 125 and 175cc awards, and Jawa the 250, 350 and 500 awards.

The Czech event saw the American Penton-mounted trophy team give its best yet performance. Clean until the very last day, they finally finished in sixth place. Interest from the other side of the Atlantic had been increasing for some time, and the Czech event saw many participants from that part of the world, including a USA-entered Dalesman works team and a trio of 500cc Yankee twins, the latter being American-built double Ossas. It was

therefore not surprising that, when announced, the 48th International would be held in the USA.

1973

An official welcome from the President of the United States – Richard Nixon – greeted visitors from the many nations who gathered in the Berkshire hills of Massachusetts to contest the sixtieth anniversary event. Centred on the small town of Dalton, the day's routes took riders through the predominantly forestry land of the Berkshire range, but this was not the original idea of the organizers. The initial intention of the American Motorcycle Association was to stage the event in Texas,

ABOVE One of the Czechoslovakian Jawas as used in 1971. The Czechs won the Trophy for the second year running and were poised to dominate the event for much of the decade

BELOW The 498cc BSA single of Dutchman Frits Selling; the same rider had earlier ridden Greeves two-strokes in the 1960s. He was a member of the Dutch Trophy team in 1971

RIGHT East German Trophy teamster Klaus Teuchert hurries his 350cc MZ up the Mountain clumb from Ramsey to Gurthrie's Memorial on the TT course, 1971 ISDT

RIGHT **Another Zündapp team in 1973 event was the British Rickman effort. Brothers Don and Derek are shown here with the bikes. Ridden by the likes of Jim Sandiford and Ernie Page their performance couldn't match the pukka (tuned!) works engines**

BELOW **One of the unit construction Triumph twins specially built for the 1973 ISDT staged near Dalton, Massachusetts**

ABOVE **Zündapp mounted West German Trophy team before the start of the 1973 ISDT in America; they couldn't repeat their success of earlier years**

but after a reconnaissance of the area, it was deemed that its near desert terrain was unsuitable for the trial, and prompted the move northward to Massachusetts. The new venue was not without its problems, for a bunch of conservationists, which included members of the New England Trail Riders Association, tried to get the International banned. The reasons given were, noise, damage to trails, the adverse effect to wildlife and the possible curtailment of future trail-riding activities. The legal battle dragged on in the Boston court, and was only resolved at the eleventh hour when the judge threw out the case on a legal technicality. The trial was saved and went ahead as planned but the legal costs nearly bankrupted the AMA.

The Americans wanted to put up a good showing, and spent heavily on the organizational side of the event, building special grandstands and viewing areas at the best vantage points. A computer was also purchased to tabulate results, but its speed and accuracy was far from satisfactory, causing many headaches. The AMA's inexperience in dealing with the complexities of the trial showed many times during the week. Marshalling was not as professional as other organizing countries, with time control crews opening and closing their posts at will. One morning, the marshals even failed to turn up to unlock the *parc fermé*, the padlock being smashed off by riders, in order to retrieve their machines. These inadequacies were far outweighed by the severe but excellent course, which reminded riders

of the damp northern European forests which they were used to.

Czechoslovakia were once again firm favourites for the World Trophy, with their all Jawa-mounted team, but much interest centred on the British team who had ousted the foreign machines of the previous year and opted to re-use Triumphs backed up by a pair of Rickmans. The Triumphs of 490 and 504cc were built at the request of the American Triumph subsidiary, in the light of the growing interest in offroad activities, and were in essence, TR5T Trophy Trails, which later became known as the Adventurer. In all, twelve of these special Triumphs were made, which used the BSA B50 Victor oil-in-frame rolling chassis, and shipped to the USA for use by British and American riders. This was the time of the BSA-Triumph group collapse, and at

the end of the trial eleven of the batch stayed in the USA to be sold off as part of the groups' assets. The one remaining machine, ridden by Malcolm Rathmell, returned to Great Britain where it was put on permanent display at the National Motorcycle Museum, and is still there to this day.

To back up the Triumphs the British team turned to the Rickman brothers to supply a pair of 125 Rickman Zündapps, to be ridden by Jim Sandiford and Ernie Page. Both Jim and Ernie considered themselves to be lucky in being offered the Rickmans, for they were promised to be up to the same standard as the West German team's mounts, but this was not to be. When sampled they were found to be nowhere near the standards promised and definitely slower than the West Germans' because over-the-counter engines had been fitted due to a shortage of tuned ones. The dispirited riders renamed their machines Rickshaw Zuncraps and set about making up the shortfall in performance by rigorous practice. This tactic paid off for both riders gained gold medals.

The trial was blessed with fine weather but the nights were frosty which saw many riders lose 50 points on the initial start-up, amongst them members of the East and West German and the Czech trophy teams. Royal Air Force pilot, Jon Tye, had a nasty shock, his 125 Monark setting off backwards after a faultless start-up. After

retiming the magneto he got away only to retire on the fifth day with big-end failure. Static noise tests were another feature which the authorities applied rigorously. The test caught no less than four Czech trophy riders on the first morning, costing them 20 bonus points each. This problem did not effect the Dalesman-mounted British military vase A team for they had lagged their silencers with asbestos tape, kindly supplied from the Quartermaster's Stores.

Eighteen nations were represented by 303 starters on the first day, but injuries and breakdowns sidelined 125 by the end of the week. The first day was easy by comparison, with 11 of the 12 trophy teams still clean. By far the biggest upset with the total withdrawal of the East Germans due to lubrication problems with the MZs. The problem was first noticed when the MZs started to lose compression, and Walter Kaaden diagnosed gummed rings. In an effort to save face, rather than to see his charges drop out one by one, Walter withdrew the whole team. Castrol later admitted responsibility saying that one of their employees supplied the wrong oil to the East Germans. As a precaution many other Castrol users changed their oil before the second day.

Day 2 saw the West Germans slip from the top of the leaderboard to third position, when Erwin Schmider lost a mark for lateness due to an ignition problem. Italy was running clean in fourth place at the end of the first

British Trophy rider John Pease (Triumph) tackling a swamp-like section of the 1973 American event. His bike is one of twelve such machines built at the request of the American Triumph subsidiary, using either 490cc or 504cc engine capacities

LEFT **In 1974 the ISDT circus moved to the picturesque town of Camerino high in the Abruzzi mountains of southern Italy. Following a good showing in the European series, Gilera machines became the standard mount for the host nation's Trophy and Vase teams**

ABOVE **One of the new Gileras. This particular machine was ridden by Alessandro Gritti. Its 123.670cc (54 x 54mm) single cylinder rotary valve two-stroke engine pumped out 21 bhp @ 9200 rpm. A larger 173.840cc (61 x 59.5mm) was also built**

day, but suffered the loss of Ivan Seravesi with two broken ribs and Emilio Capelli with a seized engine. Great Britain dropped four marks when Arthur Browning nipped his new tube while mending a puncture, the wait for a further spare putting him into the red at the next time control.

At the half-way stage the Czechs held a commanding lead over the Austrians, the only two teams still with clean sheets, followed by Sweden and Great Britain. By this stage, the sprockets of Jim Sandiford's Rickman had a few teeth missing, but the following morning he demonstrated that they could be changed in four minutes flat. Thursday saw Austrians Sommerauer and veteran Kurt Statzinger drop ten marks for lateness, and the retirement of Sweden's Jan-Eric Sallquist due to clutch failure, putting Great Britain into second position.

Friday saw the ex 500cc World Motocross champion, Jeff Smith, riding a 175 Can-Am for the Canadian team, drop out due to a puncture and a defective air bottle. All was not well with the Czech team, for Frantisek Mrazek was having trouble with a torn ligament in his hand, and Petr Cemus had once again hurt his previously damaged elbow. But the pair carried on undauntingly, to help their team once again take the World Trophy, excelling themselves on the final speed test which was run for the first time on a cross-country course. The United States won its first major award by taking the Silver Vase, the team being mounted exclusively on Husqvarnas.

After the American International Jim Sandiford announced his retirement from the ISDT. It had always been Jim's ambition to ride in the States and to win ten gold medals – 'now I have achieved both its time for me to quit', said Jim. The American event also saw, for the first time, one of the riders being chased by a bear. Metropolitan policeman, Dave Hobbs, was confronted by the angry beast on the first day. The thoughts of this encounter must have spurred Dave on for he completed the week intact, with a gold medal for his efforts.

1974

Fresh from their victory in the USA, the Czechoslovakians sent their best riders to the picturesque town of Camerino high in the Abruzzi mountains of southern Italy, to contest the 49th International Six Days Trial. With four consecutive World title wins, the Czechs wanted to field their best riders, but during the Italian round of the European championship two of their top riders were injured. Petr Cemus broke his collarbone and Frantisek Mrazek fractured his arm. Cemus healed quickly and rejoined the trophy team, but Mrazek was still unfit for the trial but nevertheless, went along – his arm in plaster – as a travelling mechanic. With the Jawas' fantastic reliability record, and the active participation of the Czech riders in every possible offroad event, prior to the International, the State-sponsored Czechoslovakian team were firm favourites to collect the World Trophy for a fifth time. Great Britain too, chose Jawas to equip its trophy team. After many years of entering British machines – to comply with the tro-

phy team rules – and then a switch to foreign bikes when the rules allowed it, the British selectors finally opted for the Jawas on the grounds of reliability, as demonstrated by the victorious Czechs. Not up to the same standard as the Czech Jawas, the British machines weighed in at some 33 lbs more and developed less power than the Czech counterparts. They were more on a par with the machines used by the Russian and Polish trophy teams. The switch, made for the correct reasons, did not achieve the desired results, the ignition system failed on Mick Bowers machine, and three other riders retired due to injuries, relegating the British team to eighth position. Another switch of team machinery was

LEFT **A Zündapp as used by the West German Trophy team in the 1974 event. The entire German squad quit half way through the week as a protest against the many accidents caused by errant moped riders and car drivers who roamed the course unchecked by the Italian organizers**

RIGHT **A sea of bikes in the Parc Fermé, ISDT Isle of Man, 1975; including Austrian KTMs, Japanese Yamahas, American Rokons, Czech Jawas, West German Maicos and Swedish Monarchs to name but a few**

LEFT **The 50th ISDT in 1975 saw the Czechs field yet another formidable Trophy team, in the hope of equalling Britain's six in a row wins back in the twenties; they were mounted on Jawas, like this 350; at the time the finest long distance trials motorcycle in the world.**

made by the Italians, last year using Austrian KTMs, finally opting to use a home product. Following a good showing in the European series, Gilera machines became the standard mount for the trophy team and one vase team. Based on the motocross machine, the blood-red disc-valve two-strokes were being tipped favourites by the patriotic local population.

Before the trial began there were many problems to be sorted out. Originally competitors were promised petrol at the tourist rate, but it was later found that the full price – nearly double – had to be paid, but the support vehicles could get the tourist concession. Because the Italians had invested heavily in the trial, they wanted to recoup every lire they could, and to this end, prices rocketed. Officials demanded hotel fees for campers, beer doubled in price and restaurants increased their charges. Car parking was another major problem in the narrow streets of Camerino. Divided into two categories – all day and one hour only – the daily parks filled quickly, leaving only the one-hour zones. When the visitors realised that the fine for overstaying the hour amounted to only 66p and rose to £1.32 if not paid

within fifteen days, they stayed put. The local police stopped writing out parking tickets when they realized that the visitors had cottoned on to the system. The local moped and scooter brigade added to the general atmosphere by removing their silencers and charging around the narrow streets like wild men.

Under cloudless skies, and temperatures in the eighties, the first riders got away at 7 am on the Monday morning, led by local hero, Giacomo Perego, on his 50cc Ancillotti, to attack the first day's run of 210 miles. The going was rough and rocky, with the heat and an altitude of 5500 ft adding to the difficulties. Riders soon encountered the day's motocross special stage, which had been hastily resited high on a mountain side, following allegations that a trophy team had been spotted indulging in unofficial practice. The second day's special test also caused an upset when the organisers added two miles to its length, after more allegations of unofficial practice. This increase caused many riders to lose marks, which included both Swedish and Italian trophy members. The clerk of the course, Luigi Secchi, announced that he was adding seven minutes' allowance

to the disputed stage, which put Italy in front, but he was met with stiff opposition from the International jury. Although out-voted, he added the allowance anyway.

Thursday morning started with a sensation. The West German team arrived at the *parc fermé* wearing their best suits and bags packed ready to go home. After seeing many riders felled by errant moped riders and kamikazi car drivers who roamed the course freely, they had had enough. Two nights before they had visited one of their team members in hospital, after one of the many head-on collisions, only to find that after six hours his injuries were still untreated. Announcing his decision to pull the team out, Erich Messmer said: 'We came here to ride for sport not to get people killed'.

The six-mile special test on Thursday saw the Czech trophy team put up one of the finest performances of the week, knocking the Italians off the top spot. And the Czechs were making sure that they were going to stay there. It had been noticed that the rear wheel of Fausto Oldrati's Gilera was breaking up, and Frantisek Mrazek was dispatched to shadow the Italian to prevent replacement. Mrazek followed Oldrati all day as the wheel progressively got worse, until the Italian lost marks for lateness. Mrazek continued his job on Friday until the Gilera rider had clocked up enough points to put the Italians out of the running. His job done, Mrazek peeled off and returned home, and Oldrati turned up at the

ABOVE **Three of these West German Hercules W2000 Wankels made history in the 1975 by being the first rotary engined machines to take part in the Six Days**

RIGHT **John Penton riding one of his own 246cc KTM engined Pentons of the USA Trophy team; he won a gold medal in the Isle of Man. But his brother Tom on a similar machine was a first day retirement**

next checkpoint with a brand new rear wheel.

The final day's motocross speed test was again a foregone conclusion, with Czechoslovakia in the lead on zero marks lost, Sweden 11 marks and Italy 28 marks. The vase was also won by the Czech B team with the Italian Gilera mounted A team runners-up. The trial will always be remembered for a number of reasons, the main ones being for the blatant favouritism shown by the organizers towards the home team, the bone-crushing severity of the rocky going and the brushes or contact with the local spectator traffic. One such incident happened to Andy Robertson of the British trophy team. After a bad start and in dire need of a smaller jet for the carburettor of his Jawa, he was caught and passed by CZ importer Dave Bickers, riding a standard CZ 175 trial bike to the rescue. A jet changed hands and Andy continued onwards only to end up going through the windscreen of a baby Fiat in one of the many head-on collisions reported.

1975

The jubilee of the International Six Days Trial saw the Czechoslovakians field yet another formidable trophy team, in a hope to equal Great Britain's six in a row wins back in the 1920s. The team was this time without their leader, for Josef Fojtik had called it a day and retired. Out also, was Petr Cemus, demoted to the club team due to the effects of a serious car smash some time previously. The captain's post this time was taken by Frantisek Mrazek, promoted – no doubt – for his excellent shadowing job in Italy, whilst unfit to ride in the event.

For the fiftieth International the teams returned to British soil once again, in honour of the very first event, way back in 1913. The venue this time was a return to the Isle of Man. The trial was again centred on Douglas, with the daily motocross tests run on the hill above the town. The daily runs took in parts of the TT course, and much of the varying terrain for which the island is famous. The big talking point before the start was of the Wankel-engined Hercules team entered by the West German factory. The trio of riders, one German, one Italian and an American, were riding the rotaries for the first time in an International but their worth had been proved by many wins in European enduros during the summer. Hercules maintained the Sachs engine's capacity was only 295cc, but the FIM doubled it to make them run in the over 500 class, an argument reminiscent of the recent Norton rotary saga.

ABOVE LEFT **Another American rider, J Hollander; with the interesting 335cc Rokon two-stroke ploughing through the Manx mud...**

...close up of the Rokon; its fully automatic two-stroke engine featured lawn mower-type hand starting

ABOVE **A group of competitors during the 1975 Isle of Man ISDT. J Fenwick (272) Jawa Canada, L Müller (261) Maico West Germany, S Zlock (270) Jawa Czechoslovakia, W Massink (276) Holland; all won medals**

It had also been noticed that the four-stroke engine was beginning to lose favour amongst the competitors. As the two-stroke became more powerful, riders tended to use it because it offered a better power/weight ratio with simplicity. To prove this point only two four-stroke singles appeared on the island, a new Yamaha 500, and a Rickman Honda 250. A few twins were apparent, mainly old Triumphs. The Metropolitan Police Club fielded a trio of Cheney Triumphs, being referred to during the week as the oldest riders on the oldest bikes. Another novel machine to debut on the island was the American Rokon 335 Auto, a fully automatic two-stroke which featured lawnmower type hand starting and Electron wheels. The wheels were its downfall as the rough going soon cracked the fragile castings,

resulting in a change to spoked wheels later in the week, and disqualification.

The American teams suffered a severe setback on the first morning when the 250cc Penton of Tom Penton brewed up only five miles from the start. By the time Tom had realized the problem it was too late to do anything about it as the fibreglass tank ruptured and burned the bike out. The Czechs suffered too, when Kvetoslav Masita lost the rear chain of his 350 Jawa in the middle of the first special test, which effectively ended the Czech bid for the World Trophy. After the special test, the organizers planned a rehearsal for the following day's acceleration and noise meter test but this was a disaster. Riders arrived so quickly that they could not be processed in time and long delays ensued. After being released, riders charged off to the finish-line, and in an effort to be on time, ignored many of the basic rules of the road. Red lights were ignored, cars passed on the inside, and pavements used to avoid traffic. The final control was eventually scrubbed, but the International jury issued a warning that any rider caught breaking the highway code in future, would be disqualified. This ultimatum quietened things down and the trial proceeded from then on in an orderly fashion. The day ended with the West German Zündapp-mounted team holding a clear lead over the Jawa-mounted Polish team, but celebrations were not in order as word came through that American, Bren Moran, riding under a

BELOW **An Austrian rider pushing his Puch in to Parc Fermé at the end of a gruelling day – completed tyre change the next morning**

RIGHT **Another unusual shot from the 1975 event; Spaniard Juan Soles carrying out running repairs to his 350 Bultaco**

The former BSA World Motocross champion, Jeff Smith, rode this 250 CanAm for his Canadian employers, Bombadier, in the 1975 ISDT; he displayed all his considerable riding skills by winning a gold medal

Canadian licence, had died in hospital after a fall on a disused railway track to the west of the island.

By Thursday the Czechs had clawed their way back into second place, but then disaster struck again on the motocross test when Zloch ran out of fuel. Dogged by West German observers, he pushed the 363cc Jawa all the way back through Douglas to the *parc fermé*. His superhuman effort kept him in the trial but forfeited his gold medal, and put the team down to third position below West Germany and Italy.

The World Championship placings stayed unaltered through to the end. The final speed test was again a mere formality, but the West Germans again paced the Italians man for man to avoid any mishaps. Even though the riders did not really need to race round the Parkfield circuit, they certainly pushed it to the limit. As the pack, sliding on knobblies, used all the road and most of the pavement to negotiate the first corner, the policeman on duty was heard to say, 'These riders can teach the TT riders a thing or two about cornering technique, I've never seen anything so hairy!'. A most spectacular performance was put up by Zdenek Cespiva, sliding his 362 Jawa round Governor's bridge on full throttle until it contacted the kerb, sending him off in the right direction. In the end, it was the West Germans who became the new World Champions with Italy gaining the vase. The Zündapp's victory in the World series was a fitting epitaph for the great sportsman and driving force behind the Zündapp factory, for when Eitel Frie-

drich Mann died his wife promised to pursue the company's interest in enduros. This she did, devoting much personal time to achieve the richly deserved result gained in the Isle of Man.

1976

After their win in the Isle of Man, the West Germans were eager to capitalize on their good fortune and sent a first-class team – again all Zündapp-mounted – to contest the 51st International Six Days Trial in Austria. After an interval of 16 years, the Austrians again took up the challenge of organizing the world's toughest offroad event. Mindful of the slating received by the organizing committee in 1960, they put on a superb event, centred on Zeltweg with its purpose-built Österreichring Auto-

A boulder-strewn gulley
during the 1975 Six
Days. Riders are: Dave
Rayner (242) GB-MZ,
Dick Mann (243) USA-
Ossa, Willie Budden
(238) GB-Jawa and
W Remner West
Germany – KTM

Unusual shot of riders being escorted around the Signpost Corner – Bedstead section prior to the start of the speed tests on the final day of the 1971 event

drome. Within the confines of the ring riders battled it out twice a day on a specially laid out motocross circuit, to earn their classification points. With so much racing during the week, many riders considered the event to be a motocross rather than a trial.

Run in fine weather, and over relatively easy terrain, most riders had a trouble free ride, but some carburation problems did occur due to the thinnesss of the air in some of the high passes. Not wishing to incur any problems the Austrians had purposely opted for the easy approach, and this could be gauged by the total of medals at the finish. Of the 322 starters, 190 riders received golds, and during the week there were only 39 retirements. One early retirement, which spelled disaster for the all KTM-mounted Italian trophy team, was Elia Andrioletti, when the gearbox of his 175 gave out. His retirement was quickly followed by that of Emilio Capelli, due again to gearbox trouble. Two men short, the Italian slipped to the bottom of the trophy leaderboard, unable to recover. That is where they stayed finishing the week in fifteenth place.

For the first three days the Czechs were out in front, leading the West Germans by the merest margin, but this situation was reversed when Kvetoslav Masita took

a tumble on the motocross circuit and lost points. As the West Germans had little opposition in the smaller capacity classes, they increased their lead on classification points, and went on to take the trophy for the second time. Meanwhile, the Czechs were having a struggle to stay in second position. Up against Gritti the Italian 250 KTM rider, and West German vase rider, Busse on his 350 KTM, the Czechs fought every inch of the way to gain points. After their many wins in the 1960s, the East Germans were once again in the running on their MZs. Following the years of inactivity and a change in rider line-up they were once again becoming competitive, and quietly crept into third place in the trophy competition. Great Britain, too, was staging a comeback, edging up through the field to finish in a creditable fourth place. Star of the British team was Mick Bowers, riding a 252 Bultaco. He led the 350 class for the first five days, but his luck ran out on the final motocross test when the Bultaco gassed up on the start-line.

A tragedy overshadowed the proceedings on the fifth day, when American Ossa rider, David Julse, hit an old lady. Hulse collapsed and withdrew when he learned that she had subsequently died from her injuries. The trial, although easy by previous standards, did result in a few broken bones for riders. Josef Chovancik, the Czech factory team rider, fell and broke his collarbone. Austrian, Reinhard Knoll, broke several bones in his left hand when he crashed, but after having them wired up he continued. His ensuing ride earned him the affection of the home spectators, for he completed the trial with his injured arm literally waving in the breeze. For this feat he received a special award, as did Canadian rider, Ted Dirstein, who finished the trial on his seriously crash damaged and deformed Yamaha.

With the trophy out of their grasp, the Czechs concentrated their efforts on the vase competition. Leading the field up to the final speed test, the Czechs nearly lost it, when Kanler got a puncture and Toman was knocked from his 500 Jawa. Kanler rode the flat tyre to the finish-line within his time limit, and Toman, after straightening his bent handlebars, reduced his deficit to finish on time. These efforts gave Czechoslovakia the Silver Vase for the fifteenth time.

So the 51st International came to an end, the easiest one for years, different in that it incorporated more tarmac road work and motocross riding than ever before. The leisurely event was best summed up by Jeff Smith, after winning a gold medal on his 250 Can-Am, when he said, 'The highlight of my week was when I got a bit carried away and fell off on a dry road. I must be getting older as I only fell off twice this year.'

J Wolforinher (Zündapp) part of the team which took the Trophy back to West Germany in 1975

1977

In contrast to the leisurely Austrian event, the 1977 International Six Days Trial was the most punishing event for years, with only 96 of the 313 starters actually finishing the course. Centred this time on Povazska Bystrica, in the Strazov Highlands region of central Czechoslovakia, the course ran through mainly forested and hilly countryside. The event was executed with typical Czech efficiency, which most riders liked, even though the going was hard. The Czechs again fielded another formidable trophy team, but this time without Zdenek Cespiva, who had retired. His place was taken by Otakar Toman, promoted from the 1976 vase team, but this time riding a 511cc Jawa. Lined up against them were the West Germans, Italians and re-emerging East Germans, all capable of winning the coveted trophy. In all, 14 countries were represented in the trophy contest, with 15 countries competing for the Silver Vase.

From the beginning it was again the Czechs who took the lead, being pushed hard by the other favourites in the running. The searing heat and rock hard tracks took their toll of both riders and machines, knocking out Mick Bowers of the British trophy squad after only 75 miles, when his Bultaco stopped with a dead engine. Ted Thompson of the same team also suffered with four separate engine seizures on his Suzuki PE250, wasting precious minutes to let it cool down. By the end of day 2 the hard going had put the retirements up to 40.

1975 Isle of Man Six Days' speed test, N Casas (65) Bultaco-Spain, E Jenson (246) Penton-USA and B Gustausson KTM-Sweden. Many observers considered riding standards around the tarmac sections outshone the TT road racers!

ABOVE After their win in the Isle of Man, the West Germans were eager to repeat the success and sent a first class team – again all Zündapp mounted – to contest the 51st ISDT in Austria; and they responded by taking the Trophy for the second year running. A 1976-model 125cc Zündapp is shown

RIGHT The 1977 Six Days – held in Czechoslovakia – was one of the most punishing for years. Centred on Povazska Bystrica, in the Strazov Highlands, the course ran through mainly forested and hilly countryside between 5/10 September

On day 3 the volatile Italians dropped a bombshell when the entire trophy team refused to start, in retaliation for the exclusion of Gian Luigi Petrogalli for outside assistance. On the first day, Petrogalli was seen by a Czech marshall to accept a length of pipe from his support crew, to straighten a bent chain adjuster. This incident was duly reportd to the organizers, and when the FIM jury met it was voted 12 to 4 in favour of exclusion. The Italian trophy team mounted solely on KTMs, were swiftly followed by the three-man KTM factory team who also withdrew in protest. The SWM mounted vase team did not join in the protest but stayed on in the hope of salvaging some Italian pride. After the trial, the Italian Motor Cycle Federation re-opened the case, and after due deliberation, meted out severe puishment to the riders and team managers for the unauthorized withdrawal.

West Germany was pushing the Czechs hard, but on day four this ceased when Paul Rottler retired with conrod failure, allowing the East Germans into second place.

Overnight torrential rain and continuing storms soon turned the dry dusty tracks into mud baths, which brought disaster to the already hard pushed riders on the fifth day. One section was so bad that it drove 132 cold and exhausted riders to defeat, including all six members of the French trophy team who had been previously intact. One of the defeated riders who went out that day was Dave Bickers, competing in his first International.

He actually survived to the finish-line but was excluded for being overtime. On returning to his quarters he said, 'I lost my soul out there today.' It was that bad.

In the vase contest the East Germans had overhauled the Italians to snatch the lead after the disastrous fifth day, putting them marginally in front of the Czech team. But on the final day, this again changed. The course was beginning to dry out, but in places it was still axle deep in mud, which favoured the larger and more powerful Jawas of the Czechoslovakians. The 75 and 100cc Simpsons of the East Germans bogged down all too frequently, and at the finish-line, after the short final stage, all four East Germans had gone over time. The Czechs again became World Champions, taking the Trophy for the thirteenth time since 1947. They also took the Silver Vase for the sixteenth time. The

Czechs did not win all the prizes for the invididual class wins in the smaller capacity categories were shared by Italy and West Germany.

Jeff Smith was again competing on a Can–Am 175 as a member of the Canadian vase team. On receiving his well earned gold medal, he recalled the catastrophic fifth day saying, 'It was the toughest single day I have ever ridden!' . . . a sentiment shared by those who fell by the wayside.

1978

Sweden hosted the 1978 International Six Days Trial, the event being centred on High Chaparral, a Wild West style theme park in Smaland, part of the southern region of the country, and the scene of a fire which devasted the Motor Museum in 1991. As Smaland is a flat region, the course was devoid of any high altitude work, being run in mainly forested areas, but the wet weather which prevailed made sure that the trial would not be an easy one. Nineteen nations were represented by 328 riders, this time attracting African and Australian competitors. Again, the vast majority of riders were amateurs who were there to ride just for the love of it, but they were up against the highly organized Czech, German and Italian professionals who would fight it out for the trophy.

ABOVE **In 1978 Czechoslovakia won the Trophy for 14th time since 1947; again their Jawa two-strokes played a big part in this success**

ABOVE RIGHT **During the late 1970s many teams and individual riders chose the Austrian KTM. This 1978 400 Enduro cost £1335 in the UK at the time**

RIGHT **Besides MZ, East Germany also had Simson; built in 75 and 100cc engine sizes, they were great bikes – except in heavy going where their small capacity and narrow powerband was at a disadvantage. A 1978 model is illustrated**

The trophy hopes of the well-motivated host nation were dashed on the first day when the automatic gearbox of Hans Hansson's 390 Husqvarna gave up. Austrian fortunes slumped too, as 175 Puch rider, Joseph Zotzek, also went out. The Americans were the surprise occupants of fourth place, but this position was in serious jeopardy when Rod Bush was seen to ride his KTM under the closed barrier of a railway crossing in front of the oncoming train. The local police wanted to press charges against Bush – which would have meant automatic exclusion – but instead, a deal was worked out by the American jury member, Kathy Wanta. The

Superbike builders Laverda were another marque which built two-stroke enduro bikes during the late 1970s. Engines came via a link with the Swedish Husqvarna concern and were of either 125 or 250cc, the latter is shown

rider signed a form of confession of guilt, paid a 300 Kronor fine, and nothing more was said.

West Germany led after the first day, but this lead was short-lived when Ebhardt Weber broke the chain of his 125 Zündapp on the Kushult motocross test. This misfortune put the Italians at the top of the leaderboard, but this again, was short-lived, as Pietro Gagni retired with ignition problems on his 175 SWM. Czecho-slovakia once again jumped into the lead, a position they held on to until the end. By day 4 the course was knee deep in mud, and the rain kept falling putting a severe strain on the riders and machines. In an effort to keep bikes going, all sorts of tricks were tried, some were spotted but many went unseen. Australian rider, Winston Stokes, got caught breaking the cylinder-head seal on his 250 SWM, in order to change the piston ring. Welshman, Ken Williams, was seen to drive his Bultaco into the team's tent for some unauthorized replace-ment. Ken insisted he had a sudden rush of gastric 'flu

and the jury believed him. They also believed the Czechs' explanation for the sudden appearance of an identical Jawa, bearing the same running number as Otokar Toman. The Czechs said it had been prepared for Toman prior to the trial, but had been rejected by him and was now being ridden by a spectator, a Czecho-slovakian, in works Jawa overalls, no doubt.

Default by a rival team is the best way of making pro-gress in the ISDT. France had been in third position behind Czechoslovakia and East Germany, but at the start up on the fifth morning, Giles Francru failed to start his Husqvarna in the one-minute period allowed, thus letting Great Britain into third place. By the last day the course was so bad in places that the marshalls were laying wooden boards over some of the deeper mud holes, said to be six feet deep in places. It was these sorts of conditions that the remaining 273 riders found themselves in when they tackled the 73-mile final leg to the Anderstorp circuit and back to the High Chaparral, but conditions were even worse on the motocross course laid out near the western town.

The final motocross speed test, or slapstick farce in a porridge pot – as Dave Wilcock of *Motor Cycle* reported it – ended the trial in utter confusion. The 50, 75 and 100cc classes raced over the circuit first and just about managed, but by the time the up to 350cc classes started, the track had deteriorated to such a degree that only half the required number of laps could be completed in the time limit. The above 350cc stint came to an abrupt end before half a lap was completed, as many riders bogged down in the churning mud. It was at this point, that West German vase rider, Paul Rottler, thinking his gold medal was lost, leapt from his bike and laid down in the mud to stop the passage of other riders. The race was well and truly over, and bedraggled riders and spectators began to drift away after extracting the remaining bikes from the glutinous mud, a task which took over an hour to complete.

The jury, quite rightly, scrapped the final speed test which left the Czechs once again the World Champions with the Italians taking the vase. The British trophy team collected six gold medals – the best performance for years – and third place behind the East German MZ-mounted team. John Knight, the British trophy rider, nearly did not get his gold medal for a hairline crack appeared in one of his KTM 350 front fork legs which marginally slowed him down to silver standard for a short time. Reg May, the British bike doctor, effected a cure which enabled John to speed up to gold standard, which he achieved by .84 seconds at the end of the week.

Simson came out with new Six Day mounts in 1979; two are seen here being tested prior to the ISDT, which that year was held in Sweden

1979

Once more the International returned to West Germany after an absence of ten years, but this time not to Garmisch. The new location was Neukirchen in the district of Siegen, the headquarters and *parc fermé* being sited in the army camp at Lager Stegkopf. The surrounding countryside, although not mountainous, was hilly and mainly forested with many marshy patches. As the sport of enduro riding was becoming more popular – the event at this stage still being refered to as a Trial – the entry list for the International grew, this time attracting 399 riders. The continuing success of the Austrian KTM company on one- and two-day events, also reflected in the entry lists for the International in that 99 riders opted to use that company's products. The Italian SWM factory received their share of publicity as 54 entrants had chosen these machines, again based on proven ability and past results. The largest entry from any country was as expected, the West Germans, with 80 riders taking part.

The Czechoslovakians, eager to capitalize on the last two trophy wins, suffered a serious setback when both Jiri Posik and Jiri Strodulka sustained severe injuries in the pre-trial recce trips. Posik recovered enough to join his team's support crew. Veteran, Josef Cisar, moved up to the trophy team and was bidding for a tenth gold medal in this his tenth ISDT.

As expected, it was the West German team – Zündapp- and Maico-mounted – which topped the leaderboard for the first two days followed by Italy, East Germany and Czechoslovakia. But this lead was short-

lived when the 750 class Maico of Heino Busse failed to start on the third morning, losing his team valuable points. The Italians, now out in front, increased their lead over the Germans when Hau Grisse and Kreutz all sustained falls in the motocross tests, losing valuable seconds and points.

Great Britain, captained by Dave Jeremiah, were having more than their fair share of troubles. John Knight had carburettor problems, Arthur Browning burnt out his clutch, and Mick Bowers broke his ankle. John went on to get a gold, and Mick, heavily strapped up, carried on to a silver, while Arthur nursed his ailing KTM to a bronze.

The Italian trophy team, all professional riders – comprised of five policemen and a mechanic, thought that they had blown their chances of the World Championship when Gualdi permitted a support crew member to re-inflate his rear tyre after mending a puncture

West Germany's BMW made a surprise return to the Six Days' in 1979 with 55bhp GS80 machines. These were a mixture of both old and new technology; but as before the famous marque injected great spectator interest in the event

on the third day. The trial manager disqualified Gualdi for accepting outside help but on reading into the re-written rules, changed at the FIM conference in Poland earlier in the year, he was reinstated. The small print catered for the possibility of inner tubes being inflated by another person, even outside the enclosed space of a time-check area. Czechoslovakia dropped to fourth place when Chovancik lost time mending a puncture, but soon jumped back to third when East German MZ rider, Vwe Kothe, crashed and lost seven minutes at a time-check.

The World Trophy was taken by the jubilant Italians, they had been in the running for years but had never quite made it since their last win on home ground at Merano in 1931. Hopes of a double for them faded on the first day when vase rider, Gagni, dropped 48 minutes on his Fantic 50 with engine trouble. West Germany, as in the World Trophy, also led the vase conflict but lost it on the fourth day when Rottler lost time over a puncture and Strossenreuther had ignition failure, letting the East Germans in to the lead. During the fifth day, the Czechs crept ahead only to lose the lead at the motocross test when four riders fell off. At the final motocross speed test, three East German riders achieved their set times but the fourth rider, Jochen

Winner of the over-750cc class at the 1979 ISDT, BMW mounted Fritz Witzel. He brought back memories of years gone by when the big four-strokes had reigned supreme in the world's toughest motorcycle competition

Schatzler on his 350 MZ, was up against Jaroslav Kmostak on his 350 Jawa. Kmostak beat Schatzler by 85 seconds and this was all that was needed to tip the balance in favour of the Czechs who returned home with the vase for the seventeenth time.

Thus another decade came to a close, the outright winners of the World Trophy being Czechoslovakia who took the trophy home on seven occasions to better their winning streak in the 1950s. The 1970s must also be remembered for the two excellent wins by the West Germans and the final triumph of the Italians who had nearly won on so many occasions. When one considers the top four professional countries, Czechoslovakia, Italy, East and West Germany, it was gratifying to see that Great Britain, although now of enthusiastic amateur status, still had enough fight to split the big four. With the decline of media interest, but with the riders being just as enthusiastic as ever, it is fascinating to review in the final chapter the developments of the International Six Days Trial over the next decade and beyond.

CHAPTER EIGHT

ISDE

The last of the International Six Days Trials was held at Brioude in central France in 1980. Of course the event continued as the biggest happening in the FIM calendar, but in 1981 it became the International Six Days *Enduro*. Many enthusiasts are likely to believe that this change of name made no significant difference to the nature of the six days. It was, however, an official recognition that its nature had changed quite dramatically and it was no longer appropriate to call it a reliability trial. Although it still retained the fundamental necessity for riders to maintain time schedules over difficult terrain and for an extended period of time, much had changed. It is not therefore the intention in the chapter to review the events of the 1980s and early 1990s in detail, but instead to sample them and to reflect on the nature of the ISDE contrasted with its predecessor.

There have been a number of evolving and fundamental changes and the authors do not feel that most of them have been for the better. The ISDE is no longer the original trial of the reliability of standard production machinery which made its predecessor so interesting for all motorcycle enthusiasts, especially in the first 45 years. A glance at the British motorcycle press reports on the 1991 event shows quite clearly that the specialist nature of the new Six Days no longer appeals to many motorcyclists. It is of marginal interest to the majority of everyday riders, of little interest to road-racing enthusiasts and of limited appeal to the one-day trials and motocross supporters. Small wonder then that in Great Britain it is of no interest at all to the media in general. In 1983, when the event was once more held, after so many years, in Wales, the lack of press response was amazing. After all, in the rest of Europe public support and media interest are still considerable. In the early days the streets of Llandrindod Wells were lined with cheering crowds during the ISDT and in continental Europe everything still stops in the villages where the competitors pass. Perhaps, for the British at any rate, the problem is that the motorcycle has not been a commonly used method of everyday transport for many years, and the man in the street cannot relate to competitive motorcycling, or at least not to the esoteric competiton which the ISDE has become. Imagine the problems involved in explaining the calculation of results, both individual and team, to an uninitiated bystander!

The ISDE is, and has been for more than a decade, the province of highly specialized machinery only of use in this type of event. It is true that the European enduro championship and the growth of the specialist sport of the enduro rider in the United Kingdom have provided a firm basis for the ISDE, but it remains of limited appeal. Moreover, as in any sport, particularly motor sport, the development of sophisticated single-purpose machinery has caused a generation of clerks of the course to produce more and more difficult routes to cater for the new bikes. In the end the enduro machines became fast, converted motocross machines which were essential to cope with the speed required on the special tests, and later an even more sophisticated breed of motocross 'plus' machinery.

We have come a very long way since the multi-purpose machines of the 1950s. At that time Great Britain was sometimes criticized for entering overweight machines which were really only slightly modified roadsters. Well, that was what the ISDT was all about and it was this 'man on the bike in the street' relationship which made it so popular and successful. The development of single-purpose machines in Europe, in particular in Czechoslovakia and Germany, began the process of change which has now overwhelmed even the famous ISDE Jawas with the motocross technology of Europe and Japan. The event has changed to match the capability of machines and this seems to be a pity. Perhaps it might have retained both its character and its widespread interest if it had been confined to truly multi-purpose machinery rather than succumbing to technology. Unfortunately, as in most branches of motor sport, the age of the computer has produced the computer machine syndrome. In general terms computers will arrive at very similar conclusions when programmed to deal with a specific problem. In this case, what is the best formula for a motorcycle to win its class in the ISDE? The result is a succession of machines which are so similar that the result is boring. What a pity it is that the days of the hand-painted Jawas, the Matchless and Ariel twins, the Gold Star BSAs, the Adlers, Gileras and Triumphs, are over. Surely it was the variety, wealth of ingenuity and, above all, the multitude of different approaches to the problem, which made the Six Days so fascinating. (As you can see, former British trophy teamster and latter-day manager Ken Heanes voices this opinion in no uncertain terms in the foreword.)

The last of the ISDTs was held at Brioude in Central France in 1980. Here Denys Lacroix (KTM) of the host nation leads other competitors in hilly terrain

Another important factor which has shaped the development of machinery and the nature of the event in recent years has been the growth of the 'Green' movement and widespread ecological awareness. Even if the minor road system of Europe had retained its 1950s' character which shaped the nature of the ISDT, access to the trails and tracks in the wild and remote areas would inevitably have been limited. The pressure on the countryside comes from an increasingly large sector of society and the ramblers, climbers, canoeists, fishermen, four-wheel-drive enthusiasts and the rally men and women are all involved in this complex situation. In short, an event today, held anywhere in Europe, must be limited to areas and routes which are not ecologically sensitive. There are very few of these!

This situation applies equally to Eastern Europe today and the route of the 1991 event held in Czechoslovakia was a pale shadow of its former self since it could not include the tough tracks which were so much a part of the old style Czech ISDTs. This severe limitation on routes open to the clerks of the courses has further emphasized the earlier tendency to rely more and more on short speed tests, usually of the motocross multi-lap type, to decide the results. In its turn, the machinery has become even more specialized to cope with this.

Unhappily, while it has changed in many other respects, the ISDE is still about breaking the rules and cheating without being caught! Such general press comment as has been aroused has usually been concerned with this aspect. Surely it is time to scrap the unenforceable rules and dispense with marked parts and the 'no external assistance' rule altogether. The ISDT was always a professional event because of the involvement of so many manufacturers, but this is now enhanced by the importance of the individual rider's contracts and the necessity to win in order to justify the manufacturer's expenditure. It seems to the authors that although the ISDE remains a team competition, the actual importance of the team, usually comprising the

David Smith (KTM)
creates his own
watersplash in the
last ISDT

products of a number of different manufacturers, is far less significant than a class win by an individual with the resulting advertising spin-off. After all, since the bikes involved are usually so similar in specification, the importance of a win to successful sales is even greater.

It may well seem that these comments are unduly critical and nostalgic, but it does appear that the ISDE is not the event that the ISDT was in many respects. However, this does not detract from the significance, importance and interest of the ISDE in the 1990s. It implies no criticism of the riders, manufacturers or organizers, all of whom have performed valiantly and expended blood, sweat and tears, not to mention very large sums of money, on the event. Perhaps it should simply be seen as different, an event derived from the ISDT and retaining as many of its features as modern times will allow. Nevertheless, it is not the same. At long last the slow and probably inevitable process of change was virtually complete by the beginning of the 1980s and the FIM finally recognized this with the change of title. It really only remained for the organizers to recognize the inevitable in 1985 and to scrap the vase competition in favour of the Junior Trophy for national teams of riders under the age of 23. So, by 1985 the ISDE, with its World Trophy and Junior Trophy, had completely supplanted the original event. Probably the ISDE is neither better nor worse than its predecessor, it

ABOVE **British rider Arthur Browning (SWM) on part of the 1980 course which included this urban setting**

RIGHT **Italian Trophy teamster Gualtiero Brissoni (SWM) during the motocross type special test in the 1980 event**

is simply different. It is not the purpose of this book to detail the course of the ISDE, that must wait for a separate volume. What follows are some scenes from the events of the 1980s as an appetizer for the future.

In September 1980 the last ISDT was held in the French Massif Central mountains. Based on the small hill town of Brioude it was very tough and reminiscent of many of the great events of preceding years. With long days over wet and rocky tracks against tight time schedules there was little time for riders to relax, and the result was settled where it should be – out on the course – rather than on final speed tests. Indeed, on the third day the conditions and the times required meant that only eight riders, all of them from either Italy or Czechoslovakia, managed to beat the clock at one check. That Wednesday is remembered as a 'flying day' when riders had no time to spare at all and had to simply pass through the checkpoints without pause. Occasionally the event proved to be too difficult. On the second day a rocky climb some 10 miles from Brioude defeated most

Jawa publicity material proclaiming the new 'Six Day Enduro', 1981

of the entry, and baulking was so bad that riders were hauled up the hill with ropes. Subsequently the marks lost as a result of this were cancelled by the jury. This last event was not without the usual controversy and near disaster. The weekend preceding the start was marked by thunderstorms and torrential rain which washed away a dam and threatened the *parc fermé* with flooding. The organizers were only given authority to go ahead at the last moment.

On the first day the jury was faced with the fact that Taiocchi, of the Italian trophy team, had been docked 60 marks for late arrival at a check. He had stopped to change a spark plug and claimed that the official clock was at fault. The jury upheld the protest but it was a dicey moment for Italy, who went on to win the trophy. Amazingly, despite their success in the major competition, the Italians lost their entire vase team because of various mishaps, and the West Germans won this contest. Another milestone in this event was the fact that the vase-winning German team included Witthoft on a BMW! So much for the argument about large and heavy machines based on road bikes! The Czechs managed second place in the trophy and third in the vase.

For Great Britain the experience at Brioude marks pretty well the nadir of ISDT experience. In the trophy Britain finished ninth out of 16 teams and in the vase thirteenth out of 15. One of the significant features of this event, as with others past and present, was the unofficial contest between the organizers attempting to enforce the regulations and the riders attempting to evade them. On some parts of the course officials lay in wait with buckets of water and brushes to wash machine parts and examine paint and seals. However, they were usually defeated by the efforts of outriders on the course riding identical machines to those of the riders they were supporting!

This account of the ISDT should really end here but life goes on! The first of the ISDEs, held on the Italian island of Elba in October 1981, was a very interesting example of the new look and philosophy which had developed over the years, and makes a fascinating contrast with the earlier ISDTs. The island has a total area of only 140 square miles, rather less than the Isle of Wight. There are only 169 miles or roads, of which only 70 have a tarmac surface. In this respect, at least, the event could have had a 1950s or 1960s format of tight times over dusty tracks, but of course there was only room for one, or perhaps two, days of the old style event. Moreover, the motocross type of machinery and the special expertise of the Italians in this branch of the sport, determined that the first ISDE would be decided on the results of daily motocross special tests. As a variation on these, each day would also feature an acceleration test. Of all the fruitless and unnecessary tests which could be devised, apart from spectator appeal, the spectacle of motocross machines drag racing on tarmac must have been the most pointless.

Nevertheless, on the fifth day Ian Thompson and Geraint Jones, of the British trophy team, put up the best times on acceleration, and the sight of 'Tonka' Thompson tearing lumps from the rear tyre of his big Maico as he tore down the strip had to be seen to be believed! Unhappily, having lost Arthur Browning from the trophy team on the second day with ignition trouble on his SWM, and Alan Brick on day 5, the team eventually finished last of the 13 national groups, with the vase team doing rather better with sixth out of 18. It must be remembered, however, that in this event the British mounted their major effort in the vase competition rather than the trophy.

In effect, the first ISDE was a glorified twice-daily motocross test with transit mileages in between, at least that was how it seemed to all of the top riders. Geraint Jones, who was almost unbeatable at that time in British national events, rode a 490cc Maico and with a gold medal under his belt, could only finish in eighteenth place in his class on the motocross times. His was the best British performance in the event.

Barring mechanical disaster the Italians were bound to win the trophy, and they did so. To emphasize this rather crazy situation, on the fifth day Eddy Orioli of the Italian team, on his 80cc AIM, was so quick on the 4½-mile motocross test that his time would have put him in fourth place in the 250–500cc class! Talent for motocross tests of this kind needs to be seen in the context of this part of the scoring system. The fastest rider in each capacity class sets the standard time and receives a zero score. All other riders in that class lose the difference between their times and the winner, converted into penalty points.

It need hardly be said that many competitors whose performance was otherwise quite excellent, finished well down the results list. At the time the Czechs pointed out that originally the ISDT was designed to demonstrate that motorcycles could equal cars at transport. After World War II the emphasis changed to prove that bikes could go where cars could not, and really tough terrain was used to prove this. For them the events held in the 1960s were the perfect tests of motorcycle quality and rider skill. Speed tests were only used to sort out ties. They were moved to protest that this event depended entirely on speed tests ridden on thinly disguised motocross machines which were barely road legal. Moreover, as the Czechs were happy to point out, only two nations, their own and East Germany, were equipped with 'domestic' machinery. No doubt these comments took account of the fact that the host nation won everything, i.e. World Trophy, Vase, Club team and Manufacturer's awards! The Czech attitude is best summed up by a comment published in a report in 1982: 'The orthodox International Six Days Trial was essentially altered in 1960 when special tests were introduced in Austria. Many organisers in the following years made things easy for themselves by letting riders quietly proceed from time check to time check and leaving everything to be decided by the special tests which, in the end, turned into motocross ... and so the event lost its original object – machine reliability and riding skill between time checks.'

Right, so having got those thoughts out of the way, it must surely have been an easy event for, after all, a very large proportion of the entry lost no time between checkpoints, but the six days has never been easy for all the entrants. It has only been relatively easy for the top competitors. In this event the author was present with the British Army team who were mounted predominantly on Cagivas. The team comprised Gwyn Barraclough (250 Cagiva), Ron Kirkland (125 Cagiva), Paddy Porter (400 Husqvarna), with Keith Hall entered at the last moment on another 250 Cagiva. The British Army has entered teams in the ISDT and ISDE for very many years. It has always been a difficult event for the riders, who have a strictly amateur status and prepare for the six days largely in their spare time. Nevertheless, they have always guaranteed to give their all to finish and their efforts epitomize those of the many riders and clubs, outside the national teams, who have always supported the event.

So, in this 'easy' first ISDE Gwyn Barraclough and Ron Kirkland won silver medals and their two compatriots bronze. More notable was the fact that Gwyn and Ron lost no marks on the road between time-checks. Under the ISDT system of earlier years this would have been gold medal standard but 'progress' had dictated that the level of ISDE medal awarded

British Army team rider Keith Hall in Elba during the 1981 ISDE. Machine is a Cagiva RX250 belonging to the British importers, the Mick Walker Group

In 1982 the Czech Jawa factory came out with this brand new 6-speed 125 two-stroke. But it couldn't regain the glory of earlier days

would be dependent on performance of the fastest rider in a class and the percentage difference between that individual and the other finishers. It hardly seems fair. Paddy Porter's Husqvarna spent the fifth day hobbling from check to check with an ever-decreasing number of spokes in the rear wheel! He originally elected to push across the line on the final speed test on the last day, but of course in the end finished in fine style despite the virtual collapse of that component! So this event, as with them all, was only 'easy' for some competitors and it seems only right to applaud the efforts of all medal winners, irrespective of their speed in the special tests.

It was hardly surprising that two years with such results resulted in much British heart searching about whether the effort involved was worthwhile. In the year of writing, 1991, this is still pertinent since Great Britain has still not succeeded in winning either of the trophies since 1953. If it is fair to compare the ISDE with the ISDT it seems almost insulting that the British trophy team should have won the Watling Trophy twice in recent years, for this award goes to the team which has

made the best effort or the greatest improvement, without actually winning anything else. Many people felt that the annual British effort could hardly be justified on grounds of national prestige or trade advantage although, providing the wrangling over breaches of the rules remains within limits, it must be of some benefit in terms of international friendship. The author believes, however, that for all nations the effort was, and is, entirely justified in both the ISDT and the ISDE by the individual rider's performances. Perhaps it is too easy to forget the achievement of all the medal winners over the years and, indeed, of those who have made gallant but unsuccessful attempts.

Other events of the 1980s are remembered for a variety of reasons: 1982 in Czechoslovakia because of the unpleasant and uncompromising attitude of the police. By the end of this event virtually every visitor seemed to have been fined for infringing local laws and, on the last night, the Swedish jury member had to be rescued from the police station where he was 'helping with enquiries' into an alleged offence by one of the Swedish riders! What a contrast this was with the 1991 event, also based on Povazska Bystrica in Czechoslovakia where the system has been transformed by political changes in Eastern Europe. Unfortunately, however, the six days Jawa

no longer reigns supreme. Noteworthy also was the fact that 'Green' pressure in that country restricted the nature of the course in 1991 to such an extent that the majority of difficult tracks and paths could not be used.

1982 was also the year in which clashes over clothing contracts forced Geraint Jones and Ian Thompson to withdraw from the British trophy team before the event. This was not the first time that contractual obligations had caused problems, nor would it be the last. Oh for the days when the black Barbour suit was the only suitable clothing and problems of professionalism were rare! Needless to say the British result was not very good. With only 11 finishers from 25 starters and not a single gold medal the teams finished thirteenth out of 15 trophy teams and eleventh out of 15 in the vase. 1982 demonstrated an attempt by Czechoslovakia to return to the original system of settling the event between time-checks on a tough course. This certainly worked for the Czechs who won the trophy for the fifteenth time. The vase also went to a nation famous for its tough, home-grown ISDT specials – East Germany with its MZs.

The return of the 'son of six days' to Wales in 1983 should have been a momentous occasion for the British at least. Unfortunately it has gone down in the unofficial records as the 'International Six Days Fiddle'. This unhappy comment, based on the most prominent problems, has obscured a rather good event in forest and moorland which produced only 19 gold medals from the entire entry. The British lost Andy Roberton from the trophy team with an injured shoulder and Aled Williams from the Vase team when he was excluded for changing machines. Britain finished fifth in both competitions. Nevertheless, this was a great improvement on previous years, but then it should have been so in an event on home territory in familiar weather conditions. More important nationally than the result was the press coverage during the week. Unhappily the results service was slow to publish the daily figures and, in consequence, British press reports were pathetically few for an international event of this size and length held on British soil, and were mainly limited to scandal. It took little effort to persuade the journalists that, in the absence of a daily progress report, there were rather more interesting aspects to publicize. Hence the general atmosphere was summed up by the headline, 'How to win in Wales – don't get caught', and the comment: 'The ISDE is associated so closely with cheating that everyone expects nothing but cheating'.

It seems highly probable that all of the competing

Like Jawa, Gilera had a new 125 enduro bike in the early 1980s. But unlike the Czech bike the Italian featured a watercooled engine. The daily motocross special tests of the ISDE favoured this type of bike, which after all was more 'motocross' than 'trials'

teams bent the rules and many broke them severely. The most popular offence was changing machines and this was generally precise and well planned. There were even suggestions that riders may have been substituted! If this seems bizarre it is certainly not confined to the ISDE. In a recent Brussels marathon it appears that the winning athlete began the event clean shaven and completed it with a full moustache! In this ISDE course cutting was also popular. In the end this conduct proved disastrous for the West German teams whose supporters opened up a route to by-pass a bog in the Tarenig forest on the Thursday. Nine of their riders accepted this offer and the result was the disqualification of two trophy and three vase team members. Even in this situation, however, the jury could only arrive at a decision by a 12 to 4 majority verdict.

This débâcle left the Swedish teams in control of the event. Hitherto noted for their sportsmanship they seemed determined to win at all costs and their progress was accompanied by hordes of supporters actively assisting their own riders and hindering the opposition. The culmination of this attitude was seen during the final speed test. Arthur Browning, of the British trophy

East German superstar Harold Sturn (MZ). Not content with Six Days success he was also a three-time winner of the European Enduro Championship

team, could have won the big four-stroke class as well as a gold medal. However, it was alleged that he was hampered in every way by Swedish supporters during the test and finally, having fallen, was pelted with clods of earth. In this way he lost the class win although he retained the gold medal.

Rightly or wrongly, all that was good about 1983 has been submerged by the memory of cheating, both successful and unsuccessful. As with laws, if rules are unenforceable they should be scrapped. If the ISDE is no longer a test of machine reliability, this should be recognized. It is a very unhappy situation which still exists today. In one report on the 1991 event and commenting on an Italian trophy team member who had just damaged his machine in an accident on the fifth day, the writer says: 'His outrider wanted to change bikes on the spot but there were too many people on the scene within seconds, so they had to limp into the next check where they swapped exhausts and handlebars'.

The events in France and Czechoslovakia in the early part of the decade contrast quite clearly with those in Elba for they represented, at least in part, an attempt to return to the formula of the tough event which tested machines and rider skill over long distances. The Welsh-based ISDE, hindered as it was by a growing lack of accessible routes, was not especially difficult since it was run largely on open moorland and forest fire

Besides MZ, the other East German ISDE medal winner was Simson...

...Rolf Hübler in action during 1984 on his 125 Simson

breaks. As the decade progressed, however, the distinction between the older style of event and the 'special test' variety became very obvious.

The 1984 event, based at Assen in Holland, had little choice of routes other than wet and sandy tracks, often deeply rutted, with occasional bogs. The area used was of course very flat. Although the rate of machine attrition was high, more significant was the feeling summed up in a contemporary report as: 'The Dutch organisers are planning to have the event won and lost in the four special tests held on each of the first five days. An acceleration test will be held at Assen, two motocross tests will be in use each day ... and, for the first time in many years a cross country test is reintroduced into the six days.'

The lead in the trophy contest alternated between the host country, Sweden and East Germany. Holland, mounted exclusively on Hondas, emerged as the winners, with Poland in second place and East Germany third. Sweden dropped back down the field after losing a rider from the team. East Germany won the Silver Vase contest. Great Britain finished fifth in the trophy contest and eleventh in the vase. The amazing achievements of the Czech team in earlier years were also under siege, and the best they could manage was tenth in both competitions after riders retired. Despite the fact that Dutch television cameras recorded daily coverage of the

Derrick Edmondson emerged as Britain's top ISDE rider during the 1980s. He is shown here (with helmet) and the 125 Yamaha he rode in the 1983 event, which was staged in Wales

event for the evening news broadcasts, rule breaking continued. An Italian rider was excluded when he was caught changing the numbers on two machines close to a checkpoint, and one four-stroke rider who started the event on a Husqvarna turned up at a later check on a Yamaha! Contractual problems over clothing almost excluded Derrick Edmondson from the British trophy team but he was reinstated at the last moment by the international jury.

The 1985 event held at Alp in the Spanish Pyrenees covered some very difficult terrain in conditions that were often hot and dusty. In fact it had all the makings of a tough ISDE which could be settled by times between checks. In fact the organizers operated slow time-schedules which enabled very large numbers of riders to stay on time, again leaving the results to be settled by special test times. It would, however, be very unfair to call it an easy event, indeed some regarded it as a classic of its time. Nevertheless, the special tests, first introduced by the FIM 25 years earlier, were the decisive factor. For the first time emphasis began to be placed on the 'overall' winner although there is no place in this team event for such a category. It has to be said that individual rider's contracts with manufacturers were beginning to devalue team success. After all, any major manufacturer was more likely to be concerned with the individual success of 'his' riders rather than national team performance.

So in 1985 it was significant that the Frenchman Gilles Lalay set the best overall performance, beating his fellow Honda rider Derrick Edmondson of the British trophy team by 104 seconds, gained over 21 motocross, cross-country and acceleration tests. Sweden won the World Trophy from Spain and East Germany. For the first time the Silver Vase was transformed into the Junior World Trophy for teams of riders under 23 years of age. Clearly this innovation was long overdue since the rule that trophy teams must use machines produced in their own countries was long gone. With almost poetic justice the East Germans won the first Junior Trophy with a team mounted on their national machinery! The British teams finished fifth in the trophy contest and ninth in the Junior Trophy.

However, if there is any doubt about the relative difficulty of the 1985 event there is little in the case of the Italian ISDE of 1986 based at San Pellegrino. It was hardly surprising that the Italian fondness for motocross special tests, seen so clearly in Elba in 1981, should have been reflected in 1986, especially as Masserini, the clerk of the course, was responsible for both events. Moreover, his choice of daily routes was severely affected by pressure from conservationists, so that cross-country routes were restricted and much tarmac was involved. Contemporary observers felt that trail and track riding very definitely took second place to motocross ability. There was also a good deal of discontent about the organization of the event, which was felt to be geared to Italian success. Certainly there were a number of occasions, including the cancellation of the entire results of the second half of the second day, when decisions seemed to favour the home teams. Geraint Jones of the British trophy team summed up his feelings by claiming that it was the easiest event in which he had ridden. The fact that once again he finished with a gold medal as the best British rider in that year, but in only eighteenth place in the 500cc class, continued to highlight the problems facing brilliant performers in difficult conditions in events dominated by motocross tests. Unbeatable in an ISDE of this kind, the Italians won both trophy competitions, the World Trophy from Sweden and Czechoslovakia and the Junior Trophy from East Germany and Czechoslovakia, and took the first three places in the club team contest, the first two in the manufacturer's and four of the five capacity classes! Despite finishing with the team intact, Great Britain only managed tenth place in the World Trophy. The Junior Trophy team finished in fourth place, an excellent result which surely suggested better performances to come.

Following the pattern set by its immediate prede-

cessors the 1987 event was also a disappointment for many. The Polish organizers centred the event on Jelenia Gura in south-west Poland but, mainly because of environmental pressure, were only given permission to use a small area, so that little variation of routes was possible and many tracks were in use every day, becoming badly rutted in consequence. The general impression was of fast, fairly easy terrain, with many riders maintaining the speed schedules without difficulty. The same motocross special test was used every day in conjunction with a daily cross-country test and these, as usual, decided the results. Despite the relatively easy routes only 6 of the 19 trophy teams finished intact and the British team, finishing in fourth place, had its best result since 1978. Particularly noteworthy was Paul Edmondson's performance which produced second place in the 125cc class. The organizers felt that Great Britain's effort, by largely amateur riders against full-time professionals, merited the award of the Watling Trophy for the most improved team. The British Junior Trophy team, having lost one rider, finished in ninth place. The overall win in both trophy contests went to East Germany's teams mounted on the faithful MZs. It was the first time for 19 years that the East Germans had been successful in the World Trophy competition.

The French won the World Trophy in their own event held at Mende in 1988. The event was certainly not easy and it indicates the problems facing ISDE organizers. Despite the problems posed by course conditions and times, both of which must be planned within ecological limitations, most of the top riders remained on time and the results depended upon the daily special test times. In consequence, success or failure was measured in seconds. For example, on the third day the French eventual World Trophy winners led the Italian team by a total of only 79 seconds. On the fourth day Paul Edmondson, who was to finish third in the 125cc class after crashing during the final motocross test, increased his lead in the class from 27 to 47 seconds. The margins were slim and remain so today. These speeds are a very far cry indeed from the days when the International Trophy would be won by the only team to finish the ISDT without time penalties between checkpoints.

The French World Trophy team proved unbeatable on the tests and won the contest from Italy and Czechoslovakia. The Junior Trophy went to Italy from Finland and West Germany. The British teams finished fifth in both competitions. The problem for the British trophy team is apparent from the class results of its members:

Rider	Medal	Position in Class
Paul Edmondson (125 Yamaha)	Gold	Third
John Deacon (510 Husqvarna)	"	Fifth
Geraint Jones (260 Husqvarna)	"	Fifteenth
Paul Fairbrother (250 KTM)	"	Twenty-four
Alan Bates (250 Suzuki)	Silver	Thirty-sixth
Wyn Hughes (260 Husqvarna)	"	Thirty-fourth

British Army teams at opening ceremony of the 1985 ISDE in Spain. Included in the picture are team manager Gordon Park and Phil Mellers (support crew). Phil rode in 1951 at Varese and 1952 at Bad Aussee for the Ariel works team

The team points total is based upon the time difference between the team members and the class leaders converted into penalty points. The team with the lowest points total wins the trophy. It is therefore clear that even if the overall calibre of riders in a team is excellent and their machines prove completely reliable, it is impossible for them to win unless every rider is capable of setting exceptionally fast times on the motocross tests.

The 1989 event marked the low point in ISDEs affected by limitations on routes and reliance on special tests. Held in West Germany and based at Walldurn, it has been described as a 'dismal' event, hit very hard indeed by 'Green' interests. In order to satisfy ecological requirements there was no really hard going and the time schedule was very slow. So effective was the pressure against the event that advertising and promotion was also at a very low level. Needless to say, all was won or lost on the usual tests and only 33 riders from the entire entry failed to finish the course. After the fifth day Geraint Jones of the British trophy team was reported as commenting that it had all been on tarmac or very fast farm tracks. The event had devalued gold

medals and proved nothing.

It should still be remembered that, even if this was the easiest ISDE, it was still not easy for all riders. The British rider Phil Cannon, who won a gold medal on his KTM, said that he had tried his hardest and earned whatever medal he won. Nor should the overall nature of the event obscure the performance of Paul Edmondson, who became the first British ISDE rider ever to win his class in the event. This was to be the first of three consecutive 125cc class wins, providing a real boost for British supporters. The World Trophy went to the Italian special test experts, from Sweden and West Germany, with Great Britain in seventh place. The Junior Trophy was won by Finland, from West Germany and France, the British team occupying twelfth place.

The Swedish event in 1990 was a brave and successful attempt to restore the image of the ISDE by returning to a tough formula with many miles of slippery rocks and tree roots in the apparently endless Swedish forests. As has often been the case the host nation dominated the event and Sweden won both trophies and four of the five capacity classes. They fielded the best club team and provided the best individual performance. On this occasion this dramatic success was the product of an excellent team, able to cope with severe conditions and tight times, in addition to achieving first-class special test results. The Swedish World Trophy team was so dominant that by the end of the fourth day, they led the

ABOVE **Gwyn Barraclough (250 Can-Am) with time card in his teeth, 1985**

LEFT **Poland in 1987; the going is very much akin to Wales with its hills and forests. But generally this type of going is getting harder and harder for organizers to find**

competition by 29 minutes. The difficulty of the event was such, especially for the riders of big four-stroke machines, that Geraint Jones said after Tuesday's run: 'It's the most difficult day of an ISDE that I've ever ridden.' Overall there were 132 retirements from the original field of 392 and among the 49 British and Irish starters 23 failed to complete the course. However, while Sweden was winning the World Trophy by a wide margin from Finland and France, Paul Edmondson was involved in a contest with Jeff Nilsson for the 125cc class award which was measured in seconds. In fact, the issue was not decided until the final test when Edmondson turned a 3-second defeat into a 61-second class win. Quite obviously the special tests were still of crucial importance.

The last of the ISDEs to date took place in September 1991. Fittingly it was staged from Povazska Bystrica in Czechoslovakia, for it serves to illustrate the most significant problems facing the modern event and the way in which the Czechs, for so long one of the greatest

Typical of the new breed enduro bike, very much a motocrosser with the bare equipment to make it road legal. Machine is a 1988 Husqvarna WRK 125. It is suited best to laid-out circuit special tests rather than true cross country work

exponents of the Six Days, have been affected. In the case of the Czechs they have also faced the transformation of their political system as part of the collapse of the Iron Curtain. The political desirability of this is obviously not in question, but it has had dramatic effects on the economies of the Eastern European states and the famous Jawa factory has suffered in consequence. For the first time in the history of the event Czechoslovakia fielded trophy teams mounted entirely on 'foreign' machinery. Indeed, the line-up of the

Junior Trophy team is particularly interesting: Jaroslav Beran (80 Gas-Gas), Redek Matoska (125 KTM), Vaclav Fojtik (250 KTM) and Martin Karas (350 four-stroke Husqvarna). The Czechs had a very mixed event. Unfortunately Bohumil Posledni, of their World Trophy team, had problems on Wednesday which eventually relegated his colleagues to tenth place. Despite losing Beran on the fourth day, following an accident, the Junior Trophy team finished fourth.

More significant, however, was that the Czechs continued to demonstrate their ability, whatever the machinery, by taking the 80cc and 500cc class wins with KTMs and the 600cc class with a Husaberg (a big four-stroke single with Swedish-designed engine and special chassis). So the Czechs at long last, and having been for so many years the advocates of nationally-produced

bow to the inevitable battle of the special tests. This in turn meant that reliance had to be placed on the specialized motocross machinery which has steadily displaced the almost indestructible Jawas.

So the result of the 1991 ISDE was decided by special test times. Sweden took the World Trophy from Germany and France, while the United States won the Junior Trophy followed by Holland and Poland. Incidentally, it was good to see 80 and 125cc Simsons included in the Polish team. The British world trophy team continued to do well, Paul Edmondson leading the 125cc class for the third consecutive year and contributing to fourth place and another Watling Trophy.

So there is no more to be said until 1992: There is little doubt that the ISDE, as opposed to its predecessor, is much more concerned with special tests and speed over short distances. As is clearly recognized, it is no longer a trial of the reliability of standard production machinery. It is virtually impossible to separate the factors which have led to the change of emphasis. It is a relationship between the technological progress in motorcycle design, the limitations imposed by environmental pressure groups upon the choice of routes and the spectator appeal of special tests. Public interest in the event has been at a low ebb in Great Britain for many years, but in the rest of Europe it remains much greater. In order to foster and maintain interest the wider public had to be given access to high profile and exciting motocross tests, frequently held on the same course every day. None of this is necessarily bad for the event but these factors have changed its nature.

Nevertheless, there are aspects of the Six Days which should receive serious consideration. Attempts should be made to eliminate cheating. If rules are unenforceable they should be amended or scrapped altogether. If it is to receive media attention and public support, no sport can afford to incorporate a built-in attitude that its regulations are there to be ignored or broken. Above all, whether it is ISDT, ISDE or simply the 'Six Days', it must remain a tough, long-distance event which tests the endurance of riders and machines. Perhaps it may be necessary, in order to preserve it, to place limitations on the type of machines which can be used and even to insist that all the bikes involved must be ridden a minimum distance to the start and be capable of returning home on the public highway after the finish.

Finally, whatever the future has in store, it is vital to salute the many thousands of riders who have taken part in 55 ISDTs and 11 ISDEs since 1913. They have demonstrated international sportsmanship, skill and endurance of the very highest order and frequently only managed to complete the course through sheer hard work and dogged determination. This event has demonstrated a relationship between man and machine of a kind not seen in any other branch of motor sport. To succeed, indeed to take part at all, you have to love motorcycles. Long may it continue.

machines for this event, have succumbed to the inevitable. Unhappily they have also been forced to accept the limitations imposed by the 'Green' movement. It seems somewhat strange that, in Eastern Europe, one of the most industrially polluted regions of the world, it should seem worthwhile to inhibit this rare six days of motorcycle sport. Nevertheless, as early as 1990 the organizers were forced to abandon their original venue near Brno, then the alternative Brezlov area, and finally to move the event to Povazska. Here the ecological pressure group enforced a massive reduction of the area to be covered and denied the use of the many difficult tracks which had made the Czech events so arduous and testing in the past. The result was that the Czechs, after years of stoutly defending the 'tough' event which could be decided on times out on the course, were forced to

Appendix

ISDT venues & results

Year	Host country	Venue	Trophy	Vase
1913	Great Britain	Carlisle	GB	
1914	France	Grenoble	Abandoned	
1920	France	Grenoble	CH	
1921	Switzerland		CH	
1922	Switzerland		CH	
1923	Sweden/Norway		S	
1924	Belgium	Chaud Fontaine	GB	N
1925	Great Britain	Southampton	GB	GB
1926	Great Britain	Buxton	GB	GB
1927	Great Britain	Ambleside	GB	GB
1928	Great Britain	Harrogate	GB	GB
1929	FICM organized	Central Europe	GB	GB
1930	France	Grenoble	I	F
1931	Italy	Merano	I	NL
1932	Italy	Merano	GB	GB
1933	Great Britain	Llandrindod Wells	D	GB
1934	Germany	Garmisch-Partenkirchen	D	GB
1935	Germany	Oberstdorf	D	D
1936	Germany	Freudenstadt	GB	GB
1937	Great Britain	Llandrindod Wells	GB	NL
1938	Great Britain	Llandrindod Wells	GB	D
1939	Austria	Salzburg	Result annulled by FIM	
1947	Czechoslovakia	Zlin	CS	CS
1948	Italy	San Remo	GB	GB
1949	Great Britain	Llandrindod Wells	GB	CS
1950	Great Britain	Llandrindod Wells	GB	GB
1951	Italy	Varese	GB	NL
1952	Austria	Bad Aussee	CS	CS
1953	Czechoslovakia	Gottwaldov	GB	CS
1954	Great Britain	Llandrindod Wells	CS	NL
1955	Czechoslovakia	Gottwaldov	D	CS
1956	West Germany	Garmisch-Partenkirchen	CS	NL
1957	Czechoslovakia	Spindleruv Mlyn	DDR	CS
1958	West Germany	Garmisch-Partenkirchen	CS	CS
1959	Czechoslovakia	Gottwaldov	CS	CS
1960	Austria	Bad Aussee	A	I
1961	Great Britain	Llandrindod Wells	D	CS
1962	West Germany	Garmisch-Partenkirchen	CS	D
1963	Czechoslovakia	Spindleruv Mlyn	DDR	I
1964	East Germany	Erfurt	DDR	DDR
1965	Great Britain	Isle of Man	DDR	DDR
1966	Sweden	Villingsberg	DDR	D
1967	Poland	Zakopane	DDR	CS
1968	Italy	San Pellegrino	D	I

1969	West Germany	Garmisch-Partenkirchen	DDR	D
1970	Spain	El Escorial	CS	CS
1971	Great Britain	Isle of Man	CS	CS
1972	Czechoslovakia	Spindleruv Mlyn	CS	CS
1973	United States	Dalton Massachusetts	CS	USA
1974	Italy	Camerino	CS	CS
1975	Great Britain	Isle of Man	D	I
1976	Austria	Zeltweg	D	CS
1977	Czechoslovakia	Povazska Bystrica	CS	CS
1978	Sweden	High Chaparral	CS	I
1979	West Germany	Lager Stegskopf	I	CS
1980	France	Brioude	I	D
1981	Italy	Elba	I	I
1982	Czechoslovakia	Povazska Bystrica	CS	DDR
1983	Great Britain	Builth Wells	S	S
1984	Holland	Assen	NL	DDR
1985	Spain	Alp La Cerdanya	S	DDR
1986	Italy	San Pellegrino	I	I
1987	Poland	Jelenia Gura	DDR	DDR
1988	France	Mende	F	I
1989	West Germany	Walldurn	I	SF
1990	Sweden	Vasteras	S	S
1991	Czechoslovakia	Povazska Bystrica	S	USA

A Austria   DDR East Germany   NL Holland   CH Switzerland   F France   S Sweden
CH Czechoslovakia   GB Great Britain   SF Finland   D West Germany   I Italy   USA United States   N Norway

International Trophy renamed World Trophy in 1970
Event renamed the International Six Days Enduro in 1981
Silver Vase renamed World Junior Trophy in 1985

For many years the British dominated the Six Days on large capacity four-stroke singles; but by 1958 machines such as the 500 Ariel were outclassed

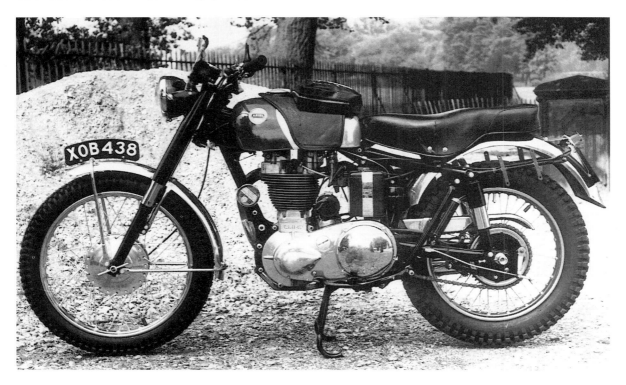

INDEX